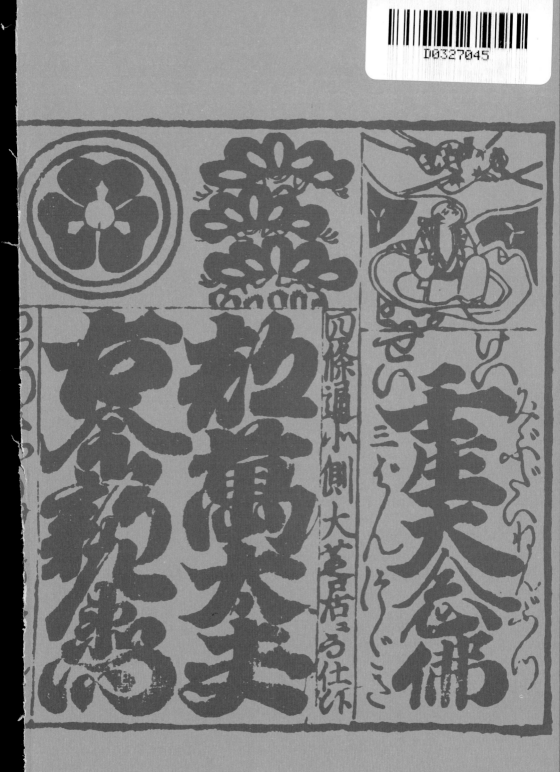

D0327045

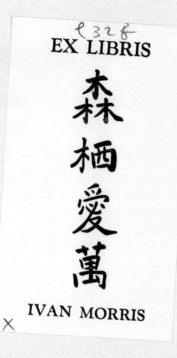

e32f

EX LIBRIS

森
栖
愛
萬

IVAN MORRIS

X

THE ACTORS' ANALECTS

THE ACTORS' ANALECTS
(YAKUSHA RONGO)

Edited, Translated and with an Introduction and Notes by

CHARLES J. DUNN and BUNZŌ TORIGOE

UNIVERSITY OF TOKYO PRESS

UNESCO COLLECTION OF REPRESENTATIVE WORKS
JAPANESE SERIES

This work has been accepted in the Japanese translation
series of the United Nations Educational, Scientific,
and Cultural Organization (UNESCO)

© UNESCO , 1969
All Rights Reserved

Published by
University of Tokyo Press, 1969
Printed in Japan

Dedicated by the authors
to their mentors
Professor F. J. Daniels
&
Professor Masakatsu Gunji

Authors' Note

Although the authors take joint responsibility for this work, it was inevitable that the labor was shared between them. Torigoe prepared all the parts in Japanese and undertook the assembling of illustrative material. Dunn wrote all the English, receiving a great deal of assistance from his partner. It is, however, unavoidable that much of the explanatory material and comment is written from the point of view of a Westerner. The authors feel that this is no great drawback, seeing that Western readers will be in the majority. On the other hand, Torigoe has tried to make the book useful for Japanese students.

Except on the cover and title page, Japanese names have been written in the Japanese order, with family name first. Dates have not been corrected to the Gregorian calendar, and the Western names for the months have not been used.

The authors especially wish to thank Professors Gunji Masakatsu and Iijima Kohei of Waseda University, the former not only for the permission he so freely gave for them to use the text and notes of his edition of *The Actors' Analects,* but also for much assistance during the preparation of the translation; the latter in his capacity as Director of the Waseda Theatre Museum, for allowing them to use illustrative materials from the collection of this great institution.

Contents

Introduction

Introduction

The work that is here translated is a collection of writings on the practice and aesthetics of acting in the *kabuki** theater in the late seventeenth and early eighteenth century in Kyoto and Osaka.

The text contains one or two references to the history of *kabuki*, but they are fragmentary and in any case not reliable, so that some account of the development of the art and a description of its externals at the time of the Analects may be of some use to the reader.[1]

The Kabuki Drama

Kabuki might be termed the popular traditional live drama of Japan, to distinguish it from the puppet drama or *jōruri*, and from the *nō* play, which, from its fixed repertory and partial simplicity, might well be called the classical drama of Japan. By the middle of the sixteenth century, peace began to take over

---

* All italicized Japanese terms used in this book that are not explained on the spot are listed in the Glossary.

[1] Those who wish to read a fuller treatment of the history of *kabuki* up to the present are recommended the works by Ernst and Scott listed in the Bibliography.

from the period of civil war that had continued, with some interruptions, for four hundred years. The Japanese, especially the townsfolk, who were embarking upon a period of increased prosperity and leisure, began to look for new means of entertainment. In the second half of the century a spirit of gaiety spread through the land, partly stimulated, it may be, by the new material civilization and ideas that were coming in from Europe through the intermediary of traders and missionaries from Portugal. There was a great deal of activity in popular dance and song, and it was in this atmosphere that two popular drama forms were born, one live and one with puppets. With the latter we are not concerned here.[2] The former, *kabuki*, developed from popular dances and seems to have crystallized around a performance that a woman named O-Kuni, from Izumo, gave at Kitano, in Kyoto, in the early years of the seventeenth century. Detailed information about her performance is lacking, and no doubt there were others in the same profession, but she is said to have teamed up with a *rōnin*, Nagoya Sanzaemon (or Sanzaburō) and become very popular as an entertainer. In the first period of *kabuki*, which ended in 1629, women played a large part, and the form during this period is generally known as " women's *kabuki*." This early form was not an entertainment of a particularly high order, and at times was not more than a shop window for prostitutes, but it seems to have included songs, dances, and a certain amount of acting. The companies were not restricted to women, and some accounts speak disapprovingly of men and women representing members of the opposite sex. The year 1629 brought about the end of women's *kabuki*, when the central government prohibited the appearance of women on the stage. Theater architecture had not advanced beyond that of the *nō* stage, and *kabuki* also used the drums and flute of the *nō* performance, as well as the *shamisen*.

---

[2] See Dunn for an account of the early puppet theater in Japan.

After the banning of women's performances there came the period of *wakashu kabuki*. *Wakashu* were young males, and they took the place of women on the stage. A lot of their attraction came from the fact that they were chosen more for their beauty than for their talent, and to a large extent the *kabuki* of this period existed to publicize young male prostitutes. At the same time, however, the dramatic content of the performances increased, partly because of the inclusion in the companies of actors from the *nō*. This period in its turn came to an end, in 1652, once more as a result of a prohibition by the government, which disapproved of the spread of homosexuality from priests and warriors, who had long practiced it, to ordinary people.

Kabuki was allowed to start up again under certain conditions, which included what was presumably intended to be a fundamental requirement, that in the future *kabuki* should restrict itself to representational drama, and also that *wakashu*, who had hitherto used elaborate styles of hairdressing, should shave off their front hair (as did the majority of males at the time) to make them less attractive. It was during this time that the specialist performance by men of female roles (*onnagata*) became established as a separate category of acting, and permanent theaters were built in the three great centers, namely Kyoto, the old capital, Osaka, the commercial city, and Edo, the new capital, which was renamed Tokyo in 1868. Government control was strict, and tended to treat the theater and the brothel districts as one, that is, as an evil not conforming to Confucian ideas of morality, but unavoidable for keeping the lower orders as contented as possible. The women performers exiled from the stage still had their place in restaurants and tea-houses, where *kabuki* actors might also perform. The *kabuki* stage itself still continued for some years to act as a place where male prostitutes could make themselves known to the public, and also helped the ladies of the town by the partly-idealized picture it gave of the high-grade courtesan (*keisei*).

One of the pieces in the *Analects*, *Mirror for Actors* (p. 38 ff.),
gives fairly lengthy summaries of some of the material that was
being used in this period, and indicates that considerable development was taking place. The simple dances which had
presumably formed a good deal of the repertory since the earliest days developed into advanced, formalized dance pieces
(*shosagoto*) of considerable beauty and complexity as more material
from the *nō* plays was brought in. But in the last decades of the
seventeenth century the line of realistic drama, which was
drawn perhaps from the comic interludes in the *nō* program,
became prominent and, under the name of *jigei*, formed a contrast
to *shosagoto*.

This occurred at about the same time that Japan entered into
the Genroku period. Strictly speaking, this was the name of
the year-period[3] between 1688 and 1704, but in the history of
Japanese culture it has become customary to include the first
two decades of the eighteenth century in the term; thus Genroku
can mean the period from 1688 to 1720. It was a time of great
brilliance in many fields. Saikaku was writing his novels, and
Bashō his poetry. The *Analects*, which date from this period
also, indicate the degree of excellence which the *kabuki* actors
had reached. In the Kyoto/Osaka area it was the time of
Sakata Tōjūrō, the superb player of lover's roles, and Yoshizawa
Ayame, generally accounted the greatest *onnagata* of all time.
The great dramatist Chikamatsu Monzaemon devoted his energies for a time during this period to the live drama, before giving
himself entirely to working for the puppets,[4] and produced a
series of plays on the theme of a courageous and virtuous *keisei*
(this is not a contradiction in terms, in the context of the period)

---

[3] The Japanese calendar uses "year-periods," and specifies years by
their number in such a period. Thus 1689 was the 1st year of Genroku, and
1969 is the 44th year of Shōwa.

[4] See Bibliography (Dunn, Keene).

which, with those of his imitators, did much to elevate *kabuki* into a serious drama form.

The history of *kabuki* subsequent to the *Analects* is very closely linked with the *jōruri* or puppet drama. Already in our text we have the first mentions of the infiltration of material from this source, and by 1750 almost the whole puppet repertory had been adopted, with more or less adaptation, and had brought with it great changes in acting and in the type of play performed. Long-drawn-out scenes of suicide, the tearful conflicts of love and duty, and much else that seems today typically *kabuki*, came in at this time and were to provide the themes for new plays until the mid-nineteenth century, when the playwright Kawatake Mokuami introduced a new style which, with ingredients from the Western drama, was to survive the Meiji restoration of 1868.

We have said that the first *kabuki* performances were on a stage which was identical with that of the *nō* play. The *nō* stage quickly became fixed in the pattern that is still the standard today, but that of *kabuki* started a series of developments which have barely come to an end even today. By the time of the *Analects*, the original *nō* stage had been reduced to only a part of the *kabuki* acting area. Entrances and exits were still usually made through the curtain at stage right, onto a section which kept the name of *hashi-gakari*, although it was no longer a gangway. But the stage had expanded in front of the *hashi-gakari* and the stage proper to form the *tsuke-butai*. The dressing-room (*gakuya*) was still a large area at the rear of the stage.

In the early days only this dressing-room and other rooms used by the staff, and the stage had been under a roof, and the audience had had to stand, or sit on grass mats, in the open. A fence surrounded the theater, with an entrance, over which was erected a symbolic watch-tower, the sign that the theater was licensed.[5] As time went by, two tiers of roofed side boxes came

---

[5] See color plate, following p. 160.

to be built along the side fences, and when the auditorium was completely roofed over, it could be fitted with thick straw mats (*tatami*) for the audience to sit on in comfort.   These mats made it possible to define the area available for each person.   Cushions could be hired, and could be used as missiles if the acting did not come up to scratch.

Such, then, were the externals of the *kabuki* theater at the time of the *Analects*.   Now let us discuss the work itself.

The Actors' Analects

Even the consideration of the title involves the reader immediately in a problem of a sort that in modern world languages can surely exist only in Japanese.   If one takes the Chinese characters with which the title is written, there is no doubt that the translation that we have given, *The Actors' Analects*, is apt. The last two characters, usually read in Japanese *rongo*, are the name of the Confucian classic translated in English as *The Analects*, and they are preceded by the word for actor.   The work is thus a guide to acting.   The pronunciation of the title, however, is noted in *kana*[6] on the first page of the original text as *Yakusha-banashi*, "Actors' tales."   This translation is also apt, since the various works are all statements by actors regarding their art. The work is thus a collection of sayings, advice and admonishments from actors to actors, brought together to form what might in the West be called an actors' bible.

The *Analects* is made up of seven chief pieces.   The first of these, *One Hundred Items on the Stage*, has in fact only seven items, to which we have added one preserved in another work.   They consist of advice and instruction by Sugi Kuhē, who is credited with having given some guidance to the great Sakata Tōjūrō, whose name constantly occurs throughout the *Analects*, and

---

[6] Almost all the Chinese characters which are used to write Japanese can be pronounced in several different ways, and the Japanese use a phonetic script (*kana*) to show which is the correct one.

serve as a useful introduction, seeing that they deal in a general way with topics—the decline of contemporary standards, the need for careful preparation, the characteristics of the various roles, and so on—that will be dealt with in later pieces in more detail.

Mirror for Actors, by Tominaga Heibē, which comes next, is of considerable interest in that it outlines some plots and gives otherwise unfamiliar details of *kabuki* of the pre-Genroku period.

With *The Words of Ayame*, which is a record by Fukuoka Yagoshirō, an actor and playwright of the early eighteenth century, of the sayings of Yoshizawa Ayame (1673–1719), the first great *onnagata*, on acting in general and the *onnagata* role in particular, the Genroku period is reached. This is the best-known of the pieces in the *Analects*, and the only one of which any part has hitherto been translated into English.[7]

The Words of Ayame contains the famous injunctions about the need for an *onnagata* to conduct himself in private as he does on the stage, and gives details of his typical career, with his start as catamite in the Dōtombori pleasure district in Osaka, where he had the good fortune to receive excellent advice from at least one patron, which helped him later. His career is characterized by great artistic integrity, with one ill-fated excursion into male roles.

Dust in the Ears, with its fanciful title taken from a work of poetry aesthetics,[8] was written down by the playwright Kaneko Kichizaemon, and does for the great player of lover's roles, Sakata Tōjūrō (1647–1709), what the previous piece does for Ayame. The next piece, *Sequel to " Dust in the Ears"* (compiler, Tamiya Shirogorō) is a series of anecdotes about various actors, but the one after that, *The Kengai Collection*, recorded by Somekawa Jūrobē, goes back to Sakata Tōjūrō as the main

---

[7] by Scott.
[8] See below, p. 12.

topic of interest. There emerges a fairly clear picture of Tōjūrō's personality. He was a hard worker, and a great observer of the world and the various occupations of the human beings who dwell in it. He had great consideration for his fellow actors, taking care not to embarrass them either on the stage or off, but he was reported to be a poor teacher, since his excellent acting was largely intuitive. Nevertheless, he seems to have been an inspiring manager, and the *kabuki* plays of the great writer Chikamatsu Monzaemon, who had Kaneko Kichizaemon as his collaborator, were written for Tōjūrō, and, in view of the way plays were prepared, may have owed more than a little to the latter's experience.

Sadoshima's Diary, the last piece of the *Analects* proper, is, as its title suggests, largely concerned with the life of the actor Sadoshima Chōgorō (1700–1757). It gives a good deal of information about the life of an actor of the time—a little later than that of the other pieces—and is followed by secret instruction on the art of the *kabuki* dance.

Finally, the edition from which our text is taken has an appendix in two parts. The first is a list of six *bon-kyōgen*, i. e. plays performed in the seventh and eighth months of 1776, in the Three Cities ;[9] the second is a classification of the actors in these plays into grades of excellence. The actors are assigned the various role-types, and their performance is then classified into grades, with the highest *shigoku jō jō kichi* (outstanding superior superior excellence), down to *jō* (superior). Although we have not translated this appendix, seeing that its date is considerably later than the pieces in the *Analects* proper, we have included the text in Japanese, and those who know Japanese will be interested to observe how the grading was done not only by the actual characters used, but also by writing these with some

---

[9] This expression, which occurs frequently in the *Analects*, refers to Edo (modern Tokyo), Kyoto and Osaka. The Japanese term could be translated literally as " three harbors."

strokes in outline or with some strokes omitted. This was the normal procedure in all sorts of ranking lists until the late nineteenth century.

The text of the *Analects* causes hardly any difficulty. The original is a wood-block printed work in four volumes comprising in all 77½ double pages, 18.5 cms. by 13.0 cms., with 9–10 lines to a single page. Volume I contains the *Preface, One Hundred Items on the Stage, Mirror for Actors, The Words of Ayame*; Volume II, *Dust in the Ears*; Volume III, *Sequel to " Dust in the Ears," Kengai Collection*; and Volume IV, *Sadoshima's Diary, Classification according to excellence of performance of the actors in the bon season plays in the Three Cities*.

We have followed Professor Gunji in basing our text on the copy of the book in the library of the Waseda Theater Museum, but have kept as far as possible the forms of the Chinese characters used in the original.[10]

The preface bears the date " late autumn of the cyclical year of the fire and monkey of the year period An-ei," i.e. 1776; the appendix is dated " on a lucky day in the 9th month" of the same year. It is to be presumed that " late autumn " and " 9th month " refer to the same publication date. The listing of the plays being performed in the " Three Cities " as *bon-kyōgen* confirms this date, since these plays were performed in the seventh month.

The date of publication is fairly remote from the period claimed for the pieces that make it up and it would be of use to

---

[10] Apart from the independent edition of *Dust in the Ears*, mentioned later (p. 12), other copies noted by Gunji are in the Tokyo National Museum, the National Diet Library, the Tokyo University Library, the Kyoto University Library and the Waseda University Library. Of these the Tokyo University Library copy is without the list of *bon kyōgen* and the actors' ratings that follow this, but has the added epilogue to *Dust in the Ears*. Other editions of some of the pieces in the collection are to be found elsewhere. *The Words of Ayame* is in Volume VI of *Shinkoku Yakusha Kōmoku* 新刻役者綱目, 1771 and *Sadoshima's Diary* and *Kengai Collection* are respectively in Volumes IV and V of *Yakusha-zensho* 役者全書, 1774.

find evidence of their existence prior to their appearance in the extant collection. One such particle of evidence has come to light in the discovery in the National Diet Library of an independent edition of *Dust in the Ears*, which is dated twenty years earlier, 1757. The main text is identical in the two cases—in fact it appears that the same blocks were used in both printings—but the earlier, independent text contains some elements missing from the version in the *Analects*. These elements are five in number, the first being a preface, in an elaborate style, which is signed by two compilers.[11] This preface recalls the work of the great teachers of the past and refers to their golden words remaining in the depth of the ears. The present work is said to be a selection from the secret writings of the former master Kaneko.[12]

The second element is an introduction in seventeen sections, of which the first two are of general interest and merit inclusion here. We have included them all as a prologue to our translation of *Dust in the Ears*.

> (*i*) *This is one of the seven writings and contains a record of all the opinions of great men of the past, set down by Kichizaemon, who was a master of the comic role[13] in the Genroku period (later, in Shōtoku,[14] he became a* tachiyaku). *It has been copied with complete accuracy from Kaneko's autograph account of what he heard, and therefore it is almost entirely in the spoken language.*
>
> (*ii*) *The reason for the title* Dust in the Ears *is as follows. There is an old book dealing with the ultimate significance of Japanese poetry-composition; it consists of questions and answers between Hosokawa*

---

[11] Rishū 李秀, formerly Zuishō 瑞笑, and Sogyoku 素玉 The former, who changed his name in 1754 and died in 1766, is more usually known as Hachimonjiya Hachizaemon V; he was a member of the firm that published the *Analects*. Sogyoku (died 1815) was his younger brother, otherwise Hachizaemon VI.

[12] Kaneko Kichizaemon.

[13] *dōke*, see Appendix I.

[14] 1711–1716.

Yūsai Hōin Genshi[15] *and Lord Karasumaru Mitsuhiro*[16] *and bears the name* Records of the Depths of my Ears.[17] *It seems that the name of the present work was given under the inspiration of this book, which is quoted in one or two places.*

The remaining fifteen sections are short notes on actors mentioned in the text, and the only noteworthy thing about them is that in (xvii) it is stated that Sugi Kuhē played until the Hōei period.[18] This is probably untrue, for although information is lacking on the details of his biography, it is generally thought that he was not active after about 1680.

Paragraph (i) carries the only direct reference to an original manuscript for any of the pieces in the collection, and serves to lessen any doubt that one might have about the authenticity of these pieces. The mention of " seven writings " will be discussed later in this section.

The third element, found in the early version of *Dust in the Ears,* but not in the text in the *Analects* is a list of contents, item by item. Rather than translate them all together, we have thought it more useful to put each one at the head of the translation of the item to which it refers.

The fourth element is a conclusion, or epilogue, in a rather ornate Chinese style, and the fifth is an advertisement at the back of the book. Translated, this reads

> Secret Notes on the Determination of an Actor's Artistic Standing. The Words of Ayame, *complete in three volumes.*
> *The above work is a collection of the sayings of the great Yoshizawa Ayame I, who was given the distinguished appellation of "supreme master of the art, absolutely unrivalled in the Three Cities," set down for posterity by the then* oyaji-gata *Miyakoya Yagoshirō*[19] *and is*

---

[15] 細川幽斎法印玄旨, 1534–1610. See also Item XII of *Dust in the Ears.*
[16] 烏丸光広, 1579–1638.
[17] *Niteiki* 耳底記.
[18] 1704–1711.
[19] Identical with Fukuoka Yagoshirō (see Appendix II).

*one of the "seven writings" by excellent authorities. We are proceeding
with the printing of this book, and we ask you to purchase it and read
it when it appears.*

Finally, there is the imprint:

*One day in the 3rd month, Spring, 1757. Kyoto, in Fuyachō Street, to
the south of the Seigan temple.
Printed by Hachimonjiya Hachizaemon, at the Ryōun-dō.*

This promised edition of the *Words of Ayame* may have never
appeared; at least, no copy of it is known. However the publication of this announcement would seem to indicate clearly, if
there was any doubt on the subject, that the *Words of Ayame*,
as well as *Dust in the Ears*, did exist in 1757. However, for *Dust
in the Ears*, we can go back considerably earlier, for at the end of
the separate edition, there is a half-obliterated date which apparently reads Kyōhō 12 (1727).

There are now two references to the "seven writings";
these must be the works that make up the present collection, and
indicate either that the *Analects* already existed more or less as
they were printed in 1776, or that, even if they existed only
separately or in manuscript, at least they were thought of as
forming a compact group. *In either case, we can be sure that they
were known and possibly fairly widely read well before the extant printed
edition.* Gunji, in his introduction to the *Analects*, quotes some
references in other works which lead to the same conclusion.
For example, the first piece, the *Hundred Items*, has only seven
items printed, the rest being said to be illegible owing to the
activities of insects.[20]   Now there is quoted in a work[21] dated
1750 an item which is mentioned as from this piece.[22]   A
short extract from the item also occurs in a work dated 1772.[23]

---

[20] See p. 36.
[21] *Kokon yakusha daizen* 古今役者大全, Vol. I.
[22] For a translation see p. 37.
[23] *Kokon yakusha rongo sakigake* 古今役者論語魁.

It is probable, therefore, that the pieces making up the collection were known about 1750 and that *Dust in the Ears* existed in 1727. These dates bring them sufficiently near to the period to which they refer to make their authenticity virtually certain.

Translation Technique

Rather than write a long analysis of the contents of the *Analects*, we rely on the reader to read the translation and form his own opinions. To this end, we have deliberately avoided committing ourselves by over-translation. Japanese is a notoriously ambiguous language; this statement can be rephrased by asserting that one of the advantages that Japanese has over other languages, especially Western ones, is that it does not have to be precise. We feel that to make a precise rendering into English when no precision exists in the original is to mistranslate. It follows that we have done our best to reproduce the stylistically none too outstanding Japanese into a similar English. We have added notes and comments, the former intended to be factual and the latter to give our interpretation of the text, although the distinction between the two has not always been strictly observed. We have also made a subject list of the major topics dealt with; the list of names of actors, etc. in Appendix II also has a reference to the place of their occurrence.

The Structure of Kabuki

Nevertheless, we think that there are some topics of special interest that we should like to develop a little in this Introduction. One concerns the structure of *kabuki*. Permanent theaters existed in Edo, Kyoto and Osaka. In Edo a great fire destroyed the old theaters in 1675, and afterwards four new ones were given a license to operate. These were named Nakamura, Ichimura, Morita and Yamamura, from the families that held the licenses. In 1714, the great scandal involving the actor Ikushima Shingorō and the lady-in-waiting Ejima brought about

the closure of the Yamamura theater, and from that time until
the end of the Tokugawa period, the remaining three were the
only official *kabuki* theaters, though their location changed from
time to time.   The incumbent member of the family was known
as the *zamoto*, and he seems to have combined the functions of
owner, manager and backer.   In the Kyoto/Osaka area the system was different from that in Edo.   Here too there was a
zamoto, but he was more or less the actors' representative, and
might change from year to year.   It would seem that the function
and prestige of the *zamoto* changed with the person holding the
title.   Sometimes the *zamoto* was a mere boy whose duties were
nominal; when Sakata Tōjūrō held this title, however, he seems
to have managed his troupe and rehearsed it.   The owner of
the theater, from whom it took its name, was called the *nadai;*
he presumably held the license to run the theater.   A third
party, usually called *kinshu*, was the backer, lending money to the
zamoto and expecting some return from the profits.

The *zamoto* himself collected the admission fees, distributed
what was due to the various parties, and apparently kept the
balance for himself.   Hence Tōjūrō was able to earn enough
money to have an imposing residence and live in style.   The
other actors worked on a yearly contract starting in the eleventh
month.   Salaries were, of course, apportioned according to the
status of the actor, and were fixed after negotiation.   Sadoshima[24] paid Ebizō 2,000 *ryō*[25] and 500 *ryō* as earnest money, but
this was the highest ever, and up to present-day film star standards.   Normally a first-class actor would have been happy with
500 *ryō* a year.

In its financial structure, Genroku *kabuki* more closely
resembles the commercial theater of the West than does modern *kabuki*.   The latter ultimately depends, of course, upon

---

[24] See *Sadoshima's Diary*, XVI, p. 154.
[25] That is, an annual salary equivalent to about £37,000 or $90,000 today;
see *Kengai Collection*, II, n. 2, p. 124.

popular support, but is cushioned from direct dependence upon audience numbers by the existence of the National Theater and the great theater/cinema combines, not to mention financial resources other than those deriving directly from the theater.[26] In Genroku times, with actors on a yearly contract, they themselves were not faced with the risk of immediate unemployment if a play flopped, but the backer was presumably able to exert considerable pressure on the management to increase audiences if takings were not sufficient for him to get his advances repaid. Sadoshima's sentiments expressed in his diary (p. 148), indicate the possibility that actors could if necessary take a reduction in salary to help defray the costs if a season was not going too well.

In 1690 there were seven approved theaters in Kyoto, arranged as indicated in the accompanying diagram.

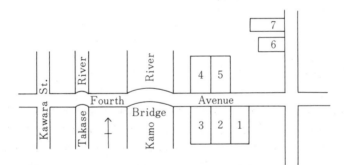

Of these Nos. 2, 5, and 6 were for *kabuki* and the rest for *jōruri*. No. 2 was named the Arashi San'emon theater, No. 5 was Murayama Matabē, and No. 6 Hoteiya Ume-no-jō. An idea of the area occupied by a contemporary theater is given by the size

────────────

    [26] The magnificent Japanese National Theater does not have to pay its way, and the firm of Shōchiku has been willing to support its less profitable traditional theater productions from the profits derived from films, etc. Actors receive fees for tuition in dancing, for example, and often have television and film earnings.

of the boundaries of No. 2, about $140' \times 75'$, and No. 5, about $180' \times 90'$. By 1762 the only ones surviving were Nos. 4 and 5, and one opposite to them, representing either No. 2 or No. 3. This last is the only survivor today, being the present Minami-za, " Southern Theater." The three Kyoto theater companies which we hear about in the *Analects*, those of Miyako Mandayū, Hayakumo and Ebisu-ya, used the three theaters mentioned, but seem to have moved round a good deal.

The theaters in Osaka are not very easy to identify, but it seems that in about 1730 they were along the Dōtombori canal as indicated in the plan. The names given for the four *kabuki*

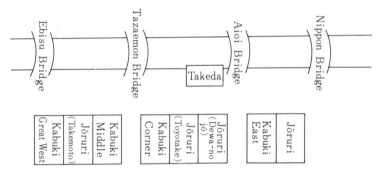

theaters are the ones by which they were best known, and theaters with the name of Middle (Naka-za) and Corner (Kado-za) are still to be found on more or less the same sites. At the time mentioned the Great West Theater seems to have had Matsumoto Nazaemon as *nadai*, the Middle, Shioya Kuemon, the Corner, Ōsaka Tazaemon and the East, Ōsaka Kuzaemon. The site marked Takeda was also known as the Hama (Shore) Theater, and was the one in which mechanical puppets, some powered by the water of the Dōtombori canal, were displayed. The whole area was (and still is) called Dōtombori, and was also the location of houses of entertainment of all sorts.

There had developed a tradition of a yearly program for all *kabuki* theaters, which was nevertheless fairly flexible, so that in any particular year the pattern might change. However, the start of the year was almost always in the eleventh month, with the *kaomise*. The actors for the year were booked in the tenth month or thereabouts, and the first productions were put on. However, the plays themselves tended to be of less importance than the " showing of faces " (*kaomise*) of the new cast that it was hoped the patrons would support for the coming season. From then on, ideally, a new program was put on every two months, but if a play was unusually successful it might run for longer, and a failure would be taken off and replaced more quickly. The greatest effort of the year was reserved for the first month, when the *ni no kawari*, or first replacement, was staged. In Kyoto/Osaka, this was normally a *keisei* piece, but in Edo very often a Soga play[27] was given. In *Sadoshima's Diary* (p. 154) it is recorded that when the Edo actor Ichikawa Ebizō came to Osaka, a Soga play was put on as the second play, no doubt because he was allowed to follow Edo custom. The *san no kawari* came in the third month. The seventh month saw the production of the *bon-kyōgen*, or plays in the season when the *bon* dances are performed throughout Japan to entertain the souls of the dead who are thought to be revisiting the earth. At this time, the tendency was to use actors of not too great reputation, since the top performers would wish to avoid the heat, and in Kyoto/Osaka a Soga play was normally given. The *bon-kyōgen* given in 1776 are listed in an appendix to the edition of the *Analects* that has been used for this translation. The first part of *Dust in the Ears* XLIV (p. 102) gives an idea of the changes that could actually occur in a year.

The daily program was very long, usually lasting from dawn to dusk, although in Osaka the first few days of the *kaomise* would be played at night, unless there was a prohibition because of the risk of fire. First, before it was really light, would come

---

[27] A play dealing with the Soga 曾我 brothers, whose avenging of their father's murder was a famous vendetta story.

the *Sambaso*, a felicitous opening piece.[28] *Sambaso* would be
followed by a *waki-kyōgen* and another short piece known simply
as *niban-me*, " second "; these were performed by actors of
not very exalted rank. All this was preliminary fare, and the
main item on the day's program, the *samban-tsuzuki*, followed.
The latter was a play in three acts, with the first two in two
scenes, and the great *keisei* plays were all in this category. The
company put all its energies into its performance, for the success
or failure of the whole program depended upon it. A *kiri-
kyōgen* brought the program to an end. The *niban-me* was very
often a *sewa-mono*, " domestic piece," set in the contemporary
scene, and often dealing with the love-suicide of a merchant
and a prostitute. This might be changed independently of the
samban-tsuzuki to add novelty during a season.

The Preparation of Plays

The *Analects* give much information about the preparation
and rehearsal of new plays. In particular, *Sequel to " Dust in the
Ears*," XXI (p. 118) is useful as showing a certain development
taking place. The first step in preparing a new play was for all
the parties to agree about its plot; the decision was not taken
merely by the actors and authors, but the backer also joined in
the discussions. Then parts were allotted and the more detailed
actions of each scene were worked out, and at this point, and
apparently not before, the words were fitted to the actions.
The authors, who until the time of Chikamatsu Monzaemon
had little status, had the responsibility not only of composing
the words and changing them to suit an actor's fancy, but also of
teaching them to the performers. It was not the custom, it
seems, to provide copies of scripts, and as *kabuki* developed and

---

[28] This is founded on the *nō* play *Okina*, and described in *Theatre in Japan*,
p. 65. This is still played on certain felicitous occasions, just as *Okina* (see
O'Neill, p. 132) is put on the *nō* stage at the New Year.
Waki-kyōgen 脇狂言 is first of two short plays in a program.

the scripts became more complicated (the earlier plays have comparatively simple lines), the actors were expected to take notes to remind them of their speeches.

The more important players worked out their actions and the others would have to fit their parts to that of the principals. This system is similar to that still prevailing in the *nō* plays, where the *shite* (principal actor) controls the whole performance, and in present-day *kabuki*, in which, in well-tried pieces, the principal actors work according to their family tradition, which can be so well-known that they themselves do not turn up at run-throughs, but leave it to stand-ins to go through the motions for them. A superior actor would learn his words beforehand, and try to find time for relaxation before a new play started, so that they should come out naturally and not have to be extracted consciously from a half-established memory, as happened with some inferior performers. The criterion was whether the words fitted the action, not the other way round. The system reminds one of the way film producers and directors decide on a story before they employ script-writers to compose the words. If a new play was under preparation it would not be put on until the principal actors were satisfied with it and with their interpretation of their part.

Genroku and Western Acting

One of the perennial questions about the actor's art in the West concerns whether he should so sink himself in his role that he really feels as the character he is representing feels. Some say, for example, that he must feel angry when his character feels angry, and glad when he is glad, whereas others maintain that to do so is fatal to the technique and that a role must be approached objectively, with careful study and patient practice.

The *kabuki* actors do not express themselves directly on this point, but insofar as the *onnagata* were expected to live like women, and since Sakata Tōjūrō, the specialist in lover's roles, always made a point of treating the *onnagata* in his company with great courtesy and kindness, as if they were real women, the tendency seems to have been to subscribe to the former view. When Tōjūrō says that the study of posture is all very well, but that he does not see the need for it, since all one has to do is to be realistic and then the posture will come naturally, he is surely saying that the actor should feel as does the character he is playing.   It is important, of course, not to overemphasize this with regard to Tōjūrō, for other anecdotes show him advocating the study of trades, standing at a shop doorway watching the preparation of foodstuffs, and planning his performances beforehand and holding rehearsals so as not to cause embarrassment to his colleagues by introducing new interpretations without warning. He seems in general, however, to have been an intuitive actor, as is instanced also by the occasion when he had to get into costume and try out his part before he could make up his mind whether a new play was worth putting on.   His alleged inability to teach points in the same direction.   But if the general tendency was toward sinking oneself in the part and acting intuitively, at least one actor seems to have made a specialist study of technique in a restricted field ; we refer to Kaneko Rokuemon, who gives very precise directions for the role of the wounded warrior, and who had obviously studied this intellectually and systematically, and had not relied upon being able to feel himself into the part.[29]

Most of the writers and those actors whose words are recorded in the *Analects* stress the importance of realism, and what they meant by this and how they sought to achieve it links up with the question discussed in the previous paragraph.   One type of realism on the present *kabuki* stage is concerned with everyday activities, like chopping radish, or filling a pipe. Whether this concern with meticulous accuracy existed in Gen-

---

[29] See *Dust in the Ears*, XXIV, p. 88.

roku *kabuki* is not certain. We suspect that much of it derives from the puppets, whose manipulators prided themselves—and still do—on their skill in making their charges perform such intricate tasks. When the puppet repertory was taken over by *kabuki*, the acting methods developed for the puppets were adopted too, and it is difficult to decide to what extent this sort of realism was in the *kabuki* before the influence of puppets became strong.[30] We have already mentioned Tōjūrō's habit of observing people at work in order to improve his performances. Another anecdote which deserves to be famous is the quarrel provoked by Arashi San'emon[31] in order to provide him with realistic dialogue and actions for a new play being worked up—an extreme measure foreshadowing the methods of the Actors' Studio.

What is certain is that *kabuki* had to some extent a didactic purpose. Part of the search for reality was linked with the desire to instruct the audience in good manners and good conduct, be it how to visit a brothel in elegant style, or how a warrior's wife should crush insolence or defend her young mistress from villainy, or the proper way of exacting revenge. For this purpose the aim was realistic exactness, although a certain amount of idealism necessarily intruded. We do not think that Western drama had this sort of purpose, and, certainly, in later times, there was no thought of instructing the lower orders in how to conduct themselves in polite drawing rooms, just as the spectator was hardly expected as a result of seeing a Shakespeare play to imitate the kings and lords of historical drama.

Both Japan and the West are faced with a dilemma with regard to the audience, even though the former seems to have expressed itself more clearly about it. This was the problem of reconciling the need to attract a large audience with the artistic

---

[30] See, however, *Dust in the Ears*, XVIII, p. 85.
[31] See *Dust in the Ears*, XXXI, p. 93.

conscience. Time and time again we read in the *Analects* that an
actor must not seek empty applause and cheap popularity. He
must try to attract the praise of other actors and not that of the
ignorant masses. Yet this was not some avant-garde theater
with small audiences, but had to have full public support to
survive. So when a rival theater was seen to be monopolizing
audiences, steps had to be taken, by putting on new plays, to
regain them. In other words, Genroku *kabuki* had to face the
same problem as any other drama that is run as a commercial
proposition—it had to find a middle way between the idealism of
the actors and writers and the practical necessity of attracting
the public. If we are to believe the accounts recorded in the
Analects, this was usually done by improving the quality of the
plays. We have some suspicion, however, that there was a
certain amount of wishful thinking involved, and that standards
were not so high as the writers would have liked their readers to
believe. The occasional references to vulgarity, to horseplay
at the end of a day's program, or at the end of a season, and the
practical joking of Nakagawa Kinnojō[32] all point in this direction.

Another difference between Genroku and modern *kabuki*
that would have made the former more familiar to Western audiences is that the plays were nearly all new. At that time,
therefore, the audience had a fresh interest in the plot as well
as in the acting, whereas today the latter is the sole point of
interest, the story being known to all. Furthermore, the actors
were not then helped (or hampered) by the rigid family
discipline which today defines within narrow limits how a role
should be played. Tōjūrō was accustomed to change his performance even during a run, and there was presumably a good
deal of improvisation. The position was, of course, changing,
and what are today typical discussions about the external dif-

---

[32] See *Sequel to " Dust in the Ears,"* XXIII, p. 120.

ferences between interpretations were already beginning, but the audiences must have derived a broader enjoyment from their theater-going than they do today, and one more like the pleasure a present-day Western audience can expect from a new play.

The system of role-types, however, may perhaps indicate two distinct ways of thought in East and West. Genroku *kabuki* actors kept to one sort of role, and if they changed, they did so with the intention of doing so once and for all, sometimes taking a new name as they did so in order to indicate the break with the past. The *Analects* is full of praise for this consistency and of blame for actors who try to chop and change. Much satisfaction is expressed at the failure of Ayame's attempt to abandon his women's roles. It is usually considered that the situation is different in the West and that actors are prepared to take many parts, but some reservations need to be made. The Japanese role-types include, of course, women's roles, and, in effect, sex imposes a more rigid division in the West between men's and women's parts than exists in *kabuki*. There have been a few female Hamlets, and Sarah Bernhardt played some male roles, but these exceptions are so rare that they do not affect the general pattern, and British pantomime dames and principal boys do not enter into this discussion. Physique, too, imposes itself, so that the normal Genroku *kabuki* career that started off with a period of playing young women's or boys' parts is comparable to that of a Western actor or actress who went on the stage at an early age. It might be argued, therefore, that in fact adult western actors, like those of Genroku *kabuki*, are either *onnagata* or *tachiyaku*, and so a sweeping statement that an actor in the West, unlike his Japanese colleague, is willing to take on any part is invalid.

Nevertheless, there is a good deal of difference between the two. The fact that Genroku *kabuki* actors thought it well, in order to achieve perfection, to live the sort of lives that were lived by the characters they played, indicates that their acting may be thought of as corresponding to that of what the West calls character actors, playing the same sort of role all the time, and in fact giving a portrayal that is only slightly an exaggeration of what they are themselves off-stage. The West, on the other hand, tends to reserve its highest praise for the great impersonators, who can apparently replace their real personalities by those of the characters they assume, putting on a new one for each role in the way that is necessary for one who aspires to play all the great Shakespeare parts.[33] Some modern *kabuki* actors approach this sort of virtuosity when they appear also in films and on television in parts that are quite different from their *kabuki* roles, but although Westerners may admire their versatility, the stern Japanese critics will find that their *kabuki* performance is impaired and praise those who keep to the narrow traditional path.

In any case, it is unfair to compare the Genroku *kabuki* and modern Western drama, if only because the range of roles available is much greater today. And in Genroku times, with runs so short, and play following play at such close intervals, it would have been intolerably uneconomical of time and effort for an actor to prepare a wide range of parts, even if they existed. The narrow specialization was as much imposed by current conditions as it was natural in a civilization where all artistic activities tend to be confined in watertight compartments. What seems clear, however, is that a Westerner looking at Genroku *kabuki* actors would not have mistaken them for anything else but actors, whereas he might not have known how to class, for example, those appearing in *nō* plays, which are much farther removed from any native Western drama than is *kabuki*.

---

[33] *The Words of Ayame*, XXIII (p. 62), indicates that Ayame at least could envisage a talent superior to that of the character actor.

The Actors' Analects

Preface

This book is a collection of teachings by actors known since days of old as famous for their skill, set down by men since dead.

One Hundred Items on the Stage, written down by the *kashagata* Sugi Kuhē, teacher of Sakata Tōjūrō I.

Mirror for Actors, written down by Tominaga Heibē, a playwright of old.

The Words of Ayame, the teachings of Yoshizawa Ayame I, set down by Fukuoka Yagoshirō.

Dust in the Ears, the teachings of skillful men, written down by Kaneko Kichizaemon.

Sequel to " Dust in the Ears," written down by Tamiya Kōon Shirogorō.

The Kengai Collection, Somekawa Jūrobē's account of his recollections, written down by Azuma Sanpachi, a playwright. Kengai is the posthumous name of Somegawa Jūrobē.

Sadoshima's Diary, the writing down of what were the requirements for actors ancient and modern by Renchi-bō. Renchi was the posthumous name of Sadoshima Chōgorō.

29

These seven writings are the secret traditions of actor families, but they have nevertheless been carved on blocks, and to them has been added as an appendix a list of merit of present-day actors in the Three Cities.

Late Autumn in 1776

Jishō at the sign of the figure 8.

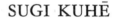

A. One Hundred Items on the Stage

SUGI KUHĒ

ITEM I

Nowadays when a *tachiyaku* turns his sword round[1] and threatens his enemy, it is but show and his heart is not in his sword-play. When he thus turns his sword-edge, he has in his heart only the thought of the praise the audience will give him. Thus it is not the enemy that he threatens with his blade; it is in effect turned towards the audience. Therefore, he does not respond to the actor playing his enemy, and, not having this element of reaction, his performance shows only weakness. It is a matter of working in partnership, and provided that one of them respects the other's performance, and his own is respected by the other, the scene is exactly right and thus naturally develops to a point at which the audience gasps with emotion. If an actor disregards those playing with him and seeks to win acclaim by himself alone, the success that he achieves is called *kojiate*.[2] The character 孤 (*ko*) means " one man " and 自 (*ji*), " by oneself." This must be avoided, avoided at all cost!

COMMENT: Kuhē here states two rules that will be found again and again throughout the Analects, *namely that the actor should not cultivate the audience*

*in order to win from it cheap praise, and that he should always consider himself
part of a team and not an individual. The strong tendency of critics of kabuki
at all periods to compare contemporary actors unfavorably with those of the
past is also evident.*

NOTES: 1. Turning the sword (lit. turning the cutting edge) was a
threatening movement of the sword, without removing it from its scabbard,
into a position from which it could be drawn and present its cutting edge to
the enemy.   2. *Kojiate* can be translated as " outrageous " but Kuhē
gives the word an imaginary etymology to fit in with his thesis, to suggest the
underlying meaning of success by individual effort.

ITEM II

Should the actor work on his acting technique both sleeping
and waking, and exert himself to the utmost at rehearsals, then
he will have no difficulty in putting out his best effort when he
appears on the stage.   The actor who puts his whole strength
into rehearsal will find that his performance, even though it
comes easily to him, will not be in the slightest degree inappropriate.   If he does not put his whole energy into rehearsal
and technique, and only gives out his full effort when on the
stage, his acting will undoubtedly seem laborious and inferior,
and the audience will very soon lose interest.   Indeed, what is
called the general rehearsal should be two days before the first
performance.   The day before this event should be spent in
complete rest, thinking over one by one those points which had
occurred in the general rehearsal of the day before, and thus
setting one's anxieties at rest.   By this means, the actor will be
relaxed on the opening day and will continue to be so, and there
will be no discrepancies in his performances.   But if he des-
perately rehearses all night through with great agitation at the
thought that next day is the first performance, it will inevitably
result that there will be a great deal of bad acting.   This item
is of the greatest importance.

COMMENT: *This idealistic advice links up with Item VIII of* Dust in
the Ears *in which Tōjūrō says that he learns his words during rehearsals, and*

then forgets them for the first performance. Actors felt that in order to give an artistic performance from the start, it was necessary to have made all one's decisions beforehand and be relaxed on the opening day. A comparison might be made with modern performances of kabuki, *in which very little attention is given in rehearsal to well-known plays, so that the opening performances are little better than dress rehearsals.*

ITEM III

The realism of a play springs from fiction; if a comic play is not based on real life, it is unnatural.

COMMENT: The authors of the various works in the Analects *were very fond of paradox, which was probably a widely used, if ineffective, didactic device. The sentiment of the second half of this Item is found again later, where it is said that it is easy enough to get laughs by senseless remarks, but that the best comic acting is based on real life. The first half is probably to be taken as signifying that it is inartistic to try to put what would now be called "photographic" reality onto the stage, but that an impression of reality is given by careful fictional writing. It may be an illustration of this point that it is often said that an* onnagata *gives a better indication of ideal feminine behavior than any woman possibly could!*

ITEM IV

Of those who act in plays, he who uses his whole heart is the one to be praised.

ITEM V

When an actor becomes outstanding, the hatred and evil words of those who have not achieved advancement can be compared to several hundred ants swarming round an earthworm; it is an extremely sordid sight. To bring himself to the level of a master performer he has polished his spirit and shown an excellence which is a measure of his innate qualities. If one joins a graft of sour persimmon[1] to a sweet persimmon tree, it is because one wishes to enjoy an earlier fruiting, but in fact it acquires the bad name of the sour sort. Should one graft a sweet persimmon to a sour, when it bears fruit it does not lose its flavor. It is impossible to know the quality of things from their first shoots, and so actors too should rely upon those with experience in their art and bear the image of the graft in their mind as they study; they will then acquire a glorious reputation.

COMMENT: *The general implication of this item is that necessary though a good teacher is (as is the stock to a graft), the fruit depends upon the pupil. So it is wrong to be envious of a successful fellow-student, whose success will have derived from his own innate ability.*

NOTE: 1. The epithet " sour " is not really applicable, for the *shibugaki* is the one that has the characteristic mouth-puckering, alum-like flavor of the persimmon that is not " sweet."

ITEM VI

Let us consider the sentiment of the various types of roles. The *keisei* places great importance on her rank and is of a fantastic disposition. The warrior's lady has a heart which pities those beneath her, and yet presents a fine appearance with her immediate reaction should she be spoken to frivolously. By portraying her thus one makes sure that she is seen to be a warrior's lady. All actors make it their first aim to fit in with other roles. In a performance in which this harmony does not exist, even though the actors be famous, the play does not achieve its desired effect. And so it sometimes happens, according to the disposition of the other actor, that the scene becomes hurried, and thus cooperation is difficult. The acting may have different artistic styles. Or it may be that it becomes hurried from being too well learned. Sometimes the pace is too leisurely. At others one is carried away by the tempo and there is a feeling of strain. Sometimes, however, even though there is a bad start, there is the possibility of retrieving the situation. At a moment of tragedy, it is unsightly for the wife of a warrior to raise her voice when weeping. Nor do men raise their voices

when they weep. As a man takes on years, he returns to fool-
ishness and thus cannot sometimes prevent himself from
weeping out loud. In the display of great grief, there is a way
of weeping that one does not show, and the way of weeping that
one stifles. The latter has regard to the fact that others are
watching, the former seems to show an unwillingness to recon-
cile oneself. Then again, when women take their lives or men
disembowel themselves, or when a wound is received, the acting
is at a higher pitch. Because the tension rises, the spoken words
in the earlier and later sections are not at the same level, and,
moreover, the voice has to grow weaker.

*COMMENT: This Item is in four parts, and would almost appear to be
four separate pieces run together. The first is concerned with the difference
between two types of female role. The second is on the often recurring theme of
the necessity for good team work between actors appearing together, and in
particular of maintaining an appropriate rhythm. The third is an analysis of
various ways of weeping, with the typically subtle example of the two sorts of
restrained weeping. The one that "one does not show" is used when events are
such that tears should surely come, but one does not show them because one still
refuses to accept defeat. The tears "that one stifles" are stifled merely for the
sake of decency and one's dignity. The good actor has to be able to express these
delicate differences. The fourth is an equally close observation of the voice of a
person weakened by a wound, with the two elements of increased tension arising
from the extreme circumstance, expressed in a higher pitch, and a feebleness
from loss of blood. It should be noted that women, when committing suicide, did
not use the man's method of disembowelling; stabbing in the throat was com-
monly used.*

ITEM VII

Not to take care over one's make-up and costume, for the
reason that the audience is small, is to do oneself harm. It would
be as if a courtesan at the top of her profession were still to attract
men even though she used no make-up. Or, to put it another
way, even though a courtesan be out of favor, when she dresses
in her finest clothes, men's hearts are still led astray in spite of

themselves. Then, if one asks another actor to take one's role in a play, or is asked to do so by another, for the deputy to take it that it will do him no harm if he plays the role without the expenditure of a great deal of energy is a great mistake. Should by any chance there be any part of the performance in which the deputy does better, even in the smallest detail, than the original actor, is it not a matter of wiping out a former shame? It is very regrettable, but true, that actors with the capability of taking major roles have, from one mistaken step at the beginning of their career, gone many leagues astray.

COMMENT: The courtesan referred to here is of course the real thing, not the keisei *of the stage. The position that she occupied in the artistic society of the time is well illustrated by the way in which her conduct is here given as an example of how an actor should carry on his profession. Just as a courtesan who for some reason is not attracting men at the moment does not give up her elegant attire, so an actor in a play that is not getting big audiences should not become negligent. In the second half of the Item, by "wiping out a former shame" is implied wiping out the shame of having been in the inferior position of having been asked to take over the other man's role. It was the sort of favor one would not ask of a senior, or even of an equal. One could do so of a junior or one of inferior skill and one might thus be giving him the chance of improving himself. If such a one does not seize such a chance if it offers he may be making the fatal mistaken step. In any case, an actor should always put out his best effort, regardless of audience reaction. Later pieces will show, however, that it is important, nevertheless, that a performance should have its moments of high achievement, with more subdued passages in between.*

We regret that the remaining items have become illegible through insect damage.[1]

NOTE: 1. This is almost certainly a comment by the publisher. We have mentioned elsewhere the survival of one other item (see p. 14), and the length and complex nature of Items VI and VII suggest that perhaps they really contain more than one item each. The following is the above-mentioned extra Item translated, numbered VIII in the translation for the sake of convenience.

ITEM VIII

For a young *onnagata* it is of the utmost importance that he should not lose his sexual attractiveness. Should it by some chance in the change of roles become necessary for him to play a *kashagata*, he should make sure that he shows some carelessness about his appearance and his wig, and indicates, quite clearly that his heart is not in it. To settle into the part, and be praised for one's close resemblance to an old woman is the beginning of the end as far as sexual attractiveness goes.

COMMENT: *This Item may run contrary to others which stress the necessity for teamwork and cooperation. It demonstrates, however, the overriding importance the actor, especially the* onnagata, *attached to complete absorption in his profession, to the extent that he should strive in every way he could to present a consistent image to the world.*

One Hundred Items on the Stage, the end.

B. *Mirror for Actors*

TOMINAGA HEIBĒ

ITEM I

It is the usual way that everything is affected by the passing of time, and the drama is especially prone to change with the years. Long ago, at the period when *kyōgen-zukushi*[1] were being played, there was a piece called *The* Rōnin *and the* Sake *Cup*, the plot of which follows.

A member of the household of Hagiyama, a *samurai* by the name of Kōsaka Uneme, is riding along on his horse to perform a mission for his lord, and admires the scenery as he goes. There follows a passage played as a *watari-zerifu*,[2] in which Uneme says " The residence yonder is the home of our master's future son-in-law,[3] so you must all proceed, once the boundary of his territory has been crossed, with correct etiquette. There must be no negligence from any of you." From each of his attendants comes a reply of agreement. From the effects room comes the sound of singing and playing in the *nō* style. He turns his horse back into its original direction[4] and as he goes grandly on his way there comes walking towards him a *rōnin*, wearing on his head a deep, woven hat.[5] He prostrates himself

38

in a doleful way before Uneme, but the attendants reprimand
him and shout that whoever he is he is unmannerly. They order
him to remove his hat and stand aside. He makes, however, no reply. The *samurai* accuse him again of impertinence
and want to go up to him but their lord says " Wait, men, wait !
I see that this man has prostrated himself before me, so he is
not completely without manners. However, I do not understand why he does not remove his hat. Now, you fellow !
You seem to have some purpose in coming before me—tell me
what sort of man you are, and what your business is with me."
The man bows low and replies : " I am overjoyed to see my
lord Uneme in good health. Formerly I was in receipt of your
kindness, but years have passed and now you will have forgotten the sound of my voice. When I heard that your lordship
was to pass this way today, I longed so much to see you that for
some time I have waited here, and while prostrating myself in
your horse's path have feared to show my face to you because I
am in disgrace. I feel ashamed and humbly beg your lordship's
forgiveness for this unmannerly headgear." As he listens to
these words Uneme thinks long and deeply and then addresses
him thus : " Haa, I remember now, you are Sir Todoroki
Ben'emon, who was once stationed with me. I too have fond
memories of you. Please excuse me for not dismounting, but I
am on an official journey.[6] I do not say that your hat is unmannerly, but I should like to see your face. If you refuse, there will
be no harm done, but come, take it off, I beg you. You can be
no other than Sir Ben'emon." " You have guessed correctly,
my lord. Indeed, this is Ben'emon, but come to this shameful
state," the other replies and removes his hat. " It is excellent
to see you safe after so long a time " says Uneme, and they
begin to relate the tale of the intervening years. " You were
sent into disgrace for a trifling thing. No day has passed but
that I spoke of you. How do you gain your living ? " he asks.
Ben'emon exclaims : " Oh, what gracious words ! Since I have

no master, the smoke barely rises morning and evening from my kitchen fire;[7] I use the *nō* singing[8] that I learnt in my old life, and with that I beg for my living. Even though I suffered bitter mortification at my dismissal, which was too severe a punishment, I have lived on up to now, placing my trust on what you said when you told me that my only course was to await the right moment. I am told that you are carrying out a mission for my lord and are acting as his representative. I feel that I am having an audience with my lord himself. It is something which I shall take away with me as a memory of this fleeting world. May you carry out your duties without the slightest incident! To take a long farewell would be a waste of your precious time, so I will straightway take my leave." Thus he moves to go on his way, with tears in his eyes. But Uneme says "Wait a moment. As you have said, today I am my lord's representative.[9] I will offer you the *sake* cup as a sign that shortly you will be relieved of your disgrace and will be re-established in your domain." The other exclaims in gratitude and once more prostrates himself. Uneme opens his fan, and uses it as a token cup for the moment, since he is on a journey on horseback. He commands his page to pour out the wine, and he too uses his fan as a wine-jar and mimes the pouring. Uneme makes a show of tasting. Then he extends it to Ben'emon and bids him drink. Ben'emon says "This is a sign of the depth of your kind feelings. Usually I do not drink, but let me partake in good measure." He mimes receiving the cup three times and drinking therefrom. "Time passes," he says, and as he rises to his feet, as if intoxicated by the wine his lord has given him, he staggers as he sings a song,[10] stammering out the praises of his native province and his thanks to his lord. Uneme sits on his horse, his face wet with tears, and leaves him: "Farewell, farewell."

This one act is said to have been a great success.

COMMENT: It is not clear whether the title of the whole play from which this was taken was The Rōnin and the Sake Cup *or whether it referred to the one act only. The play does not seem to have survived, but Gunji suggests that it dates from about 1665, a little over a decade after the resumption of* kabuki *after the ban of 1652. It is an interesting survival of a very simple type of play, with no properties required except a stage horse, a hat and fans. The name of the* rōnin *has a slightly comic ring, and might be rendered as Sir Benjamin Rattler. The conversation between the two principals has a certain sentimental tone implying that they were lovers in the past and that they still have fond memories. The erotic tone is to some extent a survival of the preceding period in* kabuki. *The next Item is a clearer example still.*

NOTES: 1. = *mono mane kyōgen zukushi* 物真似狂言尽. In 1652, *kabuki* was prohibited by the authorities because of the appearance on its stage of the boy players who had replaced the women actors in 1629. It was allowed to start again in 1653 under the name of *mono mane kyōgen zukushi*, with, as this name suggests, a drama with some claims to realism (instead of mere dances), and adult players. 2. *watari-zerifu* 渡りゼリフ (or *serifu-watari*)—a passage in which the members of a group divide the phrases of a speech between them, speaking them one after another; the last phrase is usually spoken by the group in unison. In this case the " reply of agreement " was presumably done in this style. 3. One must assume that Uneme is on some errand in connection with the marriage of his lord's daughter. 4. He had turned it round to speak to his men. 5. An *amigasa*, which irreverent Westerners liken to an inverted wastepaper basket. These were worn originally by a sect of bamboo-flute playing beggar-priests, but were adopted by *samurai* for purposes of disguise and incognito travel. 6. Since he is on an official errand for his lord his duty will not allow him to dismount until he reaches his destination. 7. He has hardly enough money to pay for fuel and food. 8. *Samurai* used to study *nō* singing as a polite entertainment fitting their station. *Nō* plays can be sung by one person without any action, just as the chanting that goes with puppet plays can be performed without the puppets. 9. He therefore can act for his lord. 10. *ko-uta* 小歌: probably here to be taken as a song from one of the *kyōgen* 狂言, comic interludes in *nō* plays, seeing that Ben'emon is a professional *nō* man. However, it might have been a popular song in the *ko-uta* style that was fashionable at the period.

ITEM II

In plays in former times the theme of male love very often occurred. Principal actors playing young men often received

larger salaries than those playing women. At that time homosexual love was the rage in all the quarters of the town. I here
record another old play. The title has been handed down as
Visiting the Family Shrine or something of the sort.

When the lord appears on his way to visit the family shrine,[1]
his entrance is in the form of a *roppō*.[2] After this a dance of the
progress and the pack-horses,[3] then a song of the period:[4]
" My lord's horses are chestnut, dappled and grey. When they
are struck they rear up like the painted moustache tips of the
Edo-reared man who holds the horse's mouth tight. The
curve of the moustache of the whiskered man, and the jingle of
harness from the curvetting horses! The spirited horses rear
and plunge, with jingle and jangle, jingle and jangle. They are
tethered and stilled, by the barrier notice against love." " Thank
you, one and all for your trouble. Rest, rest."[5] The retainers
prostrate themselves: " First, for my lord, repose in the
priests' quarters," and all go in, to the sound of singing. Some
yakko gaze at the view, and discuss the beauty of the young
men. " Yasanojō is best." " No, I've fallen for Tomoya."
Thus they are gossiping when a warrior emerges: " What
are you chattering about? Just one more word out of you about
my lord's beloved . . . "; thus does he upbraid them. They
cry out in alarm[6] and flee with not one glance behind them.
" The priests and priestesses are starting their *kagura;* a
kagura,"[7] shouts the warrior and goes within. Thereupon
Yasanojō emerges, and facing the shrine claps his hands in
worship.[8] He prays for his lord and country, and for everlasting
military fortune. As he does so the tea-expert[9] Chinsai stands
behind him, pulls at his sleeve and says in a low voice: " Let
me tell you something for your own good. You have been
imagining that my lord's love has been directed to yourself
alone but recently his nose-hairs have been growing especially
in Tomoya's direction.[10] He said that he had an errand for me
and sent me to the priest. The reason for this order was that

when I had gone Tomoya and the lord were planning to make love to each other. Look out for yourself," he says, and having thus stirred up some trouble he runs off on his errand. Yasano-jō flies into a rage, exclaiming: " How I hate that rascal Tomoya; I am mad with fury." As he utters these words, the lord calls out to him from within. Then a crowd of retainers emerge, and the lord himself appears from back-stage, and orders Tomoya to call Yasanojō but the latter makes no reply. When the lord sees this, he cries " Come here! Here, I say!" and he takes his hand and pulls him toward him. Yasanojō says not a word, but gazes into his lord's face, then suddenly shakes himself free and goes off by the *hashigakari*. " What's that about, the rogue's gone off," the lord says, and calling his sandal-boy[11] he asks him what he thinks Yasanojō is about, but the sandal-boy too looks into the lord's face, shakes himself free and takes himself swiftly off. In the same way he calls out each of his retainers in turn and puts the question to them, but all likewise shake themselves free and go off. " Well, this is a mystery. All I have left is my pack horse," so he pulls this horse to him. " Now, horse, what do you think is the reason for Yasa's suddenly leaving me?" he asks, but the horse, too, looks at his master's face and goes off. With that the curtain is drawn. Thinking of it now, it seems stupid that such a piece was a great success, but the audiences at the time thought that such plays were amusing, and the actors took a great deal of trouble over learning and playing in them.

COMMENT: Apart from its background in the current morals of the warrior class, a theme which has now virtually disappeared from the kabuki stage, this play has several interesting elements. The whole atmosphere tends toward the comic, with the exaggerated dancing of the yakko attendants, the horse, which seems to have been more like a British pantomime-horse than the elegant animals of present-day kabuki, and the indignity to which the lord is exposed at the end. This last ingredient makes one think of the comic interludes in nō programs, where the humiliation of a stupid lord is a constantly re-

curring theme. One can only think with Heibē that audiences were fairly un-complicated if such a piece as this was a great success.

NOTES : 1. Families in Japan often have a Shintō god as a protector, and will frequently visit his or her shrine. 2. Spectacular dance steps. See Appendix I. 3. When a lord made a ceremonial journey, he travelled with a retinue with litters and pack-horses. This scene must have turned such a progress into a dance. Probably it was a sort of comical *yakko* dance. 4. This song is also presented in a collection dated 1704, and survives in the repertory of some dance schools. See Gunji, p. 422, n. 3. The words show a characteristic involuted pattern, in which the separate phrases are connected phonetically rather than logically, and the song would be appreciated for its ingenuity. Its *shamisen* music was in the lively style obtained by raising the pitch of the 2nd string (*ni-agari* 二上り). Moustaches were painted on as part of the make-up. 5. These are the lord's words. 6. Our text here differs by one syllable from Gunji's. 7. 神楽, dances performed at Shintō shrines. 8. The correct way of calling a god's attention is to clap one's hands. 9. The word we have translated by " tea-expert " is *sadō* 茶道, which is here short for *sadō-bōzu*, otherwise *cha-bōzu* 茶(道)坊主. They were minor officials in warrior's households, with responsibility for the whole organization of ceremonial tea-drinking. They were also used for confidential personal business by their masters and often appear in *kabuki* in a sort of *yakko* role, as petty intriguers. 10. I.e., his eyes have been straying towards Tomoya. 11. The page who carried his lord's footwear when he was riding in a litter, etc.; another minor confidant.

ITEM III

1656. At that time, in Kyoto, there was a regulation against the wearing of hair in the long court style[1] by *onnagata*. Nevertheless one *onnagata*, Hashimoto Kinsaku by name, appeared on the stage with this hair style and, in addition, quarrelled in a box[2] with a member of the audience and drew his short sword. As a result of this offense, the closure of all *kabuki* theaters in Kyoto, without exception, was ordered.

On account of this ban, Murayama Matabē[3] appeared at the magistrate's office for more than ten years to petition for forgiveness for the theater. However, the prohibition was not lifted, and Matabē did not return to his lodgings, but camped out in front of the office and appeared every day to make his request. He was exposed to the rain and the dew, and his *kimono* and *hakama*[4] were torn and ruined, he grew thin and exhausted, so that he no longer had the appearance of a human being. During this time many of the theater apprentices and the actors became merchants or craftsmen, and also a large number of them went off into other provinces to earn their living as peddlers and the like. The few remaining boys and actors all contributed money and took food along to the front of the office and fed Matabē. However, the ban on the theater lasted for thirteen years; pardon was granted in 1668 and performances were started again on the first day of the third month. The play was one relating to *keisei*. The day was unpropitious[5] and the play would have been stopped for this reason, but bearing in mind that there is no bad day for doing a good thing, they pushed on with the opening. Since it was a thirteen years' prohibition that was being remitted, the crowds of spectators thronged to an extent which it is difficult to put into words. This was a great feat by Murayama, for which he was deserving of great honor from actors of later times.

COMMENT: *This is a fine story, fit to inspire young actors to devote themselves to their profession, but unfortunately it seems to be a considerable exaggeration of the truth. The quarrel in the box did indeed take place; the theaters in Kyoto were closed, but it was possible to persuade the authorities to allow them to reopen within a few months, on condition that the boxes were removed, and that no alcohol was served to the audience; see Gunji, p. 422, n. 3 and 4.*

The prohibition of sagegami *does not appear to be documented. It is possible, however, that it was something special to Kyoto, where the emperor had his palace, for this hair style was used by the court ladies, and it may have been thought inappropriate for actors to adopt it. Another possibility that Gunji suggests is that the reference is to a prohibition in 1656 of plays about the Shimabara brothel district in Kyoto, which included a ban on wigs.*

This Item, if nothing else, serves to illustrate the difficult relations that managements had with the authorities. Ernst has a useful account of the control exercised by officials.

NOTES: 1.   *sagegami* 下げ髪, a style in which the hair was bunched at the back and then hung straight down; a floor-length pony tail.   2.   *sanjiki* (*sajiki*) 桟敷, a raised side-box.   See Appendix I.   3.   He was the senior *ẕamoto* in Kyoto.   4.   Sort of divided skirt, still worn with Japanese dress on formal occasions.   5.   According to the Chinese-style astrologers.

ITEM IV
KEISEI *PLAYS*

These used to have special customs different from those that reign today.   The following is the construction of one sort of play that dates from that time.   A prologue appears on the stage, and announces that the visit to the *keisei* is about to begin. The *tachiyaku* Muramatsu Hachirobē is the client, and his costume is white Kaga-silk[1] with an all-over silver decoration of a wasp stinging a deer's antlers.[2]   He wears a one foot seven inch short sword with its scabbard almost falling out in front. His left hand is on his hip, and from his right dangles a fan which he holds by the rivet.   He comes slowly out from the *hashi-gakari*, and standing in the center of the stage he utters the following speech:

" By Hachiman,[3] I am going to my girl."

As he speaks he strikes the hilt of his sword with his fan. The whole audience exclaims in admiration that this is a really fine actor for such a role, and the buzz of voices goes on for some while.   In time there appears from the small exit left,[4] the landlord of an *ageya*,[5] wearing an old pale blue *hakama* and waggling his behind, a cloth tucked into his belt and holding a shell-ladle.[6]   " What, master, have you arrived? " he says. At this the audience all laugh and say "Ah, the landlord's appeared.   Just look at his face.   How comical."   So loud are the guffaws that he cannot carry on with the next speech.   After a while the laughter subsides and Hachirobē says " What, hasn't the Tayū[7] come yet? "   " She's already on her way," says the landlord and peers along the *hashi-gakari*.   " He's just said that she'll soon be here; that means that the *keisei* is going to appear."

The audience all sit as upright as they can, and now gaze in silence at the curtained entrance to the *hashi-gakari*. Then out comes the courtesan, clad in fantastic costume. It is gold brocade. At that time, *onnagata* only occasionally wore wigs; usually they tied paper up into a *hyōgo-wage*.[8] She comes out alone[9] and says " So you have come, big spender " and he greets her with joy. She and her rich client take each other by the hand, further laughter. They give an accurate performance of all the actions of greetings in the parlor and for this are cheered mightily. Now the landlord circulates the *sake* cups and as he utters his speech, " Madam, we beg, please, a dance from you to go with the drinks," some musicians immediately arrange themselves on the stage, and the *keisei* performs her dance.

There are many plays such as I have described above but I have not included any more because they are so many and all alike.

COMMENT : *This piece is not strictly drama, and hardly more than a demonstration of how a dashing hero comports himself when out on a spree. The audience was delighted to be able to study the correct behavior in such circumstances. One imagines that the men found considerable vicarious pleasure in seeing their hero enjoy himself in an activity which they could probably not afford themselves. Perhaps the respectable women liked to see a world which was otherwise closed to them. In any case, there was an immense curiosity to know what went on in the gay quarters. It may be wondered if such a scene might have overt erotic elements, other than those in the mind of the audience, but it is doubtful if there were any at this period. The actors do take each other by the hand, an act which might have seemed quite erotic at the time, but this was probably as far as it went. The great numbers of erotic prints that were produced in Japan, however, indicate that it was discretion rather than disinclination that was the restraining influence.*

NOTES : 1. A fine silk material woven in the province of Kaga 加賀, the present Ishikawa prefecture. White was at the time a smart color, especially for brothel-visiting, for which a white horse was also appropriate. 2. This motif symbolizes toughness and immunity from pain. 3. A Shintō god. His name is here used to testify to the truth of the following statement. 4. *okubyōguchi* 臆病口, one of several names of the small exit on stage left,

opposite the *hashi-gakari*.   5. House of assignation, where the client
sought his entertainment and summoned the *keisei* to him.   6. Ladle
made by fixing a clam shell to a stick.   The landlord had been busy in the
kitchen.   7. Here perhaps merely a polite term of address or reference to
a *keisei*.   8. *hyōgowage* (*hyōgomage*) was a hair-style with two side-lobes and
a rising queue that was popular with prostitutes in the 17th century and
later.   It seems that *onnagata* often tied paper up into the shape of this style,
since there were various prohibitions against attached hair.   The paper in
question (*hana-gami*, written 花紙, " flower paper " as a more elegant homo-
phone of 鼻紙, " nose paper ") was of the kind without which nobody stirred
in traditional Japan.   It was used for all sorts of hygienic purposes, and with
keisei could have a special erotic significance.   9. Just why she should
come out on stage alone is rather a mystery, for *keisei* were usually accompanied by a considerable retinue when going to the *ageya*.   It is possible that
it was here a sign of special intimacy, or just that the piece was not realistic
to that extent.

Mirror for Actors, the end.

C. The Words of Ayame

Set down by
FUKUOKA YAGOSHIRŌ

INTRODUCTION
The Great Yoshizawa was the most highly skilled *onnagata* of the past and present, so I have enquired and set down what he told various people on the subject of *onnagata* acting, and also what I heard from him myself. I have written this down and have named the thirty items[1] which this comprises *The Words of Ayame*. They should be taken as a guide to the art, kept strictly secret and not divulged to a soul. The items now follow.

COMMENT: The secret tradition, the confidential information passed on only to chosen pupils, or those who have qualified in some way, formed, and to some extent still forms, a great part of the instruction in Japanese artistic pursuits. It is, of course, not restricted to Japan, but also had its place in medieval Europe.

NOTE: 1. This total includes the introduction.

ITEM I
A certain *onnagata* asked the Great Yoshizawa how best to prepare oneself for the profession. His reply was that if an

onnagata made a success of a *keisei* role, all others were easy to perform. The reason for this is that, since he is basically a man, he possesses, by his nature, a faculty of strong action, and he must carefully bear in mind the softness of the *keisei* and her feminine charm. Thus, the greatest attention should be paid to the training for *keisei* roles.

COMMENT: *At this time kabuki was not portraying respectable merchants' wives and maidens, and the most feminine of the* onnagata *roles was the* keisei. *Others, such as the warrior's wife and elderly woman, although feminine, were less distant from the male characteristics.*

ITEM II

Karyū used to write his name with the characters 香竜 (" perfumed dragon "), but Yoshizawa was of the opinion that the character 竜 (" dragon ") was too strong for the name of an *onnagata*, and Karyū changed the way he wrote it to 歌流 (" song stream "). This Karyū on one occasion asked about dramatic techniques. Yoshizawa replied: " In the case of the wife of an elder counsellor threatening an enemy, the actor has in mind that she is the wife of a *samurai*, and so always has her place her hand on her sword in a haughty fashion. To play her as too bold in the handling of a sword, when, for all that she is a *samurai*'s wife, she does not normally wear such a weapon, is bad acting. The best way to portray her is that she should not be afraid of her sword. To have her indulge in argument, and challenge her adversary, striking the stage, and slapping her hand to her sword-hilt, is as if she were a *tachiyaku* wearing a cap." I believe that the master often made this remark.

COMMENT: *The boy actors who had replaced the women of the* kabuki *stage wore their hair long in a feminine style, and did not shave off their front hair as men were accustomed to do. In 1652, it became obligatory to shave off the front hair. Wigs were unknown at the time, and until their invention,* onnagata *and actors playing* wakashu *parts used to cover this unsightly bald patch with a cloth, often of purple color. In fact, it became so much a part of the characteristic costume of these roles that the caps were worn even over wigs. In Kyoto the custom persisted, mainly among* waka-onnagata, *at least until the end of the seventeenth century. See Shaver, Fig. 136.*

The hints on playing warrior's wives follow naturally on those in Item I, and also show the typical subtlety of Ayame's analysis of the onnagata *roles, which is continued in Item III.*

ITEM III

One of Yoshizawa's utterances was that in *onnagata* playing, her outward appearance should be coquettish, but her heart chaste. And to make a *samurai*'s wife unfeminine just because she is a *samurai*'s wife is bad acting. When one is playing the role of a strong-minded woman, one must see that her heart has some softness.

ITEM IV

One evening, Arashi San'emon II was with the Great Yoshizawa, and when *tororo*[1] was served, Yoshizawa would not take any. San'emon said that an *onnagata* had to have this sort of devotion, and was most impressed. Apparently he apologized, saying that it was a mistake to behave night and day in the way that gave one most comfort. Later San'emon met the Great Kataoka[2] and said that the reason why Ayame was called a master was because his devotion to duty was so deep.

COMMENT: We have here the first of Ayame's famous rules of conduct for onnagata. *From a practical point of view, it is obviously more efficient for an actor specializing in female roles to keep up his impersonation in his daily life, and the effect on those who met him offstage was to increase their admiration for his artistry. The tendency for Japanese artistic professions to be in water-tight compartments was also strengthened by such single-mindedness.*

NOTES: 1. *Tororo(jiru)* とろろ汁 is a jelly-like preparation made from sweet potatoes. It is unladylike to eat it because it has to be sucked into the mouth with some noise. Torigoe has also heard a suggestion from Professor Kawatake Shigetoshi that its use in male lovemaking would make it unsuitable for Ayame to eat. 2. Kataoka Nizaemon.

ITEM V

Jūjirō said that women keep their right knee upright when half-kneeling,[1] and men their left, and that it is the same when they start walking.[2] This is what he taught his pupils, but the Great Yoshizawa told him on one occasion when they were alone that although this was in fact the case, it depended upon the look of the thing, and one should not raise the knee that is on the side of the audience. If one went only by consistency, it would not be *kabuki*. It is probably good, after all, to make a mixture of half realism and half imagination. After that Jūjirō too considered the look of the thing.

COMMENT: *There is a tendency even today in* kabuki *circles to attach a great deal of importance to apparently meaningless consistency, and to criticize those who depart from it merely because they do so, without consideration of artistic effect. It is refreshing to find Ayame attacking this narrow view, and telling Jūjirō, in private, of course, so as not to embarrass him before others, to consider the general look of the thing.*

NOTE: 1. I.e., with one leg in the kneeling position, and the other with the part from the knee to the foot upright.   2. Women moved their right foot first when starting to walk, and men their left.

ITEM VI

" What should happen when a *samurai*'s wife takes her short sword and lays about her? When she is surrounded by a large force, in a scene, for example, where she protects her lord's daughter, the *samurai*'s wife should, unlikely though this may seem, be able to handle her sword more skillfully than a man can. When her loyal heart realizes the seriousness of the situation, it is then that above all she is a warrior's wife. The challenging of one playing the role of her enemy, in the drawing room, is not the same as facing the final crisis, and there I should like her handling of her sword to be much more calm than in the other situation." This advice I heard him give to Tamagashiwa, because his performance in a scene when he was beset by a large force of the enemy left something to be desired.

COMMENT : *It must be realized that* kabuki *was developing from the crude sort of performance described in* Mirror for Actors *towards a much greater subtlety. Ayame was among the first in the* kabuki *world to attempt to formulate into words the sort of thing that this implied, as we see here in the distinction he draws between a warrior's wife's use of the sword in different circumstances. Her unrealistic skill when protecting her lord's daughter can be taken as representing the intensity of her emotion.*

ITEM VII

The *onnagata* role has its basis in charm, and even one who has innate beauty, if he seeks to make a fine show in a fighting scene, will lose the femininity of his performance. Or again, if he tries deliberately to make his interpretation elegant, it will not be pleasing. For these reasons, if he does not live his normal life as if he was a woman, it will not be possible for him to be called a skillful *onnagata*. The more an actor is persuaded that it is the time when he appears on the stage that is the most important in his career as an *onnagata*, the more masculine he will be. It is better for him to consider his everyday life as the most important. The Master was very often heard to say this.

ITEM VIII

The confrontation of an enemy might very well be thought of as something that the *onnagata* would like to avoid in a play, but should the occasion arise when it is impossible to refuse, one has to take the part. When the enemy is confronted and victory is achieved, the audience will praise the *onnagata* and say " Well acted indeed ! " It is only natural that they should rejoice when the hated enemy is confronted by the *onnagata* with her supposed weakness, but for the actor to be carried away by this and become over-fond of the acclaim of the audience and want to repeat the performance over and over again is, for the *onnagata*, the road to ruin. Such a one will surely finish up by not following the true path of artistry.

COMMENT: Items VI, VII and VIII should be taken together as a state-
ment of Ayame's views in the difficulties of reconciling femininity with ability
with a sword. His basic attitude seems to be expressed in VII, namely that
sword-play and the womanly character are incompatible. Nevertheless, war-
rior's ladies must from time to time demonstrate this unfeminine skill, and the
care Ayame devoted to this type of role shows how difficult he felt it to be. In
VIII he sees the danger of an onnagata *being carried away by success in fighting*
scenes and being tempted to specialize in them. But just as a real woman
would lose her charm if she devoted all her time to military exercise, so an
onnagata *will lose his integrity if he does the same on the stage.*

ITEM IX

Among the things that I heard Ayame say to Jūjirō was
this: " My friend, I congratulate you upon the popularity that
you are enjoying from your audiences, but you must give up any
deliberate attempt to make them laugh. You should allow the
provocation of their laughter to come naturally from the action.
Trying to make audiences laugh is no part of womanly feeling."
Jūjirō's attitude showed that he was somewhat angry at this, but
when he met me later he said that he thought Ayame was the
protective deity of the *onnagata*'s profession.

COMMENT: A theme mentioned in VIII is further treated, and is one of
the characteristic injunctions of the authors of the Analects. *At all costs, one*
must not go after cheap popularity. For an onnagata *to seek applause by*
unwomanly acting activity such as sword-play or arousing laughter is a betrayal
of the art.

ITEM X

For one who is an *onnagata* to say that he might just as well
become a *tachiyaku* is to pile shame upon shame. One who says
that he might just as well change from an *onnagata* to a *tachiyaku*
cannot help being a bad *onnagata*. One who changes to *tachiyaku*
parts and does badly at them should do well when acting as an
onnagata. This is what Ayame always said, and indeed when he
became a *tachiyaku*[1] he was in fact no good. I have come to the

conclusion that this is because essentially there can be no person who can be both a man and a woman.

NOTE: 1. This occurred in 1721. In 1723 he went back to *onnagata* parts.

ITEM XI

If one who is an *onnagata* gets the idea that if he does not do so well in his chosen career he can change to a *tachiyaku*, this is an immediate indication that his art has turned to dust. A real woman must accept the fact that she cannot become a man. Can you imagine a real woman being able to turn into a man because she is unable to endure her present state? " If an *onnagata* thinks in that way," he used to say, " he is ignorant of a woman's feelings." How right the Master was!

ITEM XII

There is an *onnagata* role of the wife of a senior official who appears before her lord and delivers a judgment in place of her husband. At all costs, this should be played without making her too strong a figure. To do so would be like an actor in the role of a male senior official wearing a woman's cap.[1] This does not mean that just because she is the wife of an elder official she should be completely at ease before a number of people engaged in discussion. She might be so tensed up by this that her whole body is shaking, but if an enemy should come and hurl terrible insults at her, then she should stiffen herself and react. When it comes to situations of this sort, a woman has more that she wants to say than a man. However, in this case, he used to say, the play should be in a somewhat less natural style.

NOTE: 1. And thus appearing effeminate (see Item II).

ITEM XIII

The *onnagata* should make it a principle not to depart from

the conduct of a virtuous woman.   In this respect he should
be willing to accept the standards of a real woman.   However
popular a play might promise to be, he should refuse to take part
in it.[1]   This is the most important sort of occasion when an
onnagata might criticize his part.   This was part of Ayame's
advice to his young actors.

COMMENT :   *This can be taken as another example of the sentiment expressed
in Item IX, but at the same time it introduces a new element into the relation
between conduct on and off the stage, already touched on in Item VII.   Now,
not only must the* onnagata *live his life by feminine standards, but also he must
carry his impersonation of a modest woman onto the stage.   It should be noted
that virtue is perfectly reconcilable with the status of* keisei.   *In the first place,
the virtuous* keisei *did not usually choose her profession, or if she did, it was not
because she liked it, but for some reason of loyalty, to save a father or husband
from poverty or worse; then, she pursued her profession according to rules of
loyalty and decency.   There was all the difference in the world between a* keisei
and an adulterous wife.   All the same, Ayame's insistence that the onnagata
*should only accept virtuous roles forms a contrast with the professionalism of an
actor in the Western theater, in which the consideration might rather be whether
a role was dramatically satisfying.*

NOTE: 1.   I.e., if the new role might in some way be incompatible with
the conduct of a virtuous woman.

ITEM XIV

The *shosagoto* is the flower of *kabuki* and *jigei* is the fruit.   To
think that only *shosagoto* is likely to entertain and therefore not to
exert oneself in the presentation of *jigei*, would be like caring only
for flowers and not for the bearing of fruit.   There was the case
of Tatsunosuke who was, it is admitted, very skillful, but who,
Ayame thought, was deficient in ability in this respect.   He also
often criticized young *onnagata*, saying that the reason for the
appearance of flowers is the production of fruit, and that they
should make sure of fine flowers by careful preparation of the
ground.

COMMENT: *This is a complicated image based on the three words* hana 花,
ji 地 *and* mi 実. *Hana, " flower," is a word often used in aesthetic criticism.*
Zeami made great play with it in his works on nō, *but the use here is rather*
that found in some works on poetry, where a distinction is made between hana
and mi, *where the second word has the meaning of " fruit," " ripening " and*
also " reality." The distinction between flower and fruit is thus taken as that
between the flowering of the imagination, *i.e. non-realistic treatment, and*
realism. *The former is taken as the quality of the older style of performance,*
a non-realistic performance based on the dance, called here shosagoto; *the*
latter is that of the more recently developed jigei, *or* ji-kyōgen, *" earthy plays,"*
which were more like realistic drama. The image is further developed by the
advantage offered by using the word ji *in its sense of ground, in the last sentence*
of the translation. The object of this piece of virtuosity is to demonstrate the
interdependence of the two styles—no fruit without flower, no flower without
groundwork. See also Item X of Sadoshima's Diary.

ITEM XV

Ayame often used to say that playing with Tōjūrō was like
sailing smoothly along in a great ship. When with Kyōemon,
he was tensed up and had to pour out his energy. When
San'emon was his partner, Ayame had to pull him along, otherwise he showed a tendency to be off in his timing.

COMMENT: *Gunji points out that San'emon II died in 1701, and that this*
year was therefore the last in which Ayame could have played with him. That
year, Tōjūrō was in his fifty-fifth year, Kyōemon in his fiftieth and San'emon in
his forty-first. Ayame was twenty-nine, and even allowing for the early de-
velopment of onnagata *actors, it is a sign of his genius that he was able to*
act on an equal standing with these senior players.

ITEM XVI

An actor who thinks that all is well, provided only that he
himself makes a hit, regardless of whether the people he acts with
suffer thereby, is the same as a person who lives at his ease,
buying fine furniture and equipment, having acquired his house
without paying for it, and borrowing money without repaying
it. The man who has lent money to him is bound to be exceed-

ingly angry, and those who share the stage with a selfish actor are made to appear inferior. Ayame said that instances had occurred of actors having their whole career completely ruined by such an actor.

ITEM XVII

Samanosuke[1] said that, as in playing football,[2] one should pay great attention to passing to one's fellow player. In rejoinder, Ayame said that it was difficult to do the same in acting as in football. When one seeks to avoid upsetting the performance of the other actors, the result is that one is unable to aim at one's own success. Provided that one puts out all one's energy in an effort to improve one's ability, even though one does not achieve a great individual success, it is still possible that the cast as a whole will win acclaim.

COMMENT: *Items XVI and XVII need to be considered together if only because if taken separately they appear contradictory. It is characteristic of the style of the secret tradition that two extremes are both found equally undesirable, without the desirable mean being particularized. In these two Items the extremes of selfish acting and over-consideration for others are both blamed— the implied, and partly expressed, correct course of action being that an actor should pay due regard to his colleagues, but that an excessive subjection of his own interests to theirs can be equally bad. These sentiments may not seem particularly original today, but they are nonetheless true, and Ayame was among the first in Japan to express them.*

NOTES: 1. See Okada Samanosuke.   2. A game of ceremonious nature with a long history in Japan, and popular with the merchants at this time, in which the object was to keep the ball in the air.

ITEM XVIII

Ayame related how from the days of his childhood he was installed in the Dōtombori district.[1] He acquired the name of Ayanosuke and then came under the patronage of Tachibanaya Gorozaemon. This gentleman was a landed *samurai* from the neighborhood of Kameoka[2] in Tamba and was well-to-do. He was a person whose family line went back a considerable way, and an accomplished *nō* performer. Ayame's employer at the time was a *shamisen* player in the theater, and at a time when Ayame was being urged to devote his energies to this instrument, he was also strongly advised to profit by the fact that Gorozaemon used to come and visit him, to learn *nō*. So Ayame asked him two or three times to give him lessons, but Gorozaemon would not consent and said that he should study hard at *onnagata* acting. The reasons he gave for not teaching him were that until he should achieve general recognition at this, it would be wrong for him to do anything else. If his attention was turned to the *nō*, his ambitions towards performances in his true field would probably be diverted. Moreover, if he insisted on learning *nō*, it would have a bad effect upon his *kabuki* work. This is because his acting would become leisurely. In addition, would he not develop a tendency to give dance pieces derived from the *nō*? When he had thoroughly mastered the art of the *kabuki* dance, as well as that of the *onnagata*, if he still wanted to attempt the *nō*, he might do as he pleased. Later, under the patronage of Gorozaemon, he left his employer, and became a special pupil of San'emon. As such, he appeared at the same time as Yoshida Ayame, and it often happened that he was outshone by Yoshida. However, the latter learned a little about *nō* from a gentleman named Hokkokuya, and frequently sought to make a success of *shosagoto* based on *nō* plays, whereas Yoshizawa still struggled along with realistic pieces. After a while his name became known, while Yoshida could find no one to appear with him, and has now abandoned the profession. Yoshizawa could now see how much to the point were the words of Gorozaemon. He could not forget his kindness, and took for " house-name "[3] his name of Tachibanaya; he also told me in secret that he was given Gorōzaemon's nickname[4] of Gonshichi.

COMMENT: *The Item itself needs no explanation, because it is quite clear about the dangers of contamination of* kabuki *by* nō. *The relations between*

Ayame and his patron are of interest, since they show that what might be judged an unhealthy connection could also be of great use to the young man concerned if his patron was a good man.

NOTES: 1. Still one of the theater districts of Osaka but formerly also the haunt of prostitutes of both sexes.   2. A town to the west of Kyoto. 3. *Kamei* (家名) is equivalent to *yagō* 屋号, originally a sort of trade mark, still used by merchants.   Actors in the *kabuki* theater have always included a *yagō* among their names.   4. *Kaena* 替名, a sort of nickname used out of discretion in brothels, restaurants, etc.

ITEM XIX

When playing against an actor of little skill, the true artist's aim should be to make his companion's deficiencies appear as qualities.

ITEM XX

" Once, when I called to see Nizaemon, Sampachi[1] turned to me and said ' I don't know how you will take my saying this, but I think that it would be a good thing if you were to go to Shimmachi[2] and see what the *tayū*[3] are like. Their style has changed considerably in the last five years and the way you play them is as they were five years ago.   It is true that their ways are nowadays considerably inferior to what they were formerly, but the audiences are all seeing them as they are today and I hear that there is a lot of talk among them about whether the way you play them is as they actually are or not.'   In reply to this I said ' I am very glad to have your comments, but I think that it is good for a *tayū* to be a person of superior elegance.   If there has occurred so great a change within the mere space of five years, then they must have been of surpassing elegance twenty years ago.   I am really grateful for your excellent advice.   I should like to go further back than five years and portray them as they were twenty years ago.   It is good that *keisei* should be of the old style and somewhat fantastic.   Teashop girls and bath girls should be played as over-modern.   This is the only way to understand these roles.' When I said this, Nizaemon said that he liked my use of the term ' over-modern ' for teashop and bath girls." Ayame gave me the above account of this conversation.

COMMENT: *This slightly peevish Item shows that Sampachi knew his man when he apologized before giving Ayame advice. It also shows that Ayame was not interested in portraying* keisei *as they were, but as an ideal type. Teashop girls worked in restaurants which were often houses of assignation as well, and bath girls were of low reputation, adding to their profession that of unorganized prostitute. These Ayame did not idealize, but suggested that they be portrayed naturalistically.*

NOTES: 1. See Azuma Sampachi. 2. A brothel district in Osaka, established c. 1630. 3. *tayū* 太夫, the top rank of organized prostitute, of which there were thirty in Shimmachi in 1702, the greatest number in the " Three Cities."

ITEM XXI

" If a piece of acting comes off successfully three times in a row," he once said to his young pupils, " the actor loses his skill." This would seem to mean that the actor would be unwilling to depart from the successful pattern, and the performance would lose its freshness.

COMMENT: *This refers to successive plays with similar plots rather than a long run. Ayame does not mention another aspect of this which we know today, when actors fear to become " type-cast " and lose the chance of more varied employment; but then his thoughts are always based on artistic considerations.*

ITEM XXII

The *onnagata* should continue to have the feelings of an *onnagata* even when in the dressing room. When taking refreshment, too, he should turn away so that people cannot see him. To be alongside a *tachiyaku* playing the lover's part, and chew away at one's food without charm and then go straight out on the stage and play a love scene with the same man, will lead to failure on both sides, for the *tachiyaku*'s heart will not in reality be ready to fall in love.

COMMENT :   Once again the theme is that the onnagata *should play his role offstage as well as on.   There is also the hint that the* tachiyaku *cannot be expected to act the lover really successfully unless the* onnagata *is capable of inspiring him with love at all times.*

ITEM XXIII

" Should an *onnagata* be concealing the fact that he is married, and people talk about his wife, he should feel like blushing, otherwise he should not be performing *onnagata* roles, and will not make his way in the profession.   An actor who, regardless of the number of children he has, still keeps a child's heart is a born genius," said Ayame.

COMMENT: There is an apparent contradiction between this Item and the preceding one, but it is probably only a matter of degree.   Ayame seems to be accepting what must often have happened, namely that onnagata *married and begot children.   They should, however, keep this side of their life away from the theater, and he thinks that a father, with all the experience of life that this state implies, who still portrays a naive female with conviction, is indeed an acting genius.*

ITEM XXIV

Ayame said, " Recently, I went to Tennōji[1] to see the flower arrangement festival, and there were indeed many unusual flowers of various kinds to be seen there.   However, it is now the season when plum-blossoms are at their best.   The people who had gone to see the festival found nothing remarkable about the plum-blossoms, but at the sight of rare blooms which they could not have known about they clapped their hands and were attracted by their novelty.   Yet the only part that drew my interest was where there were some excellent arrangements of plum-blossoms.   I was filled with admiration for the skill with which the ordinary flowers were arranged.   In *onnagata* acting it is the same sort of thing—the basis of the art is not to depart from a woman's feelings.   Should he try to be out of the ordinary, or make it his first object to be unusual, or make strength the fundamental of his performance, rare though his flowers may be, it does not follow that one can ever say that they are good ones."

NOTE: 1. A district in Osaka.

ITEM XXV

" Tamagawa Handayū is not brilliant, but he is a man who has won renown for his unaffected acting. Iwai Heijirō was brilliant, but he was too subtle and he has now fallen from favor. This is something that should be borne in mind."

COMENT: *Items XXIV and XXV tell the story that acting should not strive for clever effects, but should be unaffected and true to itself. Ayame would no doubt classify offenders against this rule along with those mentioned in Item IX who seek applause by trying to provoke laughter.*

ITEM XXVI

" Kokan Tarōji had the habit of tapping his knee with his left hand. People used to criticize him for this, saying that it spoilt their pleasure. Thereupon, accepting the rightness of what they said, he made a great effort not to tap his knee. However, this made his acting lack concentration, and suddenly his performance seemed to lose about three quarters of its excellence. When he started tapping his knee again, the concentration of his acting was immediately reborn. This shows that even though a habit is a bad thing, one must not force oneself to get rid of it. If one does, it sometimes happens that one's performance loses its drive."

COMMENT: *This is an interesting indication of how closely Ayame observed his fellow human beings.*

ITEM XXVII

" Sawamura Kodenji was a player of *wakashu* parts, and in the year when he joined the theater of Fujita Magojūrō I was with

Miyako Mandayū. On one occasion, it seems, he became very
angry and came to see me. With tears pouring down his cheeks,
he told me how, in a new part, when he is fighting with spears
with Suzuki Heishichi (another *wakashu* actor from the same
company), an *onnagata*, Namie Kokan, rushes between them to
pacify them. Then a *kataki-yaku*, Kasaya Goroshirō, comes in
and shouts, 'Don't separate them, don't separate them. These
little monkeys are bloody little nuisances. Best let them do
themselves in.' These are the words he was given to say.
Kodenji went on, 'It's all very well to say it's only in the play,
but it is insulting for us who have our attractiveness to think
about to be called little monkeys. I'm going to the *zamoto*
tomorrow and complain. I won't appear.' When I come to
think about it, it was a long time ago. He felt that the words
'little monkeys' in the part would have a bad effect on his sexual
attractiveness. One cannot imagine this happening with a
wakashu actor today."

COMMENT : *One is tempted to see in this instance of an attractive young man
being treated slightingly by an adult actor, or rather, as Yagoshirō is at pains
to point out, by the person whose part the actor is playing, as a typical piece of
pique. Yagoshirō, however, takes Sawamura's words at face value, and has us
believe that his concern with his attractiveness is real and not false parade. As
an anecdote of temperament among actors this Item sounds familiar enough even
today.*

ITEM XXVIII

In a certain year[1] the Hayakumo company had as its *zamoto*
Yamatoya Jimbē. The *tachiyaku* were at the time Tōjūrō and
Kyōemon, who was still called Hanzaemon. That is, they
should have been together, but there was a plan to promote
Hanzaemon to *zamoto* of the Ebisuya theater. Since there was
thus talk of his leaving, Tatsunosuke and I both joined the
Hayakumo company. Tatsunosuke had contracted to join
Ebisuya, but this arrangement was in the way of being an ex-

change between him and Hanzaemon. However, with Tatsunosuke being released, the Ebisuya company took into its employment Ogino Samanojō and Okada Samanosuke, and to fill
their places, Jūjirō and Kamon were taken on. About this time
Tōjūrō was heard to remark that of the three theaters then opera-
ting in Kyoto, " The Ebisuya has the experienced Hanzaemon
with Samanojō and Samanosuke; Fujikawa Buzaemon is young
but there is Chōjūrō. This company has Jimbē as *zamoto* with
me and Jirozaemon, as well as you and Tatsunosuke. Thus the
two companies are well balanced, like the two horns on an ox,
and each should have material which will spur on the other.
The Mandayū company has Nakamura Shirogorō as chief
tachiyaku, with Ikushima Shingorō, Kokin Shinzaemon, Mikasa
Jōemon, and, as *onnagata*, Kirinami Senju and Asao Jūjirō. The
theatrical standards of this company are considerably lower. It
is greatly to be feared. It is possible that the two will lose the
battle for audiences and that the Mandayū company will sweep
the board. When a company is too good, it is in a dangerous
situation, since it will consider others as beneath itself." Tōjurō
said that this was one of the most important things to understand
in *kabuki* acting. As it turned out, in that year the Mandayū
theater attracted large audiences whereas the two others were
clearly unpopular. So the *zamoto* became greatly agitated and
had many discussions about the plays they were putting on, but
what Tōjūrō said was that it was wrong to get agitated. They
put on *New Mirror for Brides*[2] with Chōjūrō as Yamagata Oribe-
nosuke and their luck changed right round and the audiences
poured in. This was the first time that Chōjūrō had appeared on
the Kyoto stage, and Sawamura Kodenji, talking of his younger
brother, spoke of the cleverness of having a new actor being
made to take a big role and drawing in the public. Ayame told
this story, adding that one should consider it carefully, bearing in
mind that success was finally achieved.

*COMMENT: Although the details of the changes in the companies given in
this Item may not be entirely reliable, it nevertheless affords an interesting
glimpse of the sort of changing around that could take place.   We have also
once again the idea that a company with low artistic standards may very well
attract large audiences, an interesting forerunner of discussions such as take place
in Britain about the rival merits of commercial television and the B.B.C.   For
all their protestations, however, Tōjūrō and his companions have to do something
about increasing their popularity, and this they do in a way that presumably did
not offend their artistic integrity.*

NOTES: 1.   1701.   2.   *Shin yome kagami.*   A new, and virtually identical, version of *Yome kagami*; see *Sadoshima's Diary*, X, p. 149.

ITEM XXIX

I have heard Ayame tell pupils at rehearsals that an *onnagata*
may be more than forty years old and still be called a " young
onnagata."[1]   Or again it might be thought that he should by
rights be called just an *onnagata ;* the fact that the word " young "
is added would indicate that he performed with brilliance and
undiminished spirit.   It might be only a small thing, but they
should realize how important this word " young " is for an
onnagata.

*COMMENT: This Item would seem to indicate that apart from the normal
use of* waka-onnagata *to mean an actor specializing in young female roles, it
could be used for any* onnagata *who showed brilliance and spirit, regardless of
the age of the woman he was playing.   Naturally enough, no actor is going to
relish abandoning this claim to youth.*

NOTE: 1.   = *waka-onnagata.*

The Words of Ayame, the end.

D. *Dust in the Ears*

Prologue[1]

(i) This work is one of the seven writings and contains a record of all the opinions of great men of the past, set down by Kichizaemon, who was a master of the comic role in the Genroku period (later, in Shōtoku, he became a *tachiyaku*). It has been copied with complete accuracy from Kaneko's autograph account of what he heard, and therefore it is almost entirely in the spoken language.

(ii) The reason for the title *Dust in the Ears* is as follows: There is an old book dealing with the ultimate significance of Japanese poetry composition; it consists of questions and answers between Hosokawa Yūsai Hōin Genshi and Lord Karasumaru Mitsuhiro and bears the name *Records of the Depths of my Ears*. It seems that the name of the present work was given under the inspiration of this book, which is quoted in one or two places.

(iii) Hitsunōin Keishin is the *hōmyō* of Kaneko Kichizaemon.

(iv) The actor called Sakata Tōjurō was famous in the

Hōei period, and was the first to be named as the leading *yatsushi* of the Three Cities.

(v)   Arashi San'emon was the second holder of the name. He was the father of Shimpei of some time ago, and the grandfather of the San'emon who died recently.

(vi)   Nakagawa Kinnojō lived until the Jōkyō period and was said to be a master *tachiyaku*.

(vii)   Matsumoto Nazaemon was an *onnagata* who was famous in the Empō period. He was the founder of the Matsumoto line that until recently ran a theater in Osaka.

(viii)   Sendai Yagoshichi was a *dōke* actor of the Genroku period.

(ix)   Kataoka Nizaemon was also of the Genroku period, and played *kataki* parts. At that time there was no separate category for *jitsuaku*, which was classified with *kataki* roles. His genealogy is given in detail in *Yakusha daizen*.

(x)   Yamashita Kyōemon, whose earlier name was Hanzaemon, was a master *tachiyaku* of the same period as Sakata Tōjūrō I.

(xi)   Kirinami Senju and Sodeshima Genji were both *onnagata* of the Genroku period.

(xii)   Murayama Heiemon worked under Murayama Matahachi and became Heiemon III. He was a pupil of Sakata Tōjūrō.

(xiii)   Arashi Sanjūrō was a *tachiyaku* of the Shōtoku period. He was the father of the Arashi Sanjūrō who worked from the Kyōhō to the Enkyō period.

(xiv)   Yagoemon's[2] surname was Fukui, and in the Empō period he combined with the performance of *kashagata* parts the function of dramatist. He was very good at training actors at the beginning of their career.

(iv)   Tominaga Heibē was a dramatist of the Genroku period. He was originally a pupil of Kaneko Rokuemon and was a fellow pupil of Kaneko Kichizaemon. His genealogy also appears in *Yakusha daizen*.

(xvi)   Araki Yojibē and Fujita Koheiji were both famous in the Genroku period as *tachiyaku* actors.

(xvii)   Sugi Kuhē was a master performer of *kashagata* roles who appeared until the Hōei period. It is said that Sakata Tōjūrō had verbal instruction from him and as a result became skillful and famous.

NOTES: 1.   See p. 12.   2.   This name should be Yagozaemon.

Dust in the Ears, Book I

INTRODUCTION

[THE ORIGIN OF KABUKI[1]]

The *kabuki* that we have today was started by Nagoya Sanzaemon, a masterless warrior, it is said. The authority for this statement is *Yōshūfushi*,[2] chapter 80.

"In addition, there is *kabuki*. It started with Kuni,[3] a priestess from the Great Shrine of Izumo. She gave performances of song and dance which were modified shrine music.[4] They belonged to that type of entertainment which was of old called *shirabyōshi*,[5] and originated in an adaptation of the *kagura* style.

During the Eiroku period (1558–70) there was a man called Nagoya Sanzaemon. He had originally been a *samurai*, but had fallen on bad days. He was in the Capital, and formed an intimate relationship with the woman Kuni. They took counsel together, and evolved *kabuki* performances."

The following items are written down as I heard them.

Hitsunōin Keishin[6]

NOTES: 1. The descriptions of the Items, which we have placed in square brackets, are from the independent edition of *Dust in the Ears*; see p. 13. 2. This work was printed in 1686; its author was Kurokawa Dōyū 黒川道祐 (died 1691), and it is an account of events in Yamashiro 山城 province, which included Kyoto. The title refers to the Chinese province in which the capital Chang-an, of which Kyoto is said to be the Japanese equivalent, was situated.

Its information on the subject of *Kabuki* is unreliable.   3.   See O-Kuni, Appendix II.   4.   Kagura; see *Mirror for Actors*, II, n. 6.   5.   This was a song and dance performance to the accompaniment of a drum given by female entertainers in the 12th century and later.   The name is also applied to the performers, who wore court dress and were of fairly high social standing; *shirabyōshi* were often the mistresses of famous men.   6.   *Hōmyō* of Kaneko Kichizaemon.

ITEM I

[ON BEING UNSUITABLE AS A TEACHER; ALSO THE SHAPING OF TREES]

Yamashita Kyōemon said, " Sakata Tōjūrō is a born genius, and is recognized in the Three Cities as an actor of true worth. Among those actors who can be called great today, one cannot think that there is one who reaches the standard of Tōjūrō, nor can I claim to do so myself. However, perhaps because he is a born genius, he was unlikely to become a teacher. The reason for this can be seen if you take as an example a master gardener who takes, for instance, a pine tree and bends and shapes its branches, and makes of it a superb tree. Then there is the pine which has grown naturally into a fine tree with excellent shape. The other[1] is an excellence in which a lack of ability has been bent and shaped and made into a fine talent. Thus, because this sort of ability has been bent into shape, the person who is possessed of it has learned how to form artistry and how to teach it to his pupils. Therefore, he is to be relied upon as a teacher. The other, innate genius, is one to whom it came at birth, and since he himself has no experience of having been bent and shaped by others, he does not know how to bend and shape them himself. Therefore, as a teacher, no reliance can be placed upon him.

COMMENT: Pine trees in Japanese gardens are usually carefully trimmed into shape, and the parallel between the growth of pine trees and the development of actors is well maintained. Whether or not the conclusions that Kyōemon reaches are really valid, we are not willing to say, but it is very interesting to find any sort of discussion of teaching ability at this period. Later, there will be examples of instruction by Tōjūrō and others, from which it may be possible to obtain some hints of their efficiency as teachers.

NOTE: 1.   It might be easier to understand this clause if something like the following is placed before it.   " Thus, there are two sorts of excellence, one is natural, like Tōjūrō's."

ITEM II
[ON ROUSING LAUGHTER BY THE SERIOUS]

Another thing that he[1] said was that it did not amount to praise to have it said of one that one is good in serious parts. Since it is only a matter of saying what is written in the play, even a novice does not make too much of a fool of himself. That a skillful actor can do it goes without saying.   What everybody is unable to do is the comic part.   Naturally enough, one can cause laughter by saying some preposterous thing like " taking off an ear to blow your nose with " but there is no actor like Tōjūrō for saying something serious and making people laugh at it.

NOTE: 1.   Yamashita Kyōemon.

ITEM III
[ON THE MISTAKEN ATTITUDE OF ACTORS PLAYING SERIOUS PARTS]

Tōjūrō said, " It is realism that is comic.   This is because one performs something that happens ordinarily.   When one sees present-day actors playing a serious part,[1] they are always slapping their scabbards at each other, sticking their noses in each other's face, confronting each other with sword-drawing postures; this is not the sort of thing a *samurai* would do.   When writing speeches the same considerations should be borne in mind.   Can one call this sort of thing serious acting? "

COMMENT: *The first half of this item quotes Tōjūrō as supporting Kyōemon's statement in Item II about comedy which is based on everyday life.   There is then a shift to a discussion of one aspect of realistic acting.   One wonders what Tōjūrō would think of modern* samurai *films and television serials, which are full of just those things that he attacks here.*

NOTE: 1. The term *jitsugoto* is being used here to include the general meaning of " serious acting " and the more particular meaning of " fighting role."

ITEM IV
[ON THE LACK OF CONCERN WITH STUDYING POSTURE]

He also said, " There are some actors who carefully study the good and bad points of posture. I agree that for something to be shown before an audience, good posture is better than bad. I have not studied this point myself. Posture is not something that one can invent. It is a manifestation of the emotions. When one is joyful or angry, one's emotions show themselves naturally in the body. Can one's posture be anything other than this ? "

COMMENT: *Tōjūrō's remarks bear out what was said of him in Item I, that he was a natural actor, with no need to learn. What he says in Item V is to the same effect, and shows the impatience of the natural genius with the more plodding efforts of mediocre performers. He does not have to worry about learning posture, nor does he have to think what his function is in any one play. He just acts realistically, as he is sure others could do if they stopped fussing. One can see why Kyōemon thought that Tōjūrō was not a good teacher.*

ITEM V
[ON PLAYING THE FOIL FOR COMIC ROLES]

A certain actor remarked to Tōjūrō, "Among all the skills that you possess, you are especially praised as a master at playing the foil for comic roles." Tōjūrō replied, " What do you mean by ' foil for comic roles ? ' What I do is to act with the comic actor. Provided that he acts in a realistic sort of way, it is easy for him to play the comic part, and for me quite naturally to become the foil. If I act with the deliberate intention of playing the foil's role, the actor with the comic part will see me as merely spoiling the play." At all events he thought that one should do one's best to attach very great importance to one's acting when one is appearing against a comic role.

ITEM VI

[ON THE SMALL-DRUM PLAYING OF HONEYA SHŌZAEMON; ALSO HIS
CONVERSATION WITH SAKATA TŌJŪRŌ]

Once, when there was a subscription *nō* at Dōtombori in
Osaka, a famous small-drum player from Kyoto called Honeya
Shōemon[1] played during the third play and many people listened.
Although, of course, they thought he was a skilled performer,
they were not unduly struck by his playing. It was the opening
day of the performances, and Tōjūrō, who had studied under
Shōemon, and was exceptionally attached to him, went to pay
his respects. He took advantage of this opportunity to see the
play, and heard what the audience had to say about it. Then
he went to Shōemon's lodgings and reported to him that
although he was the only performer in the present *nō* plays whom
the Osaka audience went to see, there was no great amount of
praise or blame from them, and this he wanted to bring to
Shōemon's attention. Shōemon bade him set his heart at ease,
for he would see that he would be praised enough on the next
day. And indeed it was so, for from the second day he was
praised as the most skillful in the whole of Japan. Tōjūrō
went to see him again and told him that the favorable reports
on that day's performance were really exceptional and asked him
what he had in his mind when he played his drum. Shōemon
replied, " On the first day I was very concerned with what I
was doing, and just like you with your acting, put aside thoughts
of being praised, and concentrated on the technique of playing.
Today, with the first day safely over, I thought about getting
some applause, and showed off my skill a little. And that is why,
I think, people were praising me. It is easy enough to play on
my drum so as to get applause, but difficult to do so in a way
that satisfies my conscience." I was in the theater at the time
and heard this conversation, and could not help but agree, and

have ever since kept in mind that the great man's art resides in doing what he thinks is right, not caring whether the audience likes it or not.

COMMENT: There were two sorts of occasion when nō *plays were given, either as part of a shrine or temple festival, or, as here, as " subscription* nō," *that is, a public performance to raise funds by charging for admission. The* nō *orchestra has a flute and two (sometimes three) drums. The third, occasional, drum, is the* taiko 太鼓, *played with sticks; the others,* ō-tsuzumi 大鼓, *and the small drum,* ko-tsuzumi 小鼓, *are held in one hand and played by striking with the other. Shōemon's instrument was the last one. Nō plays are divided into five categories, and a* nō *performance should ideally have one from each, in due order. The third type, referred to here, is* kazuramono 鬘物, " wig pieces," *in which the main character is a woman.*

The theme of the necessity of being true to one's art and not courting cheap popularity, which has occurred already in the Analects, *is here developed slightly, in a direction already hinted at in Item XXVIII of* The Words of Ayame, *which describes how a special effort had to be made to increase the audience. Here Shōemon says, in effect, that he can always give a showy performance if he wants to, but that his conscience requires that the basis of his playing should be artistically sound, and that once that basis has been established, he can build on it to attract the praise of the audience. It is hardly necessary, we think, to add that the* nō *drums are instruments of great subtlety and that particular skill is required to play them.*

NOTE: 1. Nothing more is known of this man.

ITEM VII
[ON A FELLOW ACTOR'S LAUGHTER]

Tōjūrō said, " It sometimes happens that an actor is made to laugh by a piece of acting by an actor on the stage with him.[1] This I find difficult to approve of. From the time I was a learner right up to today, I have always had a rehearsal on the stage, explaining that today I will do this, tomorrow it will be thus. The reason why I take this view is that, in the case of rehearsals for a new play, on the first day both the actors playing with me, and myself, have not learned the words, and so the acting is rather rough and ready. One tries to play extremely

well, but it is very different from a play which one has grown
used to. Thus an actor performing a piece that is well known[2]
and making those playing with him laugh has not the right
spirit, has he? "[3]

NOTES: 1. A slight emendation to the text would make this mean "...
an actor is made to laugh when an actor playing with him adds a comic twist
to his acting ... " (see Gunji, p. 329, n. 28). 2. Or " an actor giving a
funny twist to a piece." 3. One must understand " even more so with
a new piece."

ITEM VIII
[ON PRACTICING ONE'S WORDS FROM THE OPENING DAY; ALSO THE EXAMPLE OF A DISPUTE]

A certain actor asked Tōjūrō the following question:
" I myself and some other actors are in some confusion on the
first day of a play, perhaps because we have not learned the words
properly yet. Your performance is as though you were doing a
play that you have become thoroughly familiar with over a
period of ten or twenty days. I should like to ask what advice
you would give on this point." His reply was: " I am the same
on the first day; I too am in confusion. But the reason that I
seem to others as if I am playing a play that I am familiar with is
that when I am practicing I commit the words well to memory,
and on the first day I forget them completely. However, I
listen on the stage to what the other actors say to me, and then
I remember my lines and speak them. The reason why I do this
is that when one encounters people in the ordinary course of
events, or fights or disputes with them, one has not the advantage of having lines prepared in advance. One hears what
the other has to say, and then, and not before, one's reply
comes to one's lips. In acting, I think that everyday life should
be the model, and that is why I commit the words properly to
memory and forget them when I appear on the first day."

ITEM IX

[ON THE PERFORMANCE OF *NŌ WAKI* ACTOR TAKAYASU TOMONOSHIN; ALSO THE GOLDEN WORDS OF THE MASTER]

There is an actor who plays *waki*[1] parts in *nō* plays, called Takayasu Tomonoshin,[2] who has the reputation of being outstanding. Once, there was a subscription *nō* at Dōtombori and the day before the opening he invited some friends to go out with him on a boating expedition. He became intoxicated and presented a very disordered appearance. On this occasion a actor named Tsuda San'eki had come down from Kyoto to pay his respects and was in the boat with him. He remonstrated with him thus: " This season of *nō* plays centers on you alone. Tomorrow is the opening day, and so you should be studying hard today, but instead you are in this sorry state. Do you not consider that it is important that tomorrow is your opening? " Tomonoshin replied: " That it is the opening day is of no importance. What is important is regular rehearsing. At rehearsal time you should put your heart in your work and learn your part thoroughly, but on the opening day you should put all that out of your mind when you go on. If one thinks that the opening day is of special importance, one has not yet made the art of acting one's own." It seems that San'eki was struck with admiration. I consider that what Tōjūrō said about remembering what one had rehearsed in a play that one had long been familiar with but forgetting the words when going on on the opening day of a new play comes to the same thing as Tomonoshin's reply that one should put things out of one's mind when going on on the first day. The words of great men agree without their being aware of it, it seems.

COMMENT: *As Kaneko suggests at the end of Item IX, it should be taken along with VIII as showing the idealistic approach to the first performance of a new play, by which great actors tried to avoid the confusion which tends to exist on such occasions. It is true that a play had more chance to settle down in Japan, where the commercial pressures were less fierce than in the West.*

Even nowadays the first day of kabuki *season is more like a dress rehearsal, and it is customary to allow clients to attend both performances for the price of one.*

NOTES: 1. The *waki* actor in a *nō* performance is usually the one who comes on first and sets the scene, and acts as the interlocutor of the principal actor. 2. Nothing more is known of this man.

ITEM X

[ON THOSE WHO SPEAK THEIR WORDS QUICKLY OR SLOWLY]

　　Somebody asked Tōjūrō the following question: "Which is better, the actor who speaks his words quickly, or the one who speaks them slowly?" His reply was: "It is said that if a quick one is bad, it is of no consequence; if a slow one is bad, it makes it worse. If there are several actors who are all bad, one can endure one among them who is a fast speaker, but a slow one is a bad actor among bad actors."

COMMENT: *It is to be presumed that the reference here is to actors who habitually speak more quickly or slowly than usual. Tōjūrō seems to have perverted to his own purpose a proverb which Gunji quotes and which might be translated "A quick one is good but makes mistakes. A slow one is bad but makes none." His comment is clear enough.*

ITEM XI

[ON UJI KAGANOJŌ AND HIS DISCUSSION WITH HIS PUPILS]

　　The pupils of the *jōruri* master, Kaganojō, once all complained to him thus. "When you, sir, are chanting, and come to a *fushi* passage, the audience goes into raptures. When we chant a *fushi* passage, however hard we try, we never get applause. Even so, it is not that we have arranged the passage for ourselves, for we have carefully learned your setting, sir. In spite of this, we get no applause; this is very mysterious." Kaganojō burst into laughter. "It is not that at all. I merely chant *jōruri* with no other object but chanting, and when it comes to the *fushi* passage, I sing the *fushi*. As you fellows start chanting, you think of being applauded, and make your performance entertaining from beginning to end, so that when you get to the *fushi*, it is no longer a passage that is more entertaining than the rest, so there is no applause. It is bad to make applause the main purpose of your chanting."

COMMENT: The Japanese puppet-play comprises three elements, a chanter to tell the story and speak the conversations, a shamisen to accompany the chanter, and the puppets to perform the actions. The art of the chanter is complicated and demanding. It is made up of various styles, one of which is the fushi. *Generally, this is the melodious, non-conversational part, and might be thought of as aria as against recitative; it provides an opportunity for virtuoso performance. The experienced Kaganojō was aware of the importance of reserving his best efforts for the* fushi; *there must be contrast in the performance. It is to be noted that applause is reserved nowadays for places in the performance where it is traditional to applaud. Thus, if the* fushi *sounds the same as the rest, the audience will not spot it and will not know when to applaud.*

ITEM XII
[ON THE THOUGHTS OF LORD HOSOKAWA YŪSAI ON PRACTITIONERS OF THE ARTS]

In *Niteiki*,[1] Hosokawa Yūsai says that to seek praise is to be artistically inferior.

COMMENT: Gunji quotes the original passage, " It is rustic art to give entertainment." This is all very well for writers of poetry, with its aristocratic tradition and amateur status, but it can only be a remote ideal for a popular drama form.

NOTE: 1. " Record from the Depth of my Ears," 3 vols; it records the words of Hosokawa Yūsai relating to Japanese poetry, and was set down by Karasumaru Mitsuhiro between 1458 and 1605; see p. 12.

ITEM XIII
[ON FORGETTING THE AUDIENCE WHEN ACTING]

Tōjūrō said, " If you wish to be praised, the best way to set about it is to forget the audience and to concentrate upon playing the play as if it was really happening."

COMMENT: Tōjūrō might seem to be giving a more practical piece of advice than just " do not play for applause," perhaps rather " do not be troubled by the presence of the audience, act naturally." The second alternative is unlikely, however, because the Analects *do not seem to refer to stage nervousness.*

ITEM XIV
[ON TAKING ARASHI SAN'EMON AS A MODEL]

Again, he said, "Arashi San'emon is a great artist. He has developed the habit of putting meaningless words in inconsequential plays. It is an amusing fact that he plays them with such a serious air that people almost believe that the plays are as he plays them. In addition his acting has a slow tempo that is quite impossible. At all events, I use my head too much about the actor's profession, and this is bad."

ITEM XV
[ON YAMASHITA KYŌEMON'S USE OF THE TERM " MASTER " TO DESCRIBE TŌJŪRŌ AND SAN'EMON]

Kyōemon said, " When I was an apprentice, I used to watch San'emon and Tōjūrō carefully, and saw that the former had an unrealistic way of acting but was all the same a master. The latter was realistic, and still a master. However, I exerted myself to put Tōjūrō and San'emon together and tried to learn from them both."

COMMENT: In Item XIV Tōjūrō rather refreshingly admits that his theories do not account for the success of San'emon's acting, which, he considers, breaks the rules. In XV we learn that in fact two schools of acting were represented by Tōjūrō and San'emon, a realistic and an unrealistic. It would have been interesting to hear more about the latter, but as far as we know, nothing from this side has been left.

ITEM XVI
[ON THE RELATIONS BETWEEN MASTER AND RETAINER AS SEEN IN THE STORY IN TWELVE PARTS; ALSO KIRINAMI SENJU AND SODESHIMA]

On one occasion, when a play on *The Story in Twelve Parts* was being prepared, with Kirinami Senju in the role of the lady

Jōruri, Sodesaki Genji[1] was Jūgoya. When he heard him
speak, Tōjūrō said, " I do not agree with Genji's interpretation
of the role. As the lady Jōruri, Senju is the mistress, and as
Jūgoya, Genji is the retainer. But as the piece is being played
now, one cannot see the difference between mistress and servant. In the bottom of his heart he sees Senju as the chief
onnagata[2] of the company and himself as second or third in rank
below. ' You see, when I get as good as that, I'll be in his place.'
In other words, he is bringing the thoughts he has in the dressing
room out onto the stage. The lady Jōruri is the mistress and
Jūgoya the servant, but however hard he tries to play the servant in a servant-like way, if he is thinking of outdoing Senju,
the thought of this will be with him all the time. If, in his role
as a servant, he is thinking of outdoing his mistress, he is not
Jūgoya, nor is she the lady Jōruri. If there were a retainer of
that sort today, there would be nothing to do but discharge
him." At this rebuke, the whole company was struck with
admiration and Genji apologized.

COMMENT : The story in twelve parts, Jūnidan 十二段, *is the legendary
story of the lady Jōruri and her love for Yoshitsune, the young hero in flight from
his enemies. This story was very popular in the 17th century, and the puppet
theater took its name* jōruri *from its heroine. For more details see Dunn.
There were also many* kabuki *versions, although it is not possible to identify
the one referred to here.*

The theme of the Item is surely applicable to all theater.

NOTES : 1. This is an error for Sodeshima Genji, q.v. 2. *tate-
oyama.*

ITEM XVII
[ON THE DEVICE USED ON THE SECOND DAY OF THE SECOND SEQUEL
TO HOTOKE NO HARA]

In the play that came on as the second sequel to *Hotoke no
hara*[1] the *keisei* Ōshū[2] who had been bought out by Umefusa
Bunzō is married to the senior retainer Mochizuki Hachirōemon.

Many days and months had passed since that event, but it was said that they had not once slept together. Bunzō thought in his heart that she must be keeping her faith to him, so as not to break the promises exchanged on so many occasions. Furthermore, he felt ashamed at what Hachirōemon might be thinking. He thought he would remonstrate with Ōshū but wished to avoid being seen, so, under cover of night and changing his appearance to that of a woman by wearing a hooded gown,[3] he crept into Hachirōemon's house. He there met Ōshū and spoke to her as he had planned. Ōshū was extremely angry: "Whether we share a pillow or not is something between Hachirōemon and myself. Once you had made me his wife, that was that and your present concern is quite unnecessary. Go away at once!" she said. Bunzō thought that the reason why she could not open her heart to him was that a number of ladies in waiting were there with her, so he would waste some time now, and when she was alone, try to talk to her in private and discover what her real feelings were. The various ways in which he tried unobtrusively to waste time were very comic and done with many actions. On the opening day, the fifteenth day of the seventh month, the audience were bored with this by-play, and there were various shouts of "Get on with it," "Pack it in," and this act finished in confusion. However, when the performance came to an end, I went to express my thanks to Tōjūrō and said, "In that comic bit you do, Chikamatsu and I wrote the words between us, but the audience does not understand it. There's nothing else for it but for you to cut out half the lines." On the sixteenth I went to see him play again. There were more people in the audience than I had expected, and they were greatly amused by the comic passage. There were many shouts of "Tōjūrō, keep it going, don't stop yet!" That evening,[4] Tōjūrō came up to me and proposed that we go and see the Daimonji bonfire together.[5] I said, "What a difference from yesterday! After all, you added more words and spun it out even more, and yet they wanted more.   Audiences in the seventh month[6] are different from what they are in the rest of the year, and it is very difficult to find out what they want."   " No, you must not blame the audience.   It was because they realized that it was Tōjūrō who was trying to be funny.   The action brings in various devices to prolong the interview so that Bunzō can discover exactly what Ōshū is really feeling.   I finally got round to thinking that the correct thing was to act the play in this spirit, and today, when I played the part with the amount of dialogue increased, the audience, just as I hoped, shouted ' Longer, longer ' and applauded.[7]   I realize now that sincerity is of the greatest importance.   I am fifty-three years old, but my art is not yet fully developed.   Does this mean that it never will be? " There was a note of despair in his voice.

COMMENT : This item reminds us of several things about the theater of the time.   Performances were during the daytime, at least in Kyoto.   The writing of plays was to some extent a negotiation between the author, or authors, and the actors.   Although Chikamatsu is credited with the authorship of several kabuki plays, in some, including this one, he had the collaboration of Kaneko Kichizaemon.   Then Tōjūrō is obviously quite free to change his words if he wishes to; the authors would not think of preventing him.

Tōjūrō blames himself for departing from his rule of natural acting, and for making the audience see that it was he himself who was trying to entertain them, instead of having the interest and amusement arise naturally from the situation and the words.   It is a typical piece of modesty for Kichizaemon to suggest that by going directly against his advice, and by lengthening the offending passage, instead of abbreviating it, Tōjūrō showed his genius.   That the latter should attain success by doing the opposite of what would seem common sense to an ordinary mortal is a commonplace of this sort of didactic material.   The close relationship between actor and audience is also to be noted.

NOTES :   1.   The play *Keisei hotoke no hara* by Chikamatsu Monzaemon, which was played in Kyoto on 24. 1. 1699.   It had a huge success, and was followed by two sequels: (i) *Hotoke no hara gonichi ryūjo ga fuchi* (see *Dust in the Ears*, XLIV), and (ii) *Tsuruga-no-tsu sankai-gura*.   Umefusa Bunzō is also known as Umenaga Bunzō.   2.   In fact she was bought out by Mochizuki to free Bunzō of her influence.   3.   *kazuki*: a *kimono* pulled up over the head, to conceal the face.   4.   In Kyoto at the time theater performances were given during the daytime, lasting until dusk.   5.   On the 16th day of the 7th month a fire in the shape of the character 大 is lit on one of the Eastern Hills of Kyoto, as part of the *bon* ceremonies.   6.   The seventh month can be very hot and oppressive.   7.   Although the text clearly has *nametari*, we have followed Gunji's suggested emendation to *hometari* in the translation.

Dust in the Ears, Book I, the end.

Dust in the Ears, Book II

[ON ARASHI SAN'EMON'S LIKING FOR SAKE; ALSO THE REFERENCE TO MOGAMI TŌHACHI AND THE SPEAR]

The late Arashi San'emon had always liked his *sake* and was so used to drinking it that even on the stage he seemed to be drinking the real article. There were many who praised him for this, saying that he was indeed a master actor, but one person who overheard this laughed and said, " When Mogami Tōhachi was run through with a spear, it really looked as if it was stuck in him. Maybe he too has real experience and is always being run through."

COMMENT: We think that this Item makes its point quite clear. The kind of material realism that comes from a close observation of everyday activity is evident in kabuki *and may be thought of as a step towards the theater of illusion; think of the cucumber sandwiches in* The Importance of Being Earnest. *In* kabuki *later than the period of the* Analects, *the tendency became stronger, but this is to some extent due to the influence of puppet plays, in which the manipulators like to display their skill in having their dolls fill pipes, and do sewing or cooking. When the* kabuki *took over the puppet repertory, they took over this sort of acting with it. However, this Item shows that pre-puppet* kabuki *too was interested in this sort of realism, and that*

*there were those who thought that it could go too far.   The next Item, too, is
on the same subject.*

ITEM XIX

[ON THE ACTOR'S NEED TO LEARN REGARDLESS OF WHETHER THE
THING LEARNT IS GOOD OR BAD]

A certain actor had a son, who was twelve or thirteen years
old and was attending school.   He said to him, "Things which
an actor need not learn are the use of the abacus, and calligraphy,
and there are also several other things that he can ignore."
Tōjūrō heard this and said, "No, no, that is not true at all.
The actor's art is like a beggar's bag.   Regardless of whether you
need it at the time or not, you should pick up everything as you
come across it and take it away with you.   You should make
use only of those things which you need, and those you do not
you should put on one side, and bring out when you need them.
There must not be anything about which you are entirely
ignorant.   Even purse-cutting should be carefully studied."

ITEM XX

[ON THE NEED TO OBSERVE CAREFULLY THE PERFORMANCE OF EVEN
AN UNSKILLFUL ACTOR]

A certain actor said, "Even watching a bad actor is good
practice for an understanding person; for he can take careful
note of the defects in the bad actor's performance, and avoid
doing them himself."

ITEM XXI

[ON ISSŌ'S FLUTE PLAYING MENTIONED IN *NITEIKI*]

In *Niteiki*, Hosokawa Yūsai reports the words of Issō, who
said that it would be wrong for him to model his flute-playing
on that of Kobue.   He was quite right, said Yūsai, for age and
youth are indeed different things.   Issō said that in his youth he
too had played brilliantly; if Kobue played in a style which he

had not taught, he should not teach it to others.

COMMENT : This item, which quotes accurately from Niteiki *(see Item XII), is in so condensed a style that it is difficult to follow. Even the identification of the personages involved is not certain, but Issō seems to have been a flute-player and Kobue to have been his pupil at some time, but to have developed a style of his own, which Issō had been urged to copy. This he refused to do, partly because he was too old, and partly, according to Shuzui's interpretation, because it would be going outside the tradition of the art for Kobue to teach something that Issō had not taught him. The points that this extract makes are, thus, that youth and age have styles of their own, and that tradition should be respected.*

ITEM XXII
[ON NAKAGAWA KINNOJŌ, WHO WAS CALLED A MASTER BY MASTERS]

Nakagawa Kinnojō was a fine actor, who was praised for his mastery by great actors like Tōjūrō, Kyōemon and others. Kinnojō said to me, " That someone should seek to be praised every day that he appears on the stage may mean that the audiences which come to see his performances are large, but, all the same, I do not like this sort of thing. I concentrate upon one or two passages and put my best efforts into them, and, for the rest, the reception I receive depends upon how hard I try."

COMMENT : This item is incomprehensible in places, and the above translation is largely conjectural. It seems to echo the sentiments of Item XI.

ITEM XXIII
[ON THE USE OF *RANJATAI* AS AN EXAMPLE]

A certain person said that in learning to appreciate perfumes, one takes *ranjatai*[1] as the ideal, and by reference to it distinguishes the others as " weak " or " strong " or " without odor,"[2] etc. With actors it is the same thing, I think—but when I asked who might be the actor whom one could take as the ideal, people who were there answered that they did not know.

NOTES : 1. 蘭奢待, the name of a famous incense wood, of which some still remains in the Imperial Repository (Shōsōin 正倉院) in Nara. It is considered to have the most refined odor of all. Perfume (incense-wood) appreciation dates from the Heian period and the methods used in training the nose have become a pattern of games and competitions still occasionally practiced today.   2.   Literal translations of adjectives used to refer to the odors of certain incense-woods.

ITEM XXIV
[ON THE PLAYING OF WOUNDED WARRIORS BY ARAKI YOJIBĒ AND KANEKO ROKUEMON]

Araki Yojibē and Kaneko Rokuemon are fine *teoi* actors.[1] Rokuemon said, " Playing a *teoi* part is not only a matter of leaning on one's sword, gasping for breath and acting as if one were in great pain.   If he thinks that his enemy is still in the vicinity, he must be very tense, directing his eyes all around, but at the same time appear to be severely wounded and indicate by his posture that he is suffering.   Again, if he thinks that his enemy has fled, he should show that then, and not until then, his wound becomes painful.   If men from his own side should run up and attend to his hurts, he should speak words of strength, but at the same time show that within himself his spirit is failing and he is growing weak.   Again, even should he lean on his sword when walking after receiving his wounds, to take short steps and bring forward his sword to lean on at each step is an ugly sight.   If he uses the sword in this way, he should take two or three steps, then bring his sword forward two or three paces from where his feet are and put it to the ground, then walk forward to a point two or three paces forward from where his sword now is ; then, bring his sword forward two or three paces in front, as before.   The length of the sword, including the hilt, should be about breast-high.   If it is shorter than that, one has to bend over to walk with it, and this does not look good." His analysis is surely accurate !   At that time he attracted large audiences with his performances as a wounded warrior.

COMMENT : *This Item indicates that careful analysis and preparation of a role characterized some actors, at least, during this period.   Rokuemon seems* to have been a real professional. *Tōjūrō might have been expected to say that one has only to imagine oneself in the situation and movements would come naturally. However, even he must have done a good deal of groundwork, as hinted in Items XIX, XXIX and XXX.*

NOTES: 1. Specializing in roles where wounds are received.

ITEM XXV
[ON THE NON-CRITICISM OF THE ART]

Kyōemon said, " The actor's duty is to work energetically and industriously regardless of the quality of the play. If he does so, even a play only two-thirds worthwhile will seem satisfactory. At all events, to play in a mood of criticism will cause harm."

COMMENT: *It looks as if Kyōemon is here talking as a manager.*

ITEM XXVI
[ON THE IMPORTANCE OF SWORD-SLAPPING FOR FUJITA KOHEIJI]

Fujita Koheiji was an actor who won fame for his portrayal of *jitsugoto* parts. On one occasion he said, " When slapping one's sword one should glare straight into one's opponent's eyes."

COMMENT: *" Sword-slapping " is a threatening gesture of putting one's hand forcibly to one's scabbard to hold it steady if one wants to draw. This advice presumably derives from actual practice.*

ITEM XXVII
[ON TŌJŪRO'S INSTRUCTION ON THE APPROACH TO THE WORK OF A DŌKE ACTOR; ALSO HIS CRITICISM OF SENDAI YAGOSHICHI]

Sendai Yagoshichi was a *dōke* actor of unequalled skill, who received a high salary in Kyoto. Thus, when I was learning to be a *dōke* my one desire was to be an actor of Yagoshichi's class. Hearing this, Tōjūrō said, " Even though you make *dōke* parts your specialty, you must be sure not to imitate Yagoshichi. The reason why I say this is that in a recent play when all were amazed at hearing that a great lord had passed away, Yagoshichi, playing a *dōke* role, exclaimed: ' By the three treasures,[1] it's like an ox getting in your ear when you're asleep.' It's not the sort of thing a *dōke* should say, however much he had the excuse that it raised a laugh. The role of a *dōke* is always that of a stupid person, who is coarse and does not know the rules of politeness. To say that an ox has got in your ear while you were asleep is rather something a *taiko-mochi*[2] might say as a smart witticism. But however smart you are, you should not talk about an ox getting into your ear while you were asleep when hearing of the death of a great lord. The common expression is ' Having water poured in your ear while you're asleep.' I should have preferred him to get his laugh by saying something like that." I said, " If what you say is correct, the audience should not have laughed." He replied, " That is an indication of his skill. They cannot help laughing at what he says." After that time, whenever I heard someone say in a play that my lady had brought into the world a young prince, I used to exclaim: " By the three treasures, it's as if someone poured water in my ear while I was asleep," and the audience would roar with laughter. That he should have considered that such a line would be particularly good came, no doubt, from his close study of his art as demonstrated in this Item.

COMMENT : *This Item indicates the care that had to be taken to get the right tone in plays of the period, and the freedom that actors had to use their own material. Our translation of Kichizaemon's joke is unfortunately not so crisp as the Japanese but it seems that he had acquired himself a useful catchphrase.*

NOTES : 1. I.e., the Buddha, the Buddhist priesthood, and the Buddhist law. This was a common expletive. 2. A sort of male entertainer, particularly at restaurant parties and the like.

ITEM XXVIII

[ON THE DEAF MAN]

In a certain work[1] it is written that a deaf man, seeing men gathered together, would watch their mouths and stand there smiling all the time.

NOTE: 1. Not identified.

ITEM XXIX
[ON THE OPEN-EYED BLIND MAN]

In a play called *Ōtsu Naraya*[1] Tōjūrō was an open-eyed blind man. It is said that he made himself look like one by holding his eyes still with their pupils in a fixed stare.

NOTE: 1. Otherwise unknown.

ITEM XXX
[ON PERFECTING THE STUTTERING ROLE]

In a play called *Muramatsu*,[1] Tōjūrō had the part of a stutterer. On the first day, whenever he stuttered, the audience thought it very funny and laughed. Rejoicing at what seemed to be Tōjūrō's excellent reception in a good play, a certain man went to see him on the evening of the first day and praised him for the great success of his stuttering. Tōjūrō did not accept this. " Why I thought of playing a stutterer on this occasion was that the audiences expect Tōjūrō in his usual plays to say things very clearly. This time I am unable to express adequately what I think, because of my stutter. I intended that the audience should think this very sad and weep, but in fact what they did today was to laugh. This was because I had not worked sufficiently hard at the part and from tomorrow I shall make them weep," he said, and just as he intended, weep they did. A certain actor went to him and asked, " How was it that you managed to get the audience to weep today? " His reply was, " Stuttering may occur when a man thinks within himself that he is a stutterer, and so, feeling ashamed that people are listening to him, he stutters from embarrassment. But it can happen when he forgets himself and stutters, as when he is happy or angry. Today I refrained from stuttering when I might have done so out of embarrassment, but restricted it to moments of joy, and anger, and when I found things funny." "But how was it that you seemed to be stuttering from start to finish?" "It is because when one says something with a stutter inside the mouth, one does not stutter. Because I was stuttering inside my mouth, to that extent my words lost their rhythm, and that is all there was to it."

COMMENT: *Items XXVIII, XXIX and XXX give further indication of Tōjūrō's careful preparation. The note on the deaf man is presumably recorded for future reference. The blindman and stutterer show Tōjūrō's observation at work. The piece on the stutterer is extremely subtle, not to say obscure. The first point is that he hoped to get the audience's tears by showing the usually fluent Tōjūrō as impeded in his speech. All he managed was to make them laugh. So, in true Tōjūrō fashion, he takes pains to lose his own identity in the part, and this time he succeeds. Whether his analysis of stuttering is correct we do not feel qualified to say, but it is certainly very interesting. To paraphrase what he says, he finds two sorts of stuttering, one from embarrassment, and one from strong emotion. Tōjūrō stuttered when emotion called for it, but did not do so overtly when embarrassment might have been the cause. However, he gave the impression of stuttering throughout, because even though he did not use the embarrassment stutter, at moments when he might have done so he changed the rhythm of his speech, which deceived the audience into thinking he was stuttering. One last ingredient in this complication is that the Japanese word refers to both stuttering and stammering.*

NOTE: 1. This play is unknown, but presumably derives from old puppet plays dealing with the same eponymous hero.

ITEM XXXI
[HOW ARASHI SAN'EMON CONDUCTED REHEARSALS FOR A NEW PIECE; ALSO HIS PLAY WITH *SAKE*-DRINKING]

The late Arashi San'emon gathered together at his house the actors who were to play with him in a piece which he was preparing, with love scenes, lovers' quarrels and so on in it. He had always been fond of *sake* and he immediately brought out the wine-cups, and although there was in the assembly a boy with whom he was on affectionate terms, he did not even look at him. Instead he went and whispered and murmured to another boy, at times stroking his cheeks and having him drink from his cup. Later he became intoxicated and no longer in control of himself. The first boy had long been of a jealous disposition and he was uttering insults of all sorts when the second boy and a *tachiyaku* calmed him down and got him to drink a cup of reconciliation. On this occasion there were also in the party Tōjūrō's father, Sakata Ichizaemon, and also Manoya Kanzaemon, the *zamoto*. So, when Tōjūrō came in he laughed out loud and exclaimed: "Ho ho, what a scene of disorder! The opening day is getting nearer. It's not the moment for quarrels with boy-friends, come on, come on; rehearse, rehearse!" San'emon replied: "That is what I thought too, so I've been rehearsing for some time already. From the moment when I handed out the first wine-cup up to the cup of reconciliation that we have witnessed, including the jealous boy and the people who calmed him down, I have remembered it all. This is the rehearsal for the next play." And in fact that is how he devised it. Ask any actor and he will say that invented scenes are bad, and truth is good. Because he believed in the correctness of this, he had the wine-cups brought out, even though normally *sake* is not served at a place where a rehearsal is taking place, in order to assist in the writing of words for the next play, and his motive for provoking a situation in which the boy could not but be jealous was the same. He said that all should do it in the same way on the stage. This was really an excellent device. It is an indication of the amount of trouble that men were prepared to take in the old days.

COMMENT: *Whether this was really a put-up job by San'emon, as he claimed, or whether the explanation he gave was just a piece of quick thinking on his part, we shall never know. It shows a scene which was presumably quite ordinary in a society in which homosexuality did not necessarily bring opprobrium.*

ITEM XXXII

Matsumoto Nazaemon said, " When I and another are performing a *shosagoto* together, should one be dancing alone, the other takes up a position in front of the musicians.[1] At such a time many actors relax and have a drink of tea or the like. I myself do not relax. Even though I am there in front of the musicians, I am performing the dance in my mind. If I did not do so, the view of my back would be so displeasing that the performance would be brought to a halt."

COMMENT: The non-habitué of kabuki is still likely to be disturbed by seeing an actor who is not engaged in dancing for the moment being brought a cup of tea. One wonders whether Nazaemon might not have been more concerned about this than some modern performers. The theme of the necessity to avoid relaxing when one is not actually speaking, or at the end of a play, is continued in the next two Items.

NOTE: 1. With his back to the audience ; the musicians would be across the back of the stage.

ITEM XXXIII

There was one called Yagozaemon. His specialty was *kashagata* and he was famous as an author. In the past plays were in one act, and the two-act and three-act plays which we have today were first written by Yagozaemon. That is, he was the author of *The Outlaw's Revenge*.[1] Fujita Koheiji made his name as a master of *jitsugoto* owing to his help. Araki Yojibē, Nakagawa Kinnojō, Kaneko Rokuemon, all were young actors at that time and later were said to have agreed that had not Yagozaemon taken them in hand, they would not have been really skillful. Yagozaemon said that among actors accounted skillful today there were many who made a habit of relaxing while other actors were speaking their lines. This is surely bad !

In the first place the play loses its pace, and then the body of the actor who is doing it is deprived of life. At all events, one should watch closely the face of the actor speaking the words, or at least listen carefully to them.

NOTE: 1. *Hinin no kataki-uchi*, c. 1664; see *Sadoshima's Diary*, VIII, p. 145.

ITEM XXXIV
[ON KATAOKA NIZAEMON AND THE NEED TO KEEP UP TENSION]

Kataoka Nizaemon said, when he was playing a *kataki* role, " Whenever a play reaches its end, in the *kataki* role there are the words 'Aa, how bitter a blow!' His evil deeds have come to light. All the warriors strike at him and at this point all the actors, including the one playing the *kataki*, play in a desultory way, because it is the end of the play. The end of a play is very important. I make a point of paying the greatest attention to this, keeping up my concentration, speaking my words with full voice, and trying not to think that it is the end."

ITEM XXXV
[ON THE FIRST APPEARANCE OF THE AUTHOR'S NAME ON THE PROGRAM]

Tominaga Heibē was a writer who came after Yagozaemon, and his was the first[1] instance of a writer's name appearing, as it does now, along with the list of actors in the program of the first performance of the year. This was at the *kaomise* late in 1680, and on that occasion it brought him a good deal of enmity from all sides. From then on the audience became quite bored with the succession of unentertaining plays that he wrote. He was urged to make another endeavor to think up a good play, but Heibē replied: " I take no pleasure in putting out bad plays but it is to the advantage of the management. Suppose that I wrote a good play for every change of program, then if the audience grew tired of seeing these good plays, grass would soon start growing in Dōtombori." I suppose you can prove anything if you try. It was a comical example of refusing to admit that one was wrong.

NOTE: 1. The translation is unaffected by our emendation of Gunji's *hajimete* to *hajimari*.

ITEM XXXVI
[ON SAKATA TŌJŪRŌ'S KNOWLEDGE OF FIRST-AID]

At the beginning of the middle act of the play *The Ten Thousand Lanterns on Mt. Kōya*,[1] when Arashi Sanjūrō stabbed himself in the belly, Tōjūrō attended to him in a very realistic sort of way. A certain actor saw this and said to Kyōemon, " Tōjūrō is always very good at first aid[2] and his performance in a part in which a wounded man is cared for is naturally good. No other actor could come up to him." Kyōemon's reply was: " For the very reason that he is good at first aid, Tōjūrō gets praise from the audience for playing such parts. Because I have never been any good at that sort of thing, I play such a part very unskillfully. The audience say that Kyōemon makes a very good job of treating the wounded, and praise me because it is something I am in fact unable to do, because I cannot do first-aid." I suppose you can prove anything if you try. However, what he said was a fact.

COMMENT: *This and the previous slightly amusing Items both deal with "proving anything if you try." Tominaga Heibē proves that he is benefitting the management by writing bad plays, and Kyōemon that it is equally true to say that an actor who knows how to do something in real life will be praised for doing it well on the stage, as to say the contrary.*

NOTES: 1. *Kōyasan mandō.* First played at the Mandayūza in Kyoto in 1696, with Sakata Tōjūrō as *zamoto.* 2. We have taken the liberty of translating *kai* (= *gekai*, " surgery ") as " first aid."

ITEM XXXVII
[ON MURAYAMA'S THANKS TO SAKATA TŌJŪRŌ]

In 1707, the Edo actor Murayama Heiemon appeared at the

Mandayū[1] theater in Kyoto.   When he left for Edo in the tenth month,[2] Sakata Tōjūrō gave a farewell party for him at his house, and I too was invited along.   Heimon turned to Tōjūrō and said, " I am most grateful to you, sir, for the help you have given me.   Ever since I went to Edo for my first *kaomise* there, I have made you my model, and in all the parts I have played, including *jitsugoto* or *nuregoto*, I have imitated your performances in every particular, for a good thing is good, no matter where.   I have now become the second or third leading actor in Edo.   This is all thanks to you."   In reply to this expression of indebtedness, Tōjūrō shook his head: " Your acting must be bad.   It is proper that a man's art should flow from his innate self as his independent style.   I think that if you make me your model, you will be inferior to me.   Work a little harder to perfect your own style! " he said, and the jollity went out of the party.

NOTES: 1. See Miyako Mandayū.   2. Of 1707.   He appeared at a *kaomise*.

ITEM XXXVIII
[ON ACTORS WHO DO NOT COME ON TILL AFTER AN INTERVAL]

Kyōemon said, " There are some who maintain that in some plays, unless you mention beforehand any actors who do not come on until after an interval, the plot will not be clear.   This opinion is not justified.   Anything that is irrelevant to the plot at the moment and that is said to help something that comes later can only hold up the scene in question.   The mouth is a very efficient instrument, and somehow or other an explanation can be given at the interval.   It is always best to keep up the interest of a play."[1]

NOTE: 1. I.e., by not disclosing the plot beforehand.

ITEM XXXIX
[ON NOT HAVING ACTORS MENTIONED BEFOREHAND]

Tōjūrō said, " If it is necessary to mention beforehand an

actor who will be making his entrance after an interval, one
should make a clear reference to him first, and then, after that,
say the words that are in the play.   The reason for mentioning
the actor beforehand is that by doing so one endeavors to get
the audience to remember about him.   If this is so it is a good
idea to make a strong point of it, by mentioning it early on, in
order to have them keep it well in mind.   And when I say that
the words that are in the play should take the second place, it is
because these words which you should be saying form part of the
the play, and so the audience will have no difficulty in remembering what they are about."

*COMMENT: Although, in Item XXXIX, Tōjūrō does not say definitely
that actors who do not come on till later should be mentioned early on, he seems
in fact to be in favor of this, thereby taking the opposite view to that of Kyōemon
in XXXVIII. Kyōemon would seem to be taking the more sensible line, in
maintaining that the suspense should be kept up, and one wonders what lay
behind the theory that Tōjūrō seems to support. In any case he says that any
reference to an actor coming on later should be made early on in order to impress
it on the minds of the spectators. These can safely miss one or two lines from the
actual play without losing the drift.*

ITEM XL

[ON PLAYS COMPOSED IN CONSULTATION BETWEEN CHIKAMATSU MON-
ZAEMON AND KANEKO KICHIZAEMON; ALSO SAKATA TŌJŪRŌ'S RE-
HEARSING FROM THE OPENING OF THE ACT; HIS HEARING THE PLAY
AGAIN: HIS HAVING THE WORDS PUT IN WHEN HE WAS COSTUMED
FOR HIS ENTRY; HIS LISTENING CAREFULLY TO THE PLOT, REGARD-
LESS OF THE SIZE OF HIS PART]

At one time when Chikamatsu and I were working together
on a new play, we called the actors into the dressing room and
told them about it.   Usually those who have good parts praise
a new play; those with bad parts make no comment on its
merits.   Those who do not know whether it is good or not
seem all the time to be looking at the faces of others, and following the crowd.   And then there are some who are ignorant,
with no feeling for plays, who get angry during the first act,

grumble at my servants, and go away out of temper without bidding anyone farewell. At that period Tōjūrō was the *zamoto*, but he made no comments on the merits or defects of the play and so there could be no comments from any other quarter. He told them to rehearse from the beginning of Act I and went away. Rehearsals started from the next day, and in four or five days the work on the first act came to an end and after that it was the day on which the opening of Act IV was rehearsed. Tōjūrō said that he would like to hear again what we had to say about the play, and this we did. He still did not comment on its merits. It was a play in which he came on wearing wooden clogs, with staff and umbrella, so he told the dressing room messenger to get these articles together; then, with the clogs on his feet, staff in hand and umbrella raised, he told us to put in the words. The play was rehearsed once right through, with Chikamatsu and me doing so, as usual. Tōjūrō said, "Yes indeed, truly a good play, is it not! When I first heard you talking about the play, and again when I heard you just now, I thought it was a bad play. But since it was obvious that you authors sincerely thought that it was a good play, I had the actors meet and discuss it. There are plays which, though I think in my heart that they are bad, are nevertheless applauded by the audience. This year I am over fifty and when I heard your account of the play I could not make up my mind about whether it was good or bad. If I knew how to judge this, I would have become a millionaire! The heart of the actor and the heart of the author are quite different from one another, and so, when I thought to have the words put in just now, I assembled my clogs, staff and umbrella, and made it a dress rehearsal right from the start. My intention was to test the whole of it. But from the words supplied by the authors just now, I realized that it was certainly a good play. I see from what happened to me just now that it would be a good thing to have dress rehearsals right from the start." These thoughts no doubt arose from his having made excellent plays in the past.[1] Whenever he heard a play being discussed, regardless of the size of his part, he listened carefully to its plot.

COMMENT: This invaluable item provides evidence of production methods and rehearsals, discussed in the Introduction (p. 20). Tōjūrō, in his privileged position as zamoto, *came late into the rehearsals, and, typically, he had to sink himself in the part before he could judge its value.*

NOTE: 1. It is not clear whether this means that he wrote plays or produced them. He is not known as a playwright.

ITEM XLI
[ON YAMASHITA KYŌEMON'S LISTENING TO THE PLOT OF A PLAY]

When Kyōemon listened to the plot of a play, regardless of whether it was good or bad, he would first praise the play, and turning to the author he would say, " Now please get on with the words." If there was a play that did not please him, he would call the author in without telling any one else, and listen to the plot again, talking over with him its merits and defects, and redoing it. Not for a moment, during the account of the action, would he say that it was bad.

COMMENT: Kyōemon shows the usual Japanese regard for another person's feelings in never criticizing the author in the presence of others.

ITEM XLII
[ON PLAYS NOT BEING THERE FOR THE PICKING UP]

Tōjūrō said, " If one is poor and wants money, one can get some by stealing. Or there may be some dropped in the street. On the other hand, if one thinks of stealing a play, or of picking one up, it is absolutely impossible to do so. An actor who does not realize this is a stupid ignoramus."

COMMENT: In Items XL and XLI Tōjūrō and Kyōemon show their regard for playwrights, though they were expected to fall in with the requirements of the zamoto *without standing on their dignity. In this Item, Tōjūrō issues a general rebuke to those actors who, unable to write plays themselves, think that they can be provided at a moment's notice. This is a period when the status of the writer was improving rapidly.*

ITEM XLIII

[HOW ALL ACTORS SEEMED SKILLFUL WHEN THEY PLAYED AGAINST SAKATA TŌJŪRŌ]

At that time all actors, whether *onnagata*, *wakashu-gata*, *tachiyaku*, *dōke* or *oyaji-gata*, who played against Tōjūrō seemed skillful. The reason for this was that Tōjūrō would instruct them in how to speak their words, in good timing and good movement. They all followed his leadership and did not go against his advice. They acted in accordance with his instruction, and thus seemed particularly good. Moreover, Tōjūrō himself had few parts and sometimes nothing to bring him before the public eye. Someone said to him, " Your plays are entertaining and popular, but the one thing that is to be regretted about them is the small number of your parts in them." Tōjūrō burst out laughing. "As long as my plays are good, please excuse my absence from the stage. The audiences know of old the qualities and defects of Tōjūrō's acting. The purpose of my theater is not at all to present myself, but to present plays," he said.

COMMENT: Ayame (The Words of Ayame, *XV, p. 57) had already said that "playing with Tōjūrō was like sailing smoothly along in a great ship." It seems that Tōjūrō had considerable powers of leadership and an ability to get willing cooperation from his cast. This must have been quite an achievement, when one considers the clashes of temperament and jealousies that must have continually arisen, especially among the* wakashu *and* onnagata (see XXXI). *On the other hand, one must not forget that the tradition of Japan is to give all-out loyalty to the person in charge. If the expression of the corporate spirit in the last sentence in this Item is reliable, Tōjūrō's modesty may have been one of his endearing qualities.*

ITEM XLIV

[ON THE MEMORIAL PLAYS FOR ŌGIYA YŪGIRI, OF SHIMMACHI IN OSAKA]

It was in the first month of the year 1678 that Ōgiya Yūgiri[1] passed away. On the third of the second month of that year, there was a first performance of a play with the title *Yūgiri departed this life in January*,[2] with Tōjūrō, as might be expected, taking the part of her patron, Fujiya Izaemon.[3] At that time Tōjūrō was thirty-two. Owing to popular demand he put it on again in the sixth month. He presented it once more on the second of the tenth, and it had large audiences until it came off on the twenty-ninth. It appeared yet again in the twelfth month: this was because he was planning to have *The Anniversary of Yūgiri's Passing*[4] from the second of the first, and he wished to have the audience reminded of her story. This was almost certainly the first and last time for the same play to be given on four occasions in the one year. Tōjūrō died in his sixty-third year, on the first day of the eleventh month of 1709. Thirty-two years had passed between 1678 and 1709,[5] and in that time there had been one play or another about Yūgiri in the program a total of eighteen times, including the original one, the First Anniversary, the Third Anniversary,[6] the Seventh,[7] the Thirteenth,[8] and the Seventeenth,[9] some of them being done over and over again. This was a play that was really out of the ordinary. And there was *The* Keisei *and the Jewel-Box*,[10] and also *The Great Temple at Sakai*,[11] *The* Keisei *and the Edo Cherries*,[12] *The* Keisei *and the Awa Whirlpool*,[13] *The* Keisei *at Hotoke-no-hara*[14] with its first[15] and second[16] sequels, *The Ceremony at Mibu*[17] with its first[18] sequel and its second (*The Autumn Ceremony at Mibu*[19])—I have not the time to list all the *keisei* plays of this sort that he was responsible for. And again, at that time, a Soga[20] piece was put on in the seventh month of every year. This was because a *keisei* piece was presented as the second play of the season, in Spring, and there were doubts about doing a Soga piece twice in a year, since it was desirable to make a change from Tora from Ōiso.[21] All things considered, he spent practically his whole life doing *keisei* pieces. This must have been because he had a special genius for the genre. The audiences forgave him,[22] and showed their support by large attendances. I suppose it is very like the present day masters of *jitsugoto* who do nothing but *jitsugoto* all their lives. However, it is very unusual to put on the same play over and over again, as Tōjūrō did. Whenever the acting art was being discussed, Kyōemon always used to say that since Tōjūrō was a master, he performed the plays he excelled at. He himself had no plays that he had mastered; at all events, Tōjūrō was an actor of great renown.

COMMENT: In case it should be thought that the drama of the period was rather monotonous in subject matter, it must not be forgotten that Edo kabuki favored warrior-plays, and that in any case the puppet drama was also flourishing at the time, with plays of all sorts, but with blood-and-thunder and religious themes still in the majority. There must have been a considerable mutual enhancing of glamor between the stage keisei and their real-life sisters.

NOTES: 1. Yūgiri 夕霧 was a *keisei* who had originally worked in the Kyoto licensed quarter of Shimabara 島原, but moved to the Shinmachi 新町 district in Osaka in 1672. She was employed in a house run by Ōgiya Shirobē 扇屋四郎兵衛, whence the name by which she is known. For a summary of the plot of a surviving play on the Yūgiri theme, see Halford, p. 210; Theatre in Japan, p. 16. 2. *Yūgiri-nagori no shōgatsu* 夕霧名残の正月. 3. 藤屋伊左衛門, a fictitious character. 4. *Yūgiri isshūki* 夕霧一周忌. 5. Counting 1678 and 1709. 6. *Yūgiri Sannenki* 夕霧三年忌, 1680. 7. *Yūgiri Shichinenki* 夕霧七年忌, 1684. 8. *Yūgiri Jūsannenki* 夕霧十三年忌, 1690. 9. *Yūgiri Jūshichinenki* 夕霧十七年忌, 1694. 10. *Keisei tamatebako* けいせい玉手箱, first played at Mandayūza, Kyoto, 1688. 11. *Sakai no ōdera—Sakai no ōdera kaichō* 堺大寺開帳, 1691. 12. *Keisei Edo-zakura* けいせい江戸桜, first played in 1698. 13. *Keisei Awa no naruto* 傾城阿波の鳴戸, first played in 1695; author Chikamatsu Monzaemon. 14. *Keisei Hotoke no hara* 傾城仏の原, 1699. After this title there occur ten characters which appear to have been carved on the block in error, with the correct version following immediately. We have ignored these in our translation, but left them in the original text. 15. *Hotoke no hara gonichi ryūjo ga fuchi* 仏の原後日竜女淵, "The Sequel to *Hotoke no hara*, The Dragon-Woman Pool," authors Chikamaksu Monzaemon and Kaneko Kichizaemon. 16. *Tsuruga-no-tsu sankai-gura* 敦賀津三階蔵, "The 3-storied Storehouse on Tsuruga Bay," 1698; see also *Dust in the Ears*, XVII. 17. *Mibu dainembutsu* = *Keisei Mibu dainembutsu* 傾城壬生大念仏, first played in 1702 in Kyoto, author Chikamatsu Monzaemon.

18. *Jorō raigō-bashira* 女郎来迎柱, "The Prostitute and the Temple-Pillar," 1702.   19. *Mibu aki no nembutsu* 壬生秋の念仏, 1702.   20. 曾我. The Soga brothers and their revenge against their father's enemy is a very widespread story in Japanese literature, and forms one of the "worlds" of *kabuki* (see Scott, *The Kabuki Theatre of Japan*, p. 203ff., although what he has to say about the theater calendar does not apply to the period of the *Analects*).   There may have been another reason for putting the Soga plays on in the seventh month, when the *bon* 盆 festivals are performed to pray for the souls of the departed.   The playing of a piece about the brothers at that time served as a way of praying for them.   The ritual element is strong in *nō* and not entirely absent from *kabuki*.   21. 大磯の虎, a *keisei* in the Soga plays.   The reference to not doing Soga plays twice in a year may allude to the Edo custom of putting such a play on in the spring, not followed in Kyoto/Osaka for the reason given in this Item.   22. For always doing the same thing.

ITEM XLV

[SUGI KUHĒ'S ADVICE TO SAKATA TŌJŪRŌ]

There was a famous *kashagata* named Sugi Kuhē. Tōjūrō, when he had turned twenty, went to Kuhē and told him he wanted to study how to act. Kuhē replied, " Since I am a *kashagata*, I have done much imitating of women. You are a *tachiyaku*, so you must imitate men. When one considers present-day *tachiyaku* actors, there do not seem to be many men among them. Nevertheless they are not *onnagata* and there is no reason at all for their lack of masculinity. You go and study how to imitate men!" Tōjūrō said that he followed this advice and learned something of the actor's art. Shortly after the above conversation took place, Kuhē was praised as a master actor unlikely to be equalled in the Three Cities.

COMMENT: *It is difficult to decide whether Kuhē's criticism of actors of his time merely shows a tendency, common enough among* kabuki *critics even today, to complain that things were much better in the past, or whether in Kyoto/Osaka at the time there was really a shortage of actors taking male parts. It is very possible that the glamor of the* waka-onnagata *and* wakashu *player attracted many actors.*

Dust in the Ears, Book 2, the end.

I have collected together and set down the words that have gathered like dust in my humble ears, and have come inevitably to think of them as *Nijinshū*.[1]

NOTE: 1. This epilogue was presumably Kichizaemon's, and explains why the collection is called *Nijinshū*, " Dust in the Ears."

E. Sequel to "Dust in the Ears"

Compiled by
TAMIYA SHIROGORŌ (KŌON)*

ITEM I

Yamamoto Kyōemon[1] always used to draw large audiences by using vulgar expressions, but in scenes where some vulgarity was necessary, Sakata Tōjūrō on the other hand would attract popular support by hinting at it. It is said that the first San'emon would say to the audience. "No doubt there are some present who have some objections: They will not be such that they will mind our showing in their presence a scene of a visit to a *keisei*. Even though they do object some will continue to watch because they realize that it is only a play, and nobody who finds the production elegant is likely to express any objection to the words."

COMMENT: *This slightly confused item shows at least that the audiences were not above enjoying a low joke. Tōjūrō seems to have been squeamish about actually uttering vulgarities. San'emon's announcement appears to indicate that there was a public opinion that controlled the amount of objectionable material in a play.*

NOTE: 1. Presumably an error for Yamashita Kyōemon.

* Kōon was Shirogorō's *haimyō*. See Tamiya Shirogorō, Appendix II.

ITEM II

Fujita Koheiji often used to say that when one slaps the scabbard of one's sword, unless one pulls back one's left leg and glares straight into one's opponent's eyes as one does so, it does not seem very effective.

COMMENT : *An almost indentical item has already appeared as XXVI of* Dust in the Ears.

ITEM III

A certain person once asked Sakata Tōjūrō what should be the spirit of the actors when a separate play is put on at the end of a program. His reply was that they should appear in the extra play with the sentiment within them that they have been reborn. It is clear that the ways of thought of a master performer are really different.

COMMENT: *The separate play at the end of a program, the* kiri-kyōgen *(see p. 20), had a theme that was quite different from that of the main, three-act play, so that Tōjūrō's remark is quite intelligible. In the interval between the long play and the one at the end of the program, the actor who has played in the first play must feel that he is reborn, to start after the interval as an entirely new man. The last sentence may seem a little exaggerated, but it should be remembered that Tōjūrō was one of that first to put into words this sort of thing, which may seem rather obvious today, and that therefore he was very different from the ordinary man.*

ITEM IV

Sakata Tōjūrō expressed the view that if an *onnagata* was a poor actor because he was too gentle, he would become a good actor some day.

ITEM V

The first Sawamura Chōjūrō, seeing an avenue of pine trees with well placed branches while on the road during one of his journeys, said, " If a man who loves naturalness plants pines of this sort and allows them to grow undisturbed, they will form an excellent landscape by themselves. Should someone interfere with this avenue, he will do it by cutting off branches, for the reason that they spoil the effect. Occasionally actors appear who attain the standard of beauty of these trees, but like them they can acquire a poor reputation owing to the activities of stupid persons. This is indeed a cause of regret."

COMMENT: *The arboricultural metaphor is here once again used to point the problem of the natural actor, whose innate talent may well be spoiled by interference from inferior instructors.*

ITEM VI

Kataki-yaku actors nowadays think only of playing at a high pitch, with no variation of intensity, and it follows that the *tachiyaku* actors are led astray by the *kataki-yaku* and they too make a show of superficial tenseness. One might compare them to two mantids eating each other. They fight with each other, if one puts out a hand, it is eaten off, if one puts out a leg, it is eaten off, so that it is natural that in the end they destroy each other. The first Nizaemon, in the early moments of a play, realized that his adversary was going to obstruct his wicked designs later on, and threw his small throwing knife at him. The *tachiyaku* actor specializing in *jitsugoto* saw through his designs, and, wishing to know the reason for his hatred, showed this knife to Nizaemon. The latter, without the slightest change of expression, praised it in the following terms. " Well, well, what excellent workmanship, you must look after that very carefully," and went off. The *tachiyaku* showed the knife to Nizaemon knowing that it was part of his evil plan, yet nevertheless Nizameon gave no hint of this, and in view of the great deal of trouble that he took over his interaction with the other part, it was a great performance. It is the same thing in football,[1] where it is said that a ball received from a skillful player is easily taken, and a *kataki-yaku* should realize this above all else, even though his part may not be very important. Therefore, it is said that Nizaemon seemed comparable to a *samurai* with a rice income of one thousand *koku*.[2] By the same reckoning, Osagawa Jūemon was worth seven hundred, and Otowa Jirosaburō three hundred.

COMMENT: *It seems that the main point of this Item is that there should be some variation in the course of a performance (cf.* Dust in the Ears, *Item XI). The implication is that to play with an unvarying degree of intensity may be all right for a* kataki-yaku, *in the playing of which, in any case, no great subtlety was to be looked for, but that the* tachiyaku *(here a* jitsugoto *actor) should not imitate the* kataki-yaku *in this, but his role, being that of the main male part, should have a certain flexibility. It was also vital to play the* kataki *and* jitsugoto *parts in a different style. A great* kataki-yaku *actor like Nizaemon, however, could and did bring a certain variation into his playing, by his cool rejoinder to the* tachiyaku's *showing him the knife. He also demonstrated at this moment how a good actor cooperates with those on the stage with him. Here he supports the* tachiyaku, *who having had the knife thrown at him, puts some variation into the intensity of the acting by showing it in a casual sort of way, instead of rantingly demanding reasons for the attack. Nizaemon plays up, and the quiet, but meaningful, exchange serves to increase the effect of the preceding and following actions.*

NOTES: 1. See *The Words of Ayame*, Item XVII for Ayame's opinion on the appropriateness of the football image. 2. *Samurai* received their stipends in rice, or rice value, measured in *koku*, a volume equal to about 5 bushels (180 liters). A stipend of 1,000 *koku* would be earned by a senior retainer, and Nizaemon is thus reckoned as very high in his profession, with the other two mentioned placed at about two-thirds and one-third respectively of his worth.

ITEM VII

Sawamura Chōjūrō I, in a play, had to realize that there was a spy concealed in a chest and pierce him with a spear. He girded up his *hakama*,[1] and silently but expressively he went boldly up to the chest and without any pause thrust in his spear. Sakata Tōjūrō said of this piece of action: " Come, come, I do not approve of the way you thrust the spear in. You should do just a little more work on it." Chōjūrō did in fact work on it that night and on the next day he girded up his *hakama* and went boldly up to the chest, but then he went back again, ungirded his *hakama*, then tiptoed quietly up to it. He listened carefully, and considered how the person hidden in the chest would be placed, and then did the job with one thrust. Thereupon Tōjūrō is said to have clapped his hands and praised him: "You really astonished me. You will be a number one actor after this." And in fact he did eventually win high praise in the Three Cities as a master performer.

COMMENT: *It seems that Tōjūrō, like many other teachers, was eager to get Chōjūrō to think out his problems for himself; a tendency to tell the pupil merely that he is wrong and that he should try again, without explaining how he was wrong, is in any case the accepted method of teaching traditional arts in Japan.*

NOTE: 1. The *hakama* or divided skirt could be tucked up into the *obi* or girdle to give freer movement in fighting, etc.

ITEM VIII

Otowa Jirosaburō said, " Sakata Tōjūrō had a habit when speaking his lines of repeating phrases in the following way: 'How charming, how charming.' 'It is I, it is I.' This was to make himself clearly heard at times when there was a large audience, and depended to some extent also upon the rhythm of the utterance. Some time later in a certain play an actor called Fushimi Tōjūrō (who had taken the name of Sakata because he looked very like him) was acting in, he was asked by another actor what sort of buddha Jizō was, and the answering words that this Fushimi Tōjūrō used were: 'He is the Boddhisattva Jizō[1] who directs the dead along the six roads of reincarnation,' and he repeated this long phrase without any reason. Maybe he thought that he had to say everything twice. It was very funny."

COMMENT: *The phrase repeated is a moderately complicated utterance, but not excessively so. The joke does not seem to have kept its comical quality, although the point that slavish imitation helps nobody is clear enough.*

NOTE : 1. Jizō 地蔵 (Sanskrit *Kṣitigarbha*) is a *bodhisattva* (one who could achieve buddhahood but renounces it to help mankind) who intercedes between man and the ruler of hell, and is the friend of children and wayfarers.

ITEM IX

Otowa Jirosaburō was not only a skillful actor but also a first class playwright. He set up a board announcing a change on the fifth day to a play from the *Taiheiki*,[1] and thereafter put on a new play every fifth day. And again, when there were four *kabuki* theaters in Osaka, the Corner theater[2] put on a play which was the first to deal with the forty-seven *rōnin*, entitled *Oni kage Musashi abumi*,[3] with Shinozuka Jirozaemon as Ōishi Kunai[4] and Mangiku as Rikiya,[5] and had a great success. So the Middle theater joined in, and the West theater had Sakakiyama Koshirō Senior and Shibasaki Rinzaemon, and the three theaters were doing the same sort of thing.[6] However, Otowa Jirosaburō, who was working at the East theater, did not merely copy the others but composed quite a different play about Kiso Yoshinaka.[7] This was well received and attracted large audiences.

COMMENT : *Jirosaburō may have been the first to use a system of fixed runs for plays, instead of keeping them on for as long as they attracted audiences. Runs for a fixed period are still the rule for* kabuki *and puppet plays although present-day managements usually think in terms of a month's season.*

NOTES : 1. *Taiheiki* is a historical romance of the late 14th century. 2. For the localities of the Osaka theaters see p. 18. 3. This title is more correctly written 鬼鹿毛武蔵鐙. The author is Azuma Sampachi, and the play (in three acts) was put on in the sixth month of 1709, and ran for 120 days. It deals with the loyal 47 retainers, and was in fact the first *kabuki* play to do so, though there was an earlier Chikamatsu puppet piece. 4. Strictly speaking the character in the play was called Ōgishi Kunai 大岸宮内 ; Ōishi was the name of the original personage, and it is interesting to find it used here, suggesting that the real names of the participants were familiar. 5. Ōishi's son. 6. The titles of the plays at the other theaters have not

been preserved.   7.   Minamoto Yoshinaka, a young general defeated and
killed in 1184.

ITEM X

Otowa Jirosaburō never played in pieces which used the
chanting that goes with the puppets.   The reason that he gave
was that in general this chanting was basically an imitation of
kabuki, and that the puppets too were being worked in a way
that copied this live theater.   On the other hand, the copying
of the puppets by *kabuki* is a cause of decline in the latter, he
said.   Sawamura Chōjūrō disliked working in *jōruri* pieces for
the same reasons, but yielding to the urgent pleas of his backer,[1]
he put on *Coxinga*[2] during its first season at the Takemoto
theater.[3]   Shinshirō played Watōnai,[4] but the role did not suit
him; Chōjūrō was Kanki.[5]   It was not a success, perhaps because his heart had not been in it from the start.   At the Middle
Theater, with Takeshima Kōzaemon (II) giving an astonishingly
good performance, it was a great success.[6]

COMMENT :   *The influences of* kabuki *and* jōruri *upon each other are
difficult to disentangle, but it is doubtful whether the influence of* kabuki *upon
the puppets was as considerable as Jirosaburō seems to be claiming here.*

NOTES: 1.   *kinshu* 銀主.   This is the Kyoto/Osaka term for the person
who provided the capital for financing a theater; another term was *kaneoya*
かねおや.   2.   *Kabuki* version of *Kokusen-ya kassen* 国性爺合戦 (*The Battles
of Coxinga*), the puppet play by Chikamatsu Monzaemon.   The original was
first played in the eleventh month of 1715, and ran for 17 months.   For a
translation, see Keene.   3.   This famous theater put on puppet-plays and
was on the Dōtombori in Osaka.   The *kabuki* version appeared early in
1716.   4.   The main character of *Coxinga*.   5.   The Tartar general
and villain in *Coxinga*.   6.   In 1717.   Kōzaemon played Watōnai.

ITEM XI

In the past in any one theater there were master portrayers
of fathers and old women[1] who used to work with great popularity.   Nowadays if it is a good part, a *tachiyaku* actor will

leave his usual roles and play a father, and a *waka-onnagata* will take older parts. This does not show true integrity. There was a *kashagata* called Kokan Tarōji who, in an interval during a play, came down from the forestage[2] in his costume and make-up as a married woman of about thirty, wearing a mauve cap,[3] and went and stood below the boxes at the back of the theater. On the first day of this play, another actor of the company who had gone round to the back of the audience saw him, and so superb was his portrayal of a woman that he thought that he was in fact one of the lady spectators and pinched her bottom, it is said. Kokan Tarōji was so accomplished a master that the Great Yoshizawa Ayame imitated him, and he was placed at the very top of the actor's rating lists.[4]

COMMENT: Dunn was very intrigued to find that unaccompanied ladies in Edo were sometimes subjected to the same dangers as they are in some parts of Europe today. The Japanese costume can accentuate feminine attractions in two main areas. The Western décolleté has its counterpart in the nape of the neck and the shoulders being more or less disclosed by the degree of lowering of the collar at the back. The hips are also fairly clearly outlined by the kimono, which tends to cling more tightly there than elsewhere, and might well attract the attention noted in this Item.

NOTES: 1. Respectively *oyaji-gata* and *kashagata*. 2. *tsuke-butai*, the forestage 3. *hirari-bōshi*, a light headcovering of mauve gauze worn by women out-of doors. See Shaver, Fig. 133. 4. The system used in the ranking lists is explained on p. 10.

ITEM XII

Actors of old placed great importance upon what they did immediately after making their entry through the curtain.[1] As they emerged they would face the audience and pose, each in his own manner and style. An actor would be considered a master right away on his entrance, and people would tell whether a play was worth watching from this sort of thing. A *kataki-yaku* named Mihara Jūdayū was short in stature, but nevertheless when he made his entrance wearing his long pair of swords and struck his vivid pose and walked his swaggering walk, he looked a big man and struck terror. Nowadays there is no style in entrances. This is just another example of the effect of the present age upon acting.

NOTE: 1. *agemaku.* The curtain leading on to the *hashi-gakari* from backstage. It gets its name of " lift curtain " from the fact that it is raised by two poles which lift it, quickly or slowly according to need, by its two bottom corners.

ITEM XIII

The actors of old did not bare their bodies. When they wanted to give the impression of stripping, they would take off their outer garments, and show a plain white garment which they had on underneath. When plunging a knife into their belly, too, they would stick it in and cut round through a layer of white material. It is the same today. Nevertheless nobody complains that it is unrealistic to cut one's belly through white cloth, because people are accustomed to seeing what is a practice handed down from the past, that white cloth should serve for skin. So that the audience should accept it as natural is, I suppose, again only natural.

COMMENT: Kabuki *today still maintains the convention, and it is a shock to see a naturalistic representation of belly-cutting on television or in a film when one is used to the propriety of* kabuki.

ITEM XIV

In the past it was rare for actors to roll up the skirts of their outer kimono from the back and tuck them into their girdle. In fighting scenes all they did was to catch up the bottom of their outer kimono. Thus, the etymology of the Edo verb *hashoru*[1] is *hashioru* (" fold the edge "). Otowa[2] used to pull his skirt to the right to tuck it up, Sakurayama Shōzaemon used to do it to the left. The first actor really to tuck garments completely up was Osagawa Jūemon. When he encountered

Kataoka Nizaemon it was a fine sight, for they were both handsome men.   They decorated their legs by fixing *sanrigami*[3] on
their white silk tights.

*COMMENT: Japanese garments tend to hamper violent movement, and
it was usual for men to lift up their skirts and tuck them into their sashes and
also to free one or both arms from the outer garments and allow these to hang
down or tuck them again into the sash. These actions became highly exaggerated
in* kabuki *acting, where a great deal of colorful effect is obtained by this sort of
partial disrobing. In real life, the loin-cloth took care of decency, but the pro-
prieties of* kabuki *require the wearing of white silk tights. The display of leg
by handsome men is still thought very fetching.*

*We regret that the translation of this piece does not keep the crispness of the
original Japanese, but we have been obliged to give a certain amount of explanation to make it at all intelligible.*

NOTES: Used in the expression *shiri o hashoru*, " tuck up one's skirts." See
Shaver, pp. 345ff.   2.   Otowa Jirosaburō.   3.   These are small triangular
pieces of paper tied over the *sanri*, which is the small bony projection just
below the knee on the outside of the leg.   It was common to apply moxa at
this point, and this paper may originally have been to hide the scar.

ITEM XV

When in a play there is a sword fight or a brandishing of
weapons, even when there is only the slightest scuffle, present
day actors do somersaults and cartwheels and barely get round
to do any actual fencing at all.   Turns and somersaults are but
copies of acrobat's tricks and are thus to be discouraged, and
leaping and springing about while using the sword is vulgar and
not something to be done by a first-class actor.   In recent years
Otowa Jirosaburō, Sawamura Chōjūrō and Yamatoyama Jinzaemon Senior very rarely acted fighting scenes with their
kimono tucked up.   They had great success just by acting the
play.   Before them, Araki Yojibē, when he was in *The Outlaw's
Revenge*,[1] was the first one to do a fighting scene when acting in a
wounded man role, and was successful because it was so unusual.

COMMENT: Otowa and the rest are praised because they achieved their effect without putting in the extra business of acrobatics or spectacular girding up of loins. The mention of Araki seems to be brought in as an afterthought while the subject of fighting is being discussed.

NOTE: 1. *Hinin no kataki-uchi*; see *Sadoshima's Diary, VIII.*

ITEM XVI

On the occasion of a brawl or a scene of fighting, large clappers are banged continuously together. This is called *kage o utsu*, "beating offstage." Formerly this did not happen. They were beaten only when a dragon was made to appear, or when there was an encounter with a demon. At first they were beaten from a position out of sight, and no doubt this is how the term arose. Nowadays the man who beats them comes out on the stage to do so. Because of this, on one occasion, a man from the country could not understand what "that man making all the noise with his banging" was for. A member of the audience, an Osaka man, replied: "That symbolizes the sound of the actor at work." The country man thought that he meant that the actor's hands and feet made a noise like that when he was acting and completely failed to understand. At any rate, both actors and spectators are now accustomed to the sound, and were the clappers not beaten they would feel that something was lacking, but at the same time I should prefer them to be hidden from the audience and beaten off-stage.

COMMENT: *Presumably the Osaka man's reply meant that the sound of the clappers was an audible symbol of the spirit of an actor, the increasing tempo of the clappers, as they lead up to a climax, representing the increasing intensity of the actor's simulated emotion.*

ITEM XVII

Kaneko Ikkō gave the following injunction to the members of his company. "On the last day of a play's run some actors play the fool. My practice is to act seriously until the very end. Why I do so is that I feel that among the audience on that day there may be people from the west and the east who have come hundreds of miles. These rare visitors from distant places will not have the chance of coming to the theater again, and to see famous actors just playing the fool would make them feel that they had wasted their journey. This is something about which actors should have a conscience."

COMMENT: *We have followed Gunji in taking it that Ikkō was referring to the last day of a run, rather than, as Shuzui suggests, the end of the day's performance. A reference to Item XXXIV of* Dust in the Ears, *however, shows that a certain amount of disorder could, in fact, take place every day. Ikkō's remarks were obviously justified.*

ITEM XVIII

Sakurayama Shōzaemon learned by heart over three thousand old poems because, he said, if you knew many old poems, it was very useful when you were composing words. For this reason he was very skillful at writing speeches and other actors used his services to a considerable extent. His *haimyō* was Ōzan, " Warbler mountain."

ITEM XIX

Kataoka Nizaemon recommended actors to learn how to write *haikai*,[1] for it was this above all that would help their art and be useful in all sorts of connections, be it the gods, Buddha, or love,[2] and would ensure that they were not ignorant either in their thoughts or their words.

COMMENT: *This and the preceding item are recommending much the same thing, for although Sakurayama learned the older poetry and Kataoka the more modern* haikai, *they are both saying that old literature contains thoughts and modes of expression that will be useful for an actor not only in composing his speeches, but in understanding the psychology of his roles.*

NOTES: 1. This term includes what is now known as *haiku* (poems of 17 syllables) as well as *renga* 連歌, " linked verse " and *haibun* 俳文, prose associated with *haikai*. 2. These are divisions of the anthologies of 31 syllable *waka* poetry, and were also applied to *haikai*.

ITEM XX

A certain old man said, "An actor has five advantages ; he is permitted to appear before illustrious personages ; he is praised by a great many persons of all ranks ; he automatically learns the old language ; by his physical activity he keeps the blood circulating in his veins and arteries ; by his acting he keeps a young appearance."

ITEM XXI

The normal way of working was that after the discussion of a new play and a decision upon it, the construction of each scene was worked out. Then the actors in a scene were called together, placed in a circle, and taught the speeches orally. They stood there until they made their exit, and then either rehearsed it again in what was termed the *kokaeshi*, " little going over," or the authors worked out the speeches for the next section, and got them fixed by repetition. The action in scenes in which a distinguished member of the company appeared was worked out by this member himself. With the revival of *kabuki*[1] the plots of plays become more difficult, and then actors were told to take their writing brushes and write down the headings ; they used to write about a line of the beginning of each speech which had been allotted to them. The complete writing down of what are called *kyōgen-bon*[2] started with Kaneko Ikkō.

COMMENT : This valuable account of the preparation of a play is discussed in the Introduction, p. 20.

NOTES : 1. A revivification of *kabuki* is generally said to have occurred at the end of the 17th century. 2. " Play books."

ITEM XXII

Actors of all roles, including *tachiyaku* and *onnagata*, can be greeted with words of praise when they come on, or the distant view can be gazed upon and extolled with decorative speech. An *onnagata* could describe a young *tachiyaku* in words such as this : " What a lovely sight, with his elegant attire and head not shaved. The bottoms of his *hakama* caught up at the side, and though it is not the Tatsuta River, famed for its ruddy tints, his countenance glows through his light make-up. On his light blue coat the cord is most smartly tied with a true lover's knot, his eye is bright and Ariwara no Narihira himself would not be far above him in charm. The more we share a pillow, the more I hate him ; I told him I would gladly give my life, would gladly cut off my little finger, and begged him not to change for I would be faithful even to the next world, but in this inconstant world, in the next existence and in later days still my body is sunk in a whirlpool of desire. I ask you, has he not indeed a lovely face ? " A boy might say, " What you can see yonder is Mt. Kurama. Should one whose heart is impure go onto that mountain, goblins large and small will become angry, let loose their evil winds and their magic winds, and immediately tear him to small pieces and leave them hanging on the tree tops. But should honorable warriors pledge themselves to Sōjōbō and pray for military prowess, they will have the power to defeat even such great generals as Fan Kuai and Chang Liang of China. It is an extremely fearful mountain, so I think it would be better if you worshipped it from afar." It is said that such speeches as these attracted large audiences. I know many others of the sort which have been told to me but I am omitting them in order to avoid over-complication.

COMMENT : Item XII has already stressed the importance of the actor's entrance. This Item shows how an entrance or a scene could be built up with elegant phrases, such as the onnagata's *description of the hero, with his attractiveness increased by his allowing his hair, usually shaved over the front of the crown, to grow unchecked. The Tatsuta river was famed for its appearance in autumn, reddened by fallen maple-leaves. Ariwara no Narihira was an early poet, famed for his love affairs. The girl "hates" her lover with a sort of love-hatred that resents his power over her, but would not wish it otherwise ; the verb* hate *becomes almost synonymous with* love. *The boy's description is of Kurama, a mountain and temple north of Kyoto, famed for the long-nosed* tengu, *"goblins," of whom Sōjōbō was one, that were reputed to live there; one of them gave training in arms to the young Yoshitsune when he was in exile.*

ITEM XXIII

The *tachiyaku* Nakagawa Kinnojō had a natural gift for comedy. In a certain play, when a messenger was talking to a secretary, Kinnojō came on with the task of offering him tea; he had to set down the cup and then withdraw. While he was close to him, he suddenly and mischievously thrust the stand the cup was on into his left hand. It was at the moment at which the messenger was stating his business that Kinnojō thrust the stand into his hand, so he could not get rid of it immediately, and his extreme embarrassment, as his expression showed his confusion, was comical. The audience found it extraordinarily entertaining, and roared their approval. It is said that Kinnojō drew great crowds by doing this sort of thing.

COMMENT: *We cannot help feeling that Kinnojō would have done well to read Item VIII of* Dust in the Ears. *Such an interview between a messenger and a secretary would have been conducted with considerable formality, and an intrusion into this of the practical joker must have indeed amused the audience, although the reception by the other actors concerned may not have been so warm.*

Sequel to "Dust in the Ears," the end.

SUPPLEMENTARY ITEMS

Kokon yakusha taizen (*see p. 14*) *has the following passage, which may be an authentic Item of* Sequel to "Dust in the Ears":

ITEM XXIV

" It is said in *Sequel to ' Dust in the Ears'* that Sakata Tōjūrō, in a play, came late one night to the licensed quarter and knocked at the gate. Miyazaki Giheita was the night-watchman and when he heard this noise he yawned and shouted ' Who's there? ' Tōjūrō would not accept this and said ' That is an early evening voice. I'll knock again.' He did so and Giheita yawned again

' Who's there? ' but received the comment ' If you say it like that, it sounds like a dawn voice.' Tōjūrō criticized him fifteen or sixteen times during the rehearsals. Because of the attention he thus gave to even minor matters as he rehearsed the play into its final form, it followed that his fellow actors tended to reach perfection by their own efforts. On the other hand, nowadays everyone is for himself and it seems that such excellent training does not exist. This must be the reason why we cannot reach a higher standard than we do."

The same Kokon yakusha taizen *has an extract which it assigns to* Kōonki, *which may be an alternative title to* Sequel to "Dust in the Ears", *seeing that* Kōon *is the* haimyō *of the compiler. For the sake of completeness we translate it.*

ITEM XXV

"In the *Kōonki* it is said that one one occasion Yamashita Kyōemon was asked about the acting of *onnagata* parts, and replied: " There are three very important rules for the *onnagata*. His acting towards a man with whom the character he is playing is in love should be very reserved and he should be reticent about it. In his acting, when it seems that the man has fallen in love first, it is better that the *onnagata* should be unrestrainedly harsh. Over and above these two rules, it is extremely important that no matter how he is urged by the writer of the play, he should refuse to act in it if it has some situation that involves a departure from womanly modesty."

F. The Kengai Collection

This volume is an account of the recollections of Somekawa Jūrōbē, a *tachiyaku*, written down by Azuma Sampachi, a playwright. Kengai is the posthumous name[1] of Somekawa Jūrōbē.

NOTES : 1. Strictly speaking, this was not his posthumous name (i. e. a name with Buddhist connotations by which one is known after death) but his *haimyō*.

ITEM I

Sakata Tōjūrō was a man of rare talent, honored as a master actor in plays involving a visit to a *keisei*. One year, it was decided that he should play Fujiya Izaemon in a *Yūgiri* piece,[1] so he gave instructions that since he would need some indoor sandals,[2] a pair should be ordered immediately. Now, when word was brought to him that they were ready and they were shown to him, Tōjūrō looked at them, pronounced them too big, and commanded that they should be remade. The man said, " I measured your foot when I ordered them, so there ought not to be any mistake." In spite of this Tōjūrō insisted that they were

122

too large, so the person in charge of purchases asked him by how much they should be made smaller. His reply was that they should be made a size smaller. They were then immediately returned with the new instructions. At the general rehearsal, he came on with them held between his toes, because they were too small.[3] On the opening day, too, he made his entrance in the same fashion. An actor (I have forgotten his name) who was at the entrance to the dressing room drew his attention to them and said, " Excuse me, but won't your feet go into your sandals? " but as he made his reply[4] to this he went on stage. A certain person found all this rather mysterious and asked him about it. Tōjūrō replied: " In this play there is an occasion when I have to take my sandals off in an *ageya* garden.[5] If my sandals are big when I take them off on the stage, they will be noticed by all the audience, who will say, ' What great clod-hoppers Tōjūrō has ' and one would not do it twice in a play of this sort." How extraordinary a grasp of things a master actor must have, when he pays attention to all sorts of things of this sort!

COMMENT : *One can only assume that the audience would not notice Tōjūrō's sandals when he was wearing them, but only when he took them off. Izaemon is Yūgiri's lover and must at all costs be made to appear an attractive man.*

NOTES : 1. See also *Dust in the Ears*, XLIV n. 1. 2. *Uazori*, a sort of sandal for wearing on wooden floors indoors, especially in such places as restaurants and brothels. 3. When a sandal is too small, one cannot get the foot into the transverse loop. Tōjūrō presumably put his big toe outside this loop, and the rest inside it. 4. Tōjūrō's reply was presumably " No, they won't," but since he went on stage immediately, the anonymous actor was unable to ask him for further explanation. 5. He took off his sandals to put on wooden clogs (*geta*), for wearing outside in the garden.

ITEM II

Sakata Tōjūrō went to a favorite restaurant of his in Gion-machi and asked how it was that in an establishment of its standing there was no tea-ceremony[1] room. The proprietor said, " I will tell you why. I have been wanting to have one now for some years, but there has always been something that has prevented it." Tōjūrō asked how much was needed and the reply was that it would take about fifty *ryō*.[2] " That is very cheap. I will provide you the money for it myself, so please see that the work is started," Tōjūrō replied and then he sent a letter to one of his patrons requesting a loan of fifty *ryō*. This person immediately arranged the matter and when his agent was to bring the money Tōjūrō asked him if he would do him a great favor and pay it all in gold *bu*.[3] Tōjūrō, thus having the whole sum in these coins, had two sheets of special paper[4] brought out, wrapped them up as if they were a gift, and went with them to the restaurant in question, where he met the proprietor. He then took the fifty *ryō* in *bu* out of his sleeve and presented them to him. The man who had provided the money went to see Tōjūrō after a day or two and they talked about this incident as it had happened. The man who had done him the favor said that, in the circumstances, it did not seem really necessary to have the money in *bu*. Tōjūrō replied that he thought it would be vulgar and unpleasant for money that one took out of one's sleeve and gave to somebody to be in *koban* and that therefore he had had it changed into *bu*.

COMMENT: This Item and the two following serve to illustrate Tōjūrō's dedication to his art, and his delicacy and tact in his dealings with others. The point about the money is that producing coins of large denomination would seem a vulgar display.

NOTES: 1. The tea ceremony is best performed in a special room, often simulating a country cottage, with a low entrance. 2. According to Morris (*The Life of an Amorous Woman*, Appendix II), this sum would be equivalent to some £900 or $2,300 nowadays. 3. This fairly large sum would normally be paid in *koban* 小判, a thin, oval gold coin valued at 1 *ryō*, but Tōjūrō had it paid in *bu*, 4 of which make up a *ryō*. 4. *Hōsho no kami*, a high quality paper normally used for memorializing officials, etc.

ITEM III

Whenever Sakata Tōjūrō was holding rehearsals, the whole company would go to his house. On one occasion, during rehearsals for a new play, the actors who were to play with him, the *onnagata* Mizuki Tatsunosuke, Yamamoto Kamon and Kaneko Kichizaemon went there together after breakfast. He was not yet up, so they waited in the adjoining room. After a while he seemed to get up, for there was the noise of a door opening, and they heard the water running as he washed his hands. Next someone apparently swept the room. Then, after an interval, they were asked to be so kind as to go through, and they all immediately went into a large room where they saw him seated on a round cushion.[1] His hair was tied at the back like a brush,[2] and he had a tobacco-tray[3] with a handle by his side. Well, they made their greetings, and then chatted about the new play and how well it had come out. He asked about its points of interest and its plot. Every day he used to look after the *onnagata* playing opposite to him and would have him accompanied home afterwards. Every day during these rehearsals he had dishes served according to the taste of each in a way which would have made them easily eaten by a real woman, and the way in which he treated the *onnagata* was such that he talked to them and so on as if they were women. He showed them great kindness and courtesy.

COMMENT: Tōjūrō was helping his onnagata *colleagues to maintain their artistic standards by treating them as women. The description of the house and furniture is meant to show his taste, and also his affluence.*

NOTES: 1. *Kagami-buton,* " mirror cushion," with the material of the bottom brought round to the top to form a sort of rim with a circle of different material in the middle, giving the effect of an oriental mirror; an alternative explanation of the term is that it was a cushion placed before a mirror. 2. *Chasengami.* The *chasen* is the brush-like bamboo whisk used to mix powdered tea with hot water in the tea-ceremony.   3. A portable tray with the equipment for smoking.

ITEM IV

When Sakata Tōjūrō got an appointment in Osaka at a high salary, he used water brought in barrels from Kyoto, and had the rice for his meals selected grain by grain. When people saw or heard of this, the word went round that indeed Tōjūrō was most remarkably extravagant. A report of this somehow reached his ears, although nobody in particular told him about it. He met a certain person and said, " People who do not know what sort of man I am must be saying that I am indeed an extravagant sort of man, as I have my rice selected grain by grain and my water brought from Kyoto. But it is not so at all. The manager[1] of this theater has laid out precious money to employ me. Should there be some stones in my rice and should I bite one and damage my teeth, I should be unable to enunciate my words[2] when I am on the stage and they would not be audible. In addition, should I drink water that my body has not become used to over the years, and have to absent myself from the stage for even one day because my stomach was upset or something of the sort, I would not be fulfilling my obligations to the manager. In this way I take care of my physical state and my health, and in addition see to it that no obstacle of any sort stands in the way of my career. And that is why I issued the instructions about my rice and water."

NOTES : 1. In this case not the *zamoto*, but the *shibai nushi* (or *kinshu*), the person responsible for the theater's finances. 2. " My words would leak out (through the gap)."

ITEM V

Once, when Nakamura Shirogorō was in the prime of youth, he was in the same company as Yamashita Kyōemon, and the latter's performance was wonderfully successful. The audience praised him for it but that evening Sakata Tōjūrō met him and told him that he had been in the audience on this opening day and that he had acted extremely badly. Kyōemon felt very aggrieved at this opinion, which was completely different from the view that all the spectators had taken, and said, "If that is so, please come to the second day." Tōjūrō agreed and joined the audience on the second day. When Kyōemon reached the dressing room after the performance, he sent a messenger to Tōjūrō's box, asking him to take the trouble to come and see him for a moment in the dressing room. Tōjūrō immediately complied and, going up to Kyōemon, addressed him in the same way as he had done the day before. " You asked me to see the play again today, and this I have done. You really are bad." Kyōemon was very upset, and after the day's program had ended, he did not go to his own home, but immediately went to Tōjūrō's residence, and said to him: "After your unfavorable criticism yesterday, I took a great deal of trouble to improve my performance today. But it still has not pleased you, and it is not in my ability to do any better. I should like the benefit of your instruction." Tōjūrō replied. " If that is so, I shall speak. Nakamura Shirogorō is a young actor, at the beginning of his career. In your present program, you come on before him. You are so great a success that what can Shirogorō possibly do following after you? Why do you not bear in mind the need to help young actors?" On receiving this admonition, Kyōemon beat his hands together in emotion.

COMMENT: *This Item shows another instance of the technique of instruction used in Japanese traditional arts. Tōjūrō merely tells Kyōemon that he is bad and Kyōemon naturally enough tries to improve his performance, but this only makes matters worse. Finally he is reduced to having to admit his inability to understand Tōjūrō's reproof, and Tōjūrō is at least kind-hearted enough to tell him that it is a question once more of cooperation.*

ITEM VI

The actor Ukon Uhē was very skillful in dance pieces with a traveling troupe. Later he appeared on the permanent stages[1] in Kyoto. Sawamura Chōjūrō too originally performed in traveling companies. After the Ise theater,[2] he moved to the permanent stages in Kyoto, where he acted in second items ; he worked very hard at these and became a skillful performer. In the past[3] the actors who appeared in these second items were of medium status.[4] In recent times second items have become like first items in that even actors of the lowest rank[5] play in them. In cases like this old precedents have become invalid. It is very pleasant to think that in Edo the old way of doing things still remains.

COMMENT: *By this time the daily program of* kabuki *was that after the preliminary* Sambasō *(see p. 20) there came the* waki-kyōgen *("first item") followed by the* niban-me *(" second item ") ; this was usually a* sewa-mono *or play of contemporary life. Next came the main three-act play, and finally a piece to close the program ; for more details, see p. 19.*

NOTES: 1. This reference is to the properly established and authorized theaters in Kyoto, as distinct from the temporary stages of the traveling troupes.   2. Ise, where a big audience could be expected from the crowds of pilgrims, ranked after the Three Cities. The reference is probably to Sawamura Chōjūrō III, i.e. Sōjūrō.   3. I.e., until about 1730.   4. I.e., more skilled than those in lower categories.   5. *Kozume*, a word used in Kyoto/Osaka to designate the lowest grade of actor.

ITEM VII

Sakata Tōjūrō often used to say that no matter what sort of role *kabuki* actors played, there was no other way to do it but with the intention of reproducing things as they are ; except that when playing the part of a beggar they should see to it that the whole performance, including the facial make-up and the clothing, is not like the original. " It is only in this role that the actor should depart from the usual principle. The reason for this is that the object of visiting a *kabuki* theater is to be entertained, and so I should strongly wish that everything should be of colorful beauty. To portray a beggar accurately even to his facial appearance is not good. It is unpleasant to have to look

at such a sight and not entertaining at all.   So you should bear
this in mind."

COMMENT: *This Item is clear enough to require no comment, but it is very*
interesting to have stated what is, we suppose, obvious enough, that kabuki *is an*
entertainment, and that though realism is good, sordid naturalism goes too far.

ITEM VIII

It is said that on one occasion Sakata Tōjūrō left the theater
with Kaneko Kichizaemon, and on the way home he stopped
on the bridge over the Takase-gawa[1] and remained there, gazing
fixedly at the running water, until quite a long time had passed.
Kaneko wondered whether he had dropped something, and
peered down with him.   A person who was with him[2] apparently thought it was rather strange and asked him if he had
dropped something.   No reply.   After a while he expressed
his admiration for the water of the Takase-gawa, saying, " How
clear it looks."   Then he walked on towards his home which
was at the time to the north of the crossing of the Fourth Avenue
and Kawara Street.[3]

When I come to think of it, there is a saying handed
down from of old that among uncontrollable things are the
the waters of the Kamogawa[4] and *sugoroku*[5] dice.

Perhaps he was thinking of this.   The great Sakata had
always been constitutionally incapable of distinguishing
between what was useful and what was not.   He was a
man who did not consider anything as of no importance.
In a street to the south of the crossing of the Fourth
Avenue and Kawara Street there was a long-established
tōfu[6] shop.   One day he noticed that inside this shop they
were preparing *tōfu*, and he stood at the entrance without
going in and sitting down, and asked searching questions
to acquire information about the process of preparing *tōfu*
for eating, and then he left, expressing his admiration.
Everybody talked about his characteristic of not ignoring

anything, however trivial, and his straightforwardness.[7]

COMMENT : *One is reminded of* Dust in the Ears, *XIX.*

NOTES : 1. This is an artificial river running through the heart of the Kyoto entertainment district.   2. A servant escorting him through the streets.   3. See plan, p. 17. Gunji has a note on its situation.   4. The large river that runs through Kyoto.   5. A game resembling backgammon.   6. A widely-used foodstuff, made of bean-curd.   7. This and other later sections are inset in the original.

ITEM IX

Sakata Tōjūrō fell in love with the mistress of a certain restaurant in the Gion,[1] and thinking to bring matters to a head immediately, the lady in question led him to a small apartment in the rear of the establishment and blew out the lamp at the entrance.   Tōjūrō immediately fled away.   The next morning he went to the restaurant and hastily sought out the lady and thanked her in these words.   " Thanks to you, I have managed to study my role in our next play.   I am going to portray an adulterer, and since I have never done such evil business, I have been very embarrassed about how to act the part.   Recently I have had two or three urgent requests from my manager,[2] who wants to open the play as soon as possible.   I have been troubled by this night and day and came to the conclusion that unless I was fortunate enough to meet such a man and find out what his feelings were, I would not learn a thing about this seducer's role.   Now my wish has been granted and I have learned how to play it.   This morning I went to my manager and told him that he could open the play on the day after tomorrow."[3]   The people who were there on this occasion beat their hands in astonishment, thinking how the methods of persons who can be called masters were out of the reach of ordinary men.

COMMENT : *This incident was developed into a play by Kikuchi Kan* 菊池 寛 *before the war.   It has been translated into English.   The theme of the Item is the now familiar one of the search for reality.   The last sentence reminds one of the stock endings of early puppet plays, and too deep a meaning should not be sought in it.*

NOTES: 1. Pleasure district of Kyoto, near the theaters. 2. *Tayū-moto*, the same as *zamoto*. 3. Note that a play was not put on until the rehearsals were satisfactorily completed.

ITEM X

When the theater was resting owing to an official ban on music,[1] Tōjūrō took two or three *onnagata* from his company to whom he was particularly attached, and invited them to accompany him to Ishiyama[2] in Ōmi. While they were feasting and drinking, there was facing them a gentleman who appeared to be a *samurai* of considerable importance, and who seemed to be visiting the temple in Ishiyama incognito. With him were five or six young lords, including some close retainers, and twelve or thirteen others attending them, of high and low rank; all were feasting and drinking *sake*. After a while a young *samurai* came over and said to him "Are you not Tōjūrō? I bring word from my lord that he would like to entertain you to a cup of *sake*." He expressed his gratitude at such good fortune and straightway joined the party behind its screen, accepting a *sake*-cup and telling many stories; thus some time was spent in a very convivial mood. When the sun was sinking in the west, he took his leave, explaining that the theater was opening tomorrow and that he would like to be allowed to return home as soon as possible. He then went back to the carpet on which his own party was seated. Shortly afterwards a young *samurai* hastened up and asked him to name anything that he wanted. He replied that he would ask him to be so kind as to tell his lord that he required nothing. Then he came back to him and said that his lord was not pleased with his reply, and that he should ask for whatever he wanted. Because of his insistence, he replied that in that case he would like to have the pine tree growing by the spot where their screen was. With that, they all got into litters and returned to Kyoto.   Some days after that, he heard a great noise of people's voices in front of his house, and, asking in the kitchen what it was all about, he was told that a pine tree had arrived.   He thought that it was a case of mistaken address, but the delivery man in charge of the pine tree came in saying, "Is this Sakata Tōjūrō's residence?" and announced that he had brought the tree which had been promised him some time ago at Ishiyama.   At this, he at length remembered the incident.   He realized that it was the present which he had received from the high-ranking lord, but he would be unable to express his thanks to him, because he did not know his name.   He exclaimed in his gratitude: "He must have generously sent me the tree because he thought that I had my heart set on it.   He looked to be an important lord, but, even so, just a small tree would have been most gratifying, but this big one is still more so.   He could not have dug it up without first consulting the temple authorities.   What a truly gracious deed!"   He gave an order to plant it immediately in his garden,[3] but there was a great to-do on the way to it.   He asked what the matter was, and the reply came that the pine tree that had come just now had become jammed against the wall and would not pass through the entrance to the passageway.   Tōjūrō grumbled at his man, "That's nothing to worry about.   If it is stuck and won't go through, you'll have to break the wall down.   A bit of plaster afterwards will put it right!"[4]   Kaneko Kichizaemon happened to be there when this happened and he used to recount it to people, expressing his astonishment at how different are the thoughts of men who have acquired the name of skilled performer.

COMMENT: Those who have had difficulty with moving a grand piano or getting a car into a suburban garage will sympathize with Tōjūrō, but probably not find his solution as remarkable as did Kichizaemon, at a time when ordinary people did not have to move large objects.

NOTES: 1.   Presumably the death of some person of high rank in the im-

perial or shogunal court had caused a period of official mourning.   2.
Ishiyama is on the shore of Lake Biwa, and has a famous temple.   3.   The
Japanese gardener was obviously already skilled in the transplanting of large
trees.   4.   The wall was probably of earth faced with plaster.

ITEM XI

During the Genroku period Nakamura Shichisaburō was
praised by all in Edo and had an excellent reputation as a skillful
actor; he was a master of lover's parts.[1]   In 1697, in the eleventh
month,[2] he came to Kyoto to join the company of Yamashita
Hanzaemon (afterwards Kyōemon) on the Fourth Avenue.
During the *kaomise*, Sakata Tōjūrō[3] had great success, but
Shichisaburō was not at all popular, and there were many reports
of his performance, all saying that he was no good.   In fact so
great was his failure that people were singing satirical songs
about him, calling him the back legs of a horse.[4]   After one or
two days the whole company came crowding in to see Tōjūrō
and talked contemptuously of Shōchō (Shichisaburō's *haimyō*),
saying that there were very bad reports about him.   For him
to have come from Edo to play lover's parts was a great mistake,
and was further proof of his lack of intelligence.   Tōjūrō
replied, " What stupidity !   Kyoto audiences are thoroughly
ignorant !   Above all, Shichisaburō is one of the greatest actors
of recent times ; at the moment there is not a single one who
stands higher than he does.   If we exert ourselves, our art will
be a little better during this year[5] because he has come to Kyoto.
Because we have done better than he has in the *kaomise*, he will
be a far tougher opponent in the second program." Tōjūrō
said this during the *kaomise* run and from the twenty-second of
the first month of the next year,[6] they put on the play *The* Keisei
and the Peak of Asama,[7] with Shōchō as Tomoe-no-jō.   In one
act of this play there is a scene where he has a lover's quarrel
with the *keisei* Ōshū while playing solitaire *go*,[8] using fragments
of a broken teacup as pieces, on a *go*-board patterned coat that

he spreads on the floor.   In this scene he surprised everybody
by his acting, which was inimitable, and the Kyoto audiences
were in raptures ; his reception was the direct opposite to what
it had been in the *kaomise*, and he had a great success.   He
acquired a great reputation and people said he was " terribly
skillful."   This play had a run of one hundred and twenty days.
The whole cast of the neighboring theater,[9] as Tōjūrō had predicted, said admiringly that the superiority of his interpretation
was really frightening.   Tōjūrō secretly summoned Kaneko
Kichizaemon to him without telling the others and gave him the
following confidential injunction.   "As I predicted during the
kaomise, we have a great competitor called Shōchō with us this
year and so all the actors will obviously have to do their best,
but above all, we shall have to work hard on our material for if
there is no thought put into new plays, the theater will suffer.
I emphasize this because our superiority in the *kaomise* might
make the authors relax their efforts."   At every change of program Tōjūrō would go and see Shichisaburō's performance,
and pronounced him a true master.   On the other hand Shichisaburō saw Tōjūrō's acting, and exclaimed bitterly :   " This
actor Tōjūrō is far better even than I had heard.   Had I seen his
acting and studied it earlier, I should have achieved a much
higher standard, but it is absolutely no good my trying to do
anything about it now."   Tōjūrō's opinion of Shichisaburō
from the performances he saw was that first of all his movements
and posture on the stage seemed absolutely correct.   Tōjūrō
derived deep pleasure from this and from the fact that his bearing
was always extremely good.   From then on the two men grew
nearer together and very often had happy meetings.   Shichisaburō worked with the Yamashita company for two years, in
1697 and 1698, and toward the end of the latter negotiations
for him to return to Edo and work in the Yamamura theater
in Kobiki-chō[10] were completed.   He gave Tōjūrō a parting
present.   Tōjūrō had already been thinking of giving him some-

thing to take with him, but when he received this gift from Shichisaburō, he thought that such a present would seem too much like a mechanical return of compliments and lacking in feeling. So he said nothing about it but went to take his leave; he saw him off and they parted on the best of terms. On the last month of that year, on the twenty-ninth day, six porters[11] appeared at the gate of Shichisaburō's house in Edo and delivered their load. Shōchō was told about this and, looking at the accompanying letter, he found that the load had come from Tōjūrō. When he opened the load, there appeared a great jar in a crate. Shōchō was consumed with curiosity about what he could have been given. Since it was a present from Tōjūrō, it must surely be something with a great deal of thought behind it, he considered. He swiftly opened the letter,[12] which read, "I hereby present you with a jar of water from the River Kamo. Please use it for your New Year's tea."[13] Shōchō was almost struck dumb with admiration. "After my meetings in Kyoto with Tōjūrō, I thought that I had got to know him thoroughly, but I obviously had not. This present shows a depth of sentiment which it would be hard to measure," he said, when relating the occurrence not only to the members of his household but to other persons as well. Even so sensitive a man as Shōchō had difficulty in divining the depths of Tōjūrō's heart. Other people were incapable even of discussing him.

COMMENT: *Tōjūrō's present is to be taken as typical of the man. Just as he was reluctant to hand over large coins to the restaurant-keeper who wanted to build a tea-ceremony room (II), so he thought that a merely expensive present would be lacking in taste. So he went to great trouble to transport the financially valueless but sentimentally invaluable water of Kamo all the way to Edo.*

NOTES: 1. *yatsushi*. 2. Gunji points out that the calendar sign in the text is in fact wrong, and should be *ushi* 丑, "ox" and not *u*, "hare." 3. Who was with Miyako Mandayū. 4. The back legs of the *kabuki* horse were traditionally played by the least skillful actor in a company. 5. Of Shichisaburō's contract. 6. The calendar sign should be *tora* 寅, "tiger." 7. *Keisei Asama ga dake*. This three-act play, reputedly written

by Shichisaburō, was first played in 1698.   It has a complicated plot involving a local family and shrine in Shinshū 信州 (Nagano 長野 prefecture),
and the love of Tomoe-no-jō for the *keisei* Ōshū.   8.   A game normally
played by two, with black and white pieces on a squared board.   9.
Where Tōjūrō was playing.   10.   After the great Edo fire of 1657,
Kobiki-chō was designated as the theater district.   11.   The load was slung
on a pole, carried by three porters at each end.   12.   Up to now he had
only read the writing on the envelope.   13.   *Ōbuku*, tea drunk during the
first half of the 1st month, containing seaweed, etc.; like most New Year
things, it was felicitous, and merited the use of special water.

ITEM XII

Yamashita Kyōemon, when giving instruction to young
actors, said " It is essential that one should endeavor to do
one's best not to have doubtful words in the speeches of the
kabuki theater.   The reason for this is that it often happens that
whole families come to see plays."   This is indeed true.

COMMENT: *This sentiment has already been encountered in* Sequel to
Dust in the Ears, *I, and occurs again in XIII.*

ITEM XIII

Sakata Tōjūrō said, " Some people even object to plays
including visits to *keisei* being performed on the stage, but I
cannot see how they can be avoided.   Even so, for some time
now, speeches which might bring forth objections have been
gradually getting more frequent and recently there have been not
a few plays in which people have gone to bed together on the
stage.   Writers who make up plots such as this ignore the teachings of men of old.   And those actors who accept all that the
authors write, no matter what it is, and perform it, are guilty
of the same crime."   This is what Tōjūrō said, when he foresaw
that when twenty or thirty years had passed, the conduct of actors
would deteriorate, and I think every day how apt his remark
was.   Should there be in a play the likelihood of objection being
made, there should be some way of dealing with it before the

objection is actually raised. It is impossible for parents and children, brothers and sisters to go to see present plays together. This is truly most disturbing.

COMMENT: *The remark by Tōjūrō about the deterioration of acting is referred to again in* Sadoshima's Diary, *XII*.

ITEM XIV

Sakata Tōjūrō used always to say to young actors, "As long as *kabuki* actors play with the spirit of just being *taiko-mochi* for other men, they will not become skillful. If they sink so low as that, then the relations between actor and actor will become extremely distant."

COMMENT: Taiko-mochi *were male entertainers at parties, whose sole object was to make their clients laugh, and pander to their whims. Actors, however, should remain faithful to their art. If not, they will not be able " to look each other in the face."*

The Kengai Collection, the end.

G. Sadoshima's Diary

— RENCHIBŌ*

ITEM I

The custom of performing the *roppō* is said to have started with a certain man who had sprung from a distinguished warrior family in Shinshū. He was extremely fond of entertainment of all sorts and therefore left the service of his lord and went to Kyoto. This was the time when the *rōnin*, Nagoya Sanzaemon, who had married the priestess O-Kuni from Izumo, was doing theatrical performances with her at Kitano in Kyoto. So he joined up with Sanzaemon, and did the *roppō* as a dance performed when visiting the Edo *sancha* girls.[1] In Edo it is called the *tanzen* and in Osaka the *deha*. A tradition was formed, and after his time the *tachiyaku* Araki Yojibē drew large audiences by dancing the *roppō*. Up to his time, it was not performed, as it is today, with *tasuki*[2] on, but with each arm stretched out forwards in turn. Even today, this old way of doing it persists in Edo. It was passed from Yojibē to Arashi San'emon I, and he developed it and made it what it is today. After him, an actor of old,

---

* Renchibō was the buddhistic name of Sadoshima Chōgorō.

138

Yamatoya Jimbē, had some success when he devised the " crip-
pled *roppō*." Arashi San'emon II passed it on to San'emon III
and he constantly performed it. Then I did some work on it.
It is very difficult to describe its movements in writing, and it
is taught only orally.

COMMENT: *The* roppō *is a very characteristic ingredient of* kabuki, *and*
roppō *exits down the* hanamichi *are still extremely effective. Though there
may be some connection between brothel-visits and* roppō, *Gunji thinks that one
cannot place reliance upon Sadoshima's account.*

NOTES: 1. The *sancha* girls 散茶女郎 of Edo were prostitutes of the third
rank; see Gunji, p. 424, n. 20. Sadoshima is claiming that the predecessor
of the *roppō* was used when visiting these girls. 2. A cord used to hold
up the ends of the sleeves of a kimono, when working or in violent activity.
Gunji mentions the possibility that the phrase *tasuki o mawashi* might mean
" whirling the *tasuki*."

ITEM II

The first time that I danced the *roppō* was in a theater in
Dōtombori in Osaka, and I was asked by the *zamoto* to perform
it during the opening program. Up to then it had been done
by actors like San'emon and Jimbē, and I declined, saying that
I could not possibly think of following on after them; however,
he insisted, and I found it hard to refuse. So I took a lot of
trouble devising a striking appliqué-work costume and did the
roppō at the performance on the first night.[1] Halfway through,
there were cries of " Pack it in " from the audience, and five or
six cushions[2] came flying in. This was the signal for a whole
rain of them from all over the house. I carried on regardless
and finished the performance. When we returned to the dressing room, the whole cast were clapping[3] at a job well done,
but I had no heart at all for this sort of thing and did not join
in. On the second and third days, there were the same cries
from the audience, the seventh day went by, then the day performances started and even then they still hurled in their cushions
as ferociously as ever. I was most unhappy but thought that

I would never forgive myself if I failed in my *roppō* at this *kaomise*, and that the shame of it would be with me ever afterwards, so I persisted and tried my utmost to improve my performance. Then, suddenly the reception I was given improved, with shouts of " Bravo." Every day after that reports of my performance were more and more favorable, and I heard from all sides that my reputation was saved. This all shows the necessity for work and persistence. Some people asked me whether or not I would have saved my reputation if I had not improved my performance of the first day. I have asked this question of myself but I do not know the answer.

NOTES: 1. In Osaka the first seven performances of the *kaomise* started at sunset at this time.   2. Lit. " half-mats," i.e. equivalent perhaps to half the standard 6′ × 3′ floor mat, or perhaps with each dimension halved, i.e. 3′ × 1.5′; these were hired by theater-goers, as in *sumō* meetings even today. 3.   No doubt the rhythmical clapping still performed on felicitous occasions.

ITEM III
     Ever since my fifth year I was taught dancing by my father Dempachi. He took me to Edo and had me do a *go*-board doll act on a *go*-board. We had engagements all over the place, and worked from Spring to the ninth month. I attracted the attention of a certain gentleman and was frequently summoned by him to dance my *go*-board dance. So great was his regard for me that he ordered some pottery figures of myself sitting on a *go*-board to be made in Karatsu in Hizen,[1] and they pleased him so much that he had three of them made and delivered to him. When we were traveling to Kyoto in the tenth month of that year, the word got around about my *go*-board doll dance, and I was asked to do it at every inn we stayed at. I always complied with these requests. When I reached my ninth year, I was no longer able to perform on a *go*-board. Dempachi then devised the trick with the seven changes of costume and taught me that. In later years it was to become my specialty

and to be known as " Chōgorō's seven changes." It is impossible for me to express with my pen all that I owe to my father. My memory of him is now as part of the past. At the end of this collection I append his secret tradition of the dance.

I left the world and took up my residence before the gate of Kenninji,[2] where I spent my whole day reading the Lotus Sutra,[3] with no object in life but to seek to follow the way of the Buddha. One day when making my daily visit to Chōmyōji[4] in the new quarter of the Third Avenue, I saw in an antique shop one of these Karatsu-ware figures of myself at the age of five as a *go*-board doll. As it had childhood memories for me, I swiftly reached an agreement about a price, bought it and took it home. At some time in the past my lord must have presented one of them to a person in close attendance on him whom he had taken a liking to, and no doubt this was the history of the one I bought. As I gaze long upon it, I remember the struggles and toil that my father had, and it seems to invite my tears.

COMMENT : The go-board was a sort of low table with a square top on which the game of go *was played. The go-board doll was a mechanical puppet that danced either on an actual* go*-board, or a small table of the same size. The young Chōgorō imitates the dancing of such a doll and is very popular. This Item gives a hint, in spite of the gratitude that he expressed to his father, of the difficult life such a boy would have had, constantly on the move and performing even in inns.*

NOTES: 1. In the present Saga 佐賀 prefecture in Kyūshū. 2. A Zen temple in Kyoto. 3. One of the most important Buddhist scriptures. 4. A temple of the Nichiren sect of Buddhism in Kyoto.

ITEM IV

One year I went to the Ise theater and found that there was an extraordinary shortage of musicians. And of course the instruments and so on were not complete, so that although there was a small drum there was not a large one. We should be very embarrassed without one so I used my ability with tools, and, cutting some bamboo, I joined it together and made a large drum, and then so arranged things as to produce what was called " one man with two drums,"[1] in which a player could play very quickly on both, hence the name. It is rather amusing that somehow or other it became a turn in itself.

NOTE: 1.   This appears to have been a contraption incorporating both types of drum, on which one player could play more or less simultaneously, thus " very quickly."

ITEM V

Sawamura Sōjūrō became Chōjūrō in Edo, and later changed his name again to Suketakaya Takasuke, his *haimyō* being Tosshi. He came from a very distinguished family in Kyoto and in his youth he entered government service, but even though he sprang from an ancient line, he was by nature too self-indulgent, for he fell from grace and finally became an actor in a *kabuki* theater. For a while at first he did not settle down, as he did later, but wandered from place to place, not able to get proper employment. He played the flute in theatrical companies that traveled through the provinces, or went off to do some temporary work as required. After that he acted in a theater in Ise.[1] At that time he was called Sawamura Tōgorō,[2] and I got to know him for the first time when I went to Ise. I watched his performance very closely, and considered that he was different from other traveling players, and that his acting was noteworthy from all points of view. After my attention had been drawn to him as one who was not unlikely in the course of time to reach the top of his profession, I secretly summoned him one evening, and asked him, were he going to remain an actor, whether it would not be a good idea to go to Edo and make an effort there. In reply he told me that he had ambitions in this direction, but no great confidence in his abilities. I said that I would take over his responsibilities in Ise and advised him to go to Edo that year-end; he did so that winter. After a short while, he changed his name to Sōjūrō, and he gradually acquired an excellent reputation, finally being rated second after Ebizō. Afterwards I went to Edo, and even though I had formerly been in the same company as he, he had now reached an eminence such that it would have been up to me to bow low and give him my humble greetings, and he need not have paid the slightest attention to what had happened in the past. But Tosshi thanked me in the dressing room, in front of everybody, saying " Well, well, what an unexpected meeting! When I think back to the time when you and I were together, it seems a long while ago. At that time some years ago I relied upon your aid and thanks to you I have, in the ensuing period, made a place for myself in the world." In fact, turning to Ebizō and the other distinguished men there, he made public expression of his indebtedness, saying that he had incurred a great obligation. I thought at the time how different from the ordinary are the ways of thinking of outstanding men. The majority of people do not disclose what happened in the past, but lose all gratitude, because they have now reached a high position; there are not many men who would thus recall past history in front of so many people. After this he came to Osaka and acquired the reputation of being a skillful actor. In the autumn of that year he appeared before the Kyoto audiences for ten days at the theater of the southern side,[3] and so good was the reception accorded to him that the prices of the boxes were put up, and so large were the audiences that it was the busiest season for some time. He returned to Edo and in the following autumn he went once again to Kyoto and while he was there received renewed praise for his brilliant acting. Later he returned once more to Edo. While in Kyoto he wrote a treatise about the interpretation of *onnagata* roles. This is called *Tosshi's Forty-Eight Articles.*[4]

NOTES: 1. In 1715. 2. Some authorities say Zengorō 善五郎.
3. The surviving *kabuki* theater in Kyoto is still called Minamiza 南座,

" Southern theater," see p. 17.   4. See Gunji, p. 367, n. 7.

ITEM VI

Of recent years actors playing in *shosagoto* have been wearing a stupendous number of costumes one over the other, and in moments when they have not been dancing, they have faced the musicians ranged across the stage, turning their backs to the audience, and have been divesting themselves one by one of these kimono. The intention behind the taking off in *shosagoto* pieces of the top costume (and revealing a new one underneath) is that however entertaining such a play is, when the audience has been watching it for some time, there is a tendency for their eyes to grow a little tired of it, and to arouse them from the resulting somnolence a change of costume is put in. However, for a time now actors have been taking pride in excessive layers of costume, and have been removing these with such frequency that their preoccupation with this activity has become rather an eyesore. During the time spent in divesting and arranging the next costume, the audience's eyes have nothing to look at. After all, it is better there should be no interruption in the action.

ITEM VII

Takeda Izumo, from Osaka, wrote requesting that I should teach his children[1] to perform *roppō*. I went to Osaka to comply with his wish, and he was particularly pleased that I did so. Now, when I came to give the children instruction, their dancing and their use of their heads did not come up to my expectations. Then I suddenly had an idea and suggested to them that the control and rhythm found in the dancing of the *roppō* were the same as those used in the movements of a cock's head. Then they immediately grasped the point and the lesson went off perfectly. In teaching, there is no better way than by using similes. But even so, even this method must use practical examples to be of any use. After my class in *roppō*, various tales were told about people of the past and one of these concerned the Takemoto Chikugo theater, which at the time referred to was working on a new *jōruri* play being prepared for a new program. The whole numerous Takeda clan were working, each at his own job, constructing properties and everything necessary. In the midst of this activity a man who had been asked to make some properties said to Izumo : " Could you come for a moment," and called him into the next room. In reply Izumo asked what he wanted him for. " The willow tree is ready. I should like you to look at it," he answered. Izumo said, " It is no use my looking at it. As long as it bears some resemblance to a real willow that's all that matters." Indeed, one of the admirable characteristics of the Takeda family that has been handed on from generation to generation is that their attitude of mind is always exceptional. How true are the teachings of the men of the past, that the whole theatrical art, from the acting of the part down to the making of properties, is nothing but the reproducing of reality. Be it evil or good, if it is something in which everyday things appear, the most important thing for the actor is his approach to those everyday things.

COMMENT : Sadoshima gives the impression of being rather fulsome in his praise, not only in this Item. One can imagine Takeda saying, " Don't bother me with detail; as long as it looks something like a willow, it will do !" but even so, the main point is there, namely that realism was the goal. Provided that the property willow looks like a real one, it will do. As long as the roppō *looks like something concrete, it will be all right. Note, too, that Sadoshima tries to use a more effective teaching method than the more usual paradox or negative criticism.*

NOTE: 1. Presumably not his own children, but those attached to a children's theater which he appears to have been running.

ITEM VIII

Young people may think that performances of the play *The Outlaw's Revenge*[1] started in the not so far distant past with Anekawa Shinshirō,[2] but in fact it was first acted long ago by Araki Yojibē.[3]   He used to appear at the time in the following costume and make-up: a sick man's wig, greased to make it very black; his face made up to look handsome, with white paint applied very thick; his dress a kimono of white unpatterned material. This had sleeves with a wide opening, and had a lining of plain red silk.   His round, pale-blue sash was tied at the front.   His arms and legs were made very white and this gave him an excellent appearance.   I heard this description of him from my father Dempachi.

My humble opinion is that what Sakata Tōjūrō said about the interpretation of the role of the outlaw was not after all his own idea.   What Tōjūrō said agrees exactly with the description that the men in the past have left of Araki Yojibē's costume and make-up in *The Outlaw's Revenge*.   The thought also occurs to me regarding Anekawa's interpretation of the role of the outlaw, that the expression " as different as snow and ink " is really apt.   Because Shinshirō's acting of the outlaw was good, people always talk of him in connection with it, but his interpretation was extremely vulgar.   This is not to blame Anekawa.   My argument takes into account the interpretation given to the role by the men in the past. His acting, too, when compared with theirs, was vulgar. In the words of Kamura Utaemon, who has come to test a new sword, there occurs: " You say you are a *kataki-uchi* but it's only because you want to save your life."   He then makes a ferocious attack on him.   Thereupon the outlaw draws his sword from the bamboo in which it has been concealed, and thrusts it into him, saying, " This Aoe Shimosaka cuts sweetly through two bodies, their hands tied behind their backs," and laughs a long laugh.   How Araki played it in its first presentation was that halfway through the speech " This Aoe Shimosaka cuts sweetly through two bodies, their hands tied behind their backs " he took the inthrust sword with both hands, and pulled it over to the left. Then, lowering his voice, he finished his speech as before with a long laugh. The question of which was right and which was wrong is something that later actors should ponder over.

COMMENT: *The authors too have been made to ponder over this rather obscure Item. It seems that the outlaw is not really a " non-human," i.e. one who for some crime had been deprived of his human status, but a warrior Shundō Jirōemon* 春藤次郎右衛門, *who was seeking for the object of his revenge Kamura Utaemon. The latter comes across him by chance when he is out looking for something or someone to try out his sword on. A " non-human" was just what he wanted, but Shundō draws his sword from the section of bamboo in which it had been concealed. It was made by a famous swordsmith Shimosaka from Aoe in the present Okayama* 岡山 *prefecture, and had been tested by cutting through two bodies with their hands tied behind their backs, in which position, of course, the arm-bones made the test more difficult. The bodies of executed criminals were often used for this purpose. The sword was thus certified whereas Kamura's had not been tested yet. The only difference between the acting accounts seems to be that Araki twisted the sword in the wound. Such varying interpretations are a source of much discussion among* kabuki *experts. The alleged vulgarity of Anekawa's performance possibly lay elsewhere than in this scene.*

Another point of interest in this Item is that we have a rare precise reference to make-up, with the face made very white, to give, apparently, a handsome pallor, to contrast with the black hair of the " sick wig "; a sick man did not shave the top of his head, and the hair thus grew long and bushy. The plain but smart costume matched the make-up. The sash, a cylindrical cord rather than a flat strip, was tied at the front to show that he was living alone, with no wife to tie it at the back for him.

NOTES: 1. *Hinin no kataki-uchi.* See also *Dust in the Ears,* XXXIII, p. 94. 2. In 1723. 3. Yojibē is more correctly written 与次兵衛, as later in this Item.

ITEM IX

One thing that my father Dempachi used continually to say to me when I was young was that actors were not people who " gave eyes to money," but the most vital thing in their whole life was to make their name more widely known. He would emphasize this to me most strongly, over and over again, till my ears were almost deafened.   I have kept this injunction in mind during the years that have passed since my childhood and therefore, no matter where people come from to ask me to work for them, I never go into the question of payment, but, if I am requested to do so, I decide upon a contract to go anywhere, without further discussion.   Pay should be distributed to each according to the work he does, and there should be sufficient for an adequate amount to be given to everybody that is employed. It follows that the wages available do not come up to requirements.

When there is a lack of support for the theater throughout the year, and there do not seem to be sufficient funds to pay the year's bills, I appreciate the situation and take a reduction in my own salary.   The manager[1] does not need to increase his fame, as an actor does, but what is above all vital for him is the earning of money.   The thinking of actors and that of backers is quite distinct.   Even so, I have recently been hearing rumors that many negotiations have failed over the question of a small amount of pay.   I do not understand this spirit.   When actors in the past entered into disputes about whether they would appear or not it was always on some question involving their role or the acting.   Nowadays, it seems, such disputes are very often concerned with pay.   The behavior of both sides[2] has become despicable.

COMMENT: One can only applaud Sadoshima's idealistic sentiments, and remind oneself that it is not unknown for the cast of a play in the West to forego their salaries and agree to share the takings in order to save a play.

NOTES: 1. *Shibai-nushi,* who put up the money, i.e. *kinshu.*   2. Actors and management.

ITEM X

Shosagoto, and this applies, of course to straight plays[1] too, should not be represented with added work on them by other hands. In recent years there has been a certain amount of vying of one theater with another, arising from hearing that something was going to be played in the theater opposite, and hastily putting a play with the same theme into rehearsal in order not to be outdone. What pleasure can audiences get from seeing the same thing in two places? It is the same as with poetry, which has the court lady with her elegant appearance, and also the aged form of a woodcutter bearing his load of firing. In one day's program of plays, too, there must be the discussion between the stern warriors, the rivalry between *keisei*, and again the comic ingredient; in other words it is the characteristic of this art that two similar things should not be placed side by side. This can be seen in successful old plays such as *Hotoke no hara*,[2] *The Peak of Asama*,[3] *The Inaba Pine*,[4] and *Mirror for Brides*.[5]

COMMENT: We find the connection between the first sentence and the rest of the Item far from clear, especially since it was the custom to present sequels of successful plays with only little change from the first version. Perhaps his general remark about not altering pre-existing shosagoto *led him to think of the authors attached to one theater making slight variations in the play put on at the " theater opposite," and putting it on in theirs. The rest of the Item has a fairly obvious train of thought. That competition between theaters should have meant that patrons had no choice of program seems to indicate that program-planners have not changed much over the centuries, seeing that competition between television channels often has the same result nowadays.*

NOTES: 1. *Jigei ;* see *The Words of Ayame*, XIV.   2. *Keisei Hotoke no hara ;* see *Dust in the Ears*, XVII.   3. *Keisei Asama ga dake ;* see *Kengai Collection*, XI.   4. *Keisei Inaba no matsu*, first played on the third day of the third month of 1705 in Kyoto.   5. *Yome kagami*, first played at the *Mandayūza* in Kyoto, in 1691 (see *The Words of Ayame*, XXVIII, p. 66).

ITEM XI

One year I went to the theater at the place called Miyauchi in Bitchū,[1] and I had the idea of visiting the grave of Kaneko Rokuemon (Kichizaemon's teacher), who passed away at this spot, and with that intention I made some enquiries about how to

get there.   I finally discovered the direction in which it lay, and,
forcing my way through rough grass, I found the small stone
stupa that marked it.   I made offering of flowers and water,
then paid someone from the vicinity to cut the *susuki*[2] and other
plants from in front of the grave.   I found a narrow board and
set it upright, writing on it with my traveling brush[3] the in-
scription "The grave of Kaneko Rokuemon."   A Chinese
poet[4] said that Heaven and Earth are the temporary lodging of
all things, but actors in particular have no settled abode, and
theirs is an unhappy lot, with no knowledge of where they will
come to their end.

NOTES: 1. Near the present city of Okayama 岡山. The Kibitsu
吉備津 shrine in whose grounds the plays were staged still preserves many
relics of the local *kabuki*.   2. "pampas-grass."   3. I.e., brush
forming part of writing equipment that can be carried with one on a journey.
Its name *yatate*, "quiver (for arrows)," is an abbreviation of *yatate-suzuri*,
writing equipment for carrying in a quiver.   4. Li Po 李白.

ITEM XII

Among actors performing in *shosagoto* nowadays there are
many who take a rest during intervals in the dancing, and have
assistants[1] fanning them on left and right, or drink tea.   I am
very doubtful about this.   The time that is spent with one's
back to the audience is even more important than the dancing at
the front of the stage.   Men in the past, too, have said that
great pains should be taken to avoid a feeling of inappropriate-
ness at such times.[2]   Thus if an actor cannot play without taking
refreshment or being fanned, it would be better for him not to
perform in *shosagoto*.   I make a point of writing this because
actors today do not criticize themselves and nobody follows the
teachings of men of the past.   When my father Dempachi was
teaching me, he warned me most strictly, from when I was five,
against this drinking of tea.   In recent years persons deeply
interested in *shosagoto* have been coming to me and asking me

about it, and I have given as my first piece of advice a warning against drinking tea in the intervals of dancing and having oneself fanned on left and right. A certain actor, playing in the *shosagoto*, *The Stone Bridge*,[3] for example, fell flat on the stage at the end of his dance, and the stage assistants came up and carried him away to the dressing room. In the first place, this is an insult to the audience, and in addition, by indicating that *kabuki* might be such a vulgar thing as that, this one man has lowered the reputation of all those involved in the art, and this damages the theater as a whole. This *kabuki* of ours is essentially something in which such ill conduct should not occur. But there are few people in it who know much about the past, and recently every year has brought a worsening of behavior. Sakata Tōjūrō said that there had been a decline as Genroku came to an end and Hōei[4] began, and that when twenty or thirty more years had passed, there would be a very considerable falling off in the theater. From the time he made this remark, he would speak of it with grief. He was indeed right, for from the middle of Kyōhō,[5] behavior in *kabuki* has gradually declined, and now the deterioration is quite beyond dispute. Should by some rare chance there be someone now to follow the precepts of the past, there would be many who would do nothing but insult him, as being the most stupid of idiots. Even during his lifetime Tōjūrō would continually express his grief at the bad ways into which actors had fallen. No need to say what things are like today!

COMMENT: *The behavior of the actor in* Shakkyō *was shocking, we suppose, for either or both of the following two reasons: (i) to collapse in pretended exhaustion insults the audience by its implication that the actor resents, and therefore does not hesitate to show, the effort he has put into his performance, and (ii) because* Shakkyō *is a serious work, any attempt (if indeed that was the intention) to arouse laughter by such inappropriate behavior was despicable.*

Sadoshima seems to be a blind admirer of the past, but he is certainly no worse than many present-day kabuki *critics, and it is probable that he had cause for complaint.*

NOTES: 1. *Kōken*, also found on the *nō* stage, their task being to watch their principals, and see that there are no mishaps.   2. See *Dust in the Ears*, XXXII.   3. *Shakkyō*, taken from the *nō* play of the same name, often played on the *kabuki* stage since about 1690. For a summary see O'Neill, p. 158.   4. The year 1704 divided Genroku from Hōei. 5. About 1725.

ITEM XIII

In the doll theater, one who bore the name of Ishii Hida of Osaka must be mentioned with respect.   At the beginning puppets had had clothes attached only to a head, and the hands and feet were played entirely by the manipulator's hands.   These puppets were the same as have existed until recently as children's toys, under the name of *dekonobō*.[1]   This Ishii thought that to thrust a grown man's hand out from the sleeve looked extremely unpleasant, so he devised a way for making hands for dolls and attaching them.   Others profited from his experience, and fitted feet, made fingers move, manipulated eyes and moved eyebrows.   Thus now puppets are made which have every sort of capability.   Ishii was the originator of these developments. Today the name of Hida remains only as the name of one of the ' Shore ' theaters.[2]

COMMENT: This Item must not be taken as accurately reporting the development of puppet movements, although his description is correct in very broad outline. Sadoshima brings it in here as an example of a praiseworthy effort towards realism.

NOTES: 1. This name, or other similar ones, is quite a common term for puppets.   2. These were in Dōtombori in Osaka. They were small theaters, and one of them is mentioned on p. 18.

ITEM XIV

Until the Genroku and Hōei periods, the work on a following play was started while the first play of the new year was still being performed; then, when it was seen that it was unlikely that anything would go wrong, the boards announcing the new play were displayed. Next the parts for each type of role were worked out, and when two or three of the principal actors had agreed that the rehearsals had reached a satisfactory level, posters announcing that the new program would start on such and such a day were stuck up. It seems that nowadays it happens quite often that a board announcing a change of program is put up, then suddenly a fresh one is displayed announcing a different program altogether. The reason for this is that the board announcing the new program has been put up before the rehearsals for the new plays have reached completion; then, when they get round to having a conference, and try to agree upon a distribution of parts, by some unforeseen chance there are numerous difficulties, and they cannot reach a final decision. So they hastily change the plays, and new boards have to be put up. Rehearsals are hurriedly started two or three days before the opening, and the whole company is in a state of great confusion, like birds flying off disturbed by human feet. This slipshod way of doing things must make one ponder about the differences between the present and the past.

ITEM XV

When one listens to young actors talking nowadays there are many of them who continually say about other people's actions things like " So-and-so's acting is old-fashioned," or " If he does that, up-to-date people won't accept it." I am completely unable to fathom what they are talking about. One cannot divide the acting of parts into old-fashioned and up-to-date when it comes to the portrayal of the sentiments of old and young, men and women, exalted and lowly. Smartness in dress involves fashions which change with the times, and thus costumes appropriate to the various periods should be used on the stage. There cannot be new styles when it comes to feelings about things. The distinctions between wigs according to types of role are already fixed. Some might say that an old man's hair is out-of-date, but it would hardly do to have it completely black !

COMMENT : *To us today, Sadoshima's comment seems unfair, because we feel that there can be a new approach to a play dealing with the past without sacrificing realism, but then we are aware of possible differences in psychological approach that were probably not in the minds of the young actors in question.*

ITEM XVI

There are various appellations given to actors according to their acting, such as *kōsha*, *neoi* and *meijin*.[1] But one who was virtually unequalled in the past or present was Ichikawa Ebizō. I apply to him the appellation of fantastic master. He was the outstanding actor, whom others were quite unable to emulate. When I was residing in Edo, Hakuen (Ebizō's *haimyō*) said to me on one occasion that if I would be his manager[2] he would go to Kyoto at any time. So, one year, when I was thinking of running a company at Dōtombori in Osaka, I sent Hakuen a letter to open negotiations, and in his reply he wrote that he would require a salary of two thousand *ryō* for the year, and a booking fee of five hundred *ryō*.[3] I was very intrigued by this, since as far as I had heard, there had never in the history of the *kabuki* theater been an actor with a salary of two thousand *ryō*, and what he was asking was really exceptional. I therefore got together the five hundred *ryō* deposit and sent it off to him. He probably thought that it would come to nothing, for when he came to Osaka he said as much when he made his greetings. I said, " This is the first time ever that an actor has had a salary of two thousand *ryō*. Since you insisted on this amount when you wrote to me, I trust that you will do something exceptionable, in keeping with the size of the sum." I merely thought that he was an eccentric.[4] At the *kaomise*, he gave the *uirō* seller's scene,[5] and no doubt because of its novelty, it had a great success. But when a Soga play[6] was put on in the second program, it was a complete failure, and advantage was taken of the illness of his son

Danjūrō to stop its run soon after the tenth day. Then when the dressing-room and the front[7] got round to discussing the third program, and what should be in it, all sorts of things were suggested, but we came to no conclusion. At this point Hakuen suggested that we put on *Narukami*[8] next. I said that if we did this play, there would be no need for a plot to be thought up. I joined the old play on to an introduction. In the fourth act, there is a point where a servant kills the hermit Narukami and for the conclusion I thought up the part where the ghost of Narukami attaches itself to the Princess Kumo-no-taema, and there follows the dance of the skeleton. Hakuen had an inborn fear of being killed with a sword in a play, so he did not perform scenes of this sort. He had the idea of making me play this, and asked me to perform the skeleton scene in pantomime. I said that if there was nothing else for it, I would be killed, and so the discussion was brought to an end, and the rehearsals completed. When it came to the first day, he became the samurai with the name of Kumedera Danjō,[9] and acted the scene where he came as a messenger; he indeed seemed to be a real warrior. This performance acquired for him a great reputation in Osaka, and it was said that nobody else could have done this impersonation. There was indeed great admiration for his skill. The fourth act was the one in which we two actors played the hermit Narukami; since the part was traditional to his family, the acting was second nature to him. Reverberations of the " thunder god " not only reached the neighboring provinces, as was to be expected, but also there came to Osaka a great number of people even from distant parts especially to see Ebizō's *Narukami*. It was universally well received, and the crowds were packed so tight that one could not force one's way through them. Many connoisseurs of the art from Kyoto came to Osaka to see his performance. His only regret was that he did not, nevertheless, play the part in the Capital. What a fantastic genius he had, thus to excel even when not in view of the audience! Try as I may, I cannot avoid using this word " fantastic." But what is one to make of a *kabuki* actor not liking parts in which he is killed? This must be termed fantastic, too!

COMMENT : Sadoshima seems to have made no attempt to bargain, but, as he implies, he had in mind the great obligation such a large salary, agreed on beforehand, would lay upon Ebizō to give superb performances.

NOTES: 1. *Kōsha*, " effective actor," is much the same as *jōzu*, " skillful " ; *neoi*, " scion of a tradition," is one skillful by heredity ; *meijin*, "master." 2. *tayū-moto*, the same as *zamoto*. 3. See *The Kengai Collection*, II, n. 2 for the modern equivalent of the *ryō ;* also p. 16. 4. " . . . and that he was not really worth it." 5. *Uirō* was a sort of medicine, and the scene of the *uirō* seller was originally an independent play. It was later included in *Sukeroku* 助六 (see Halford, p. 321 ; *Theatre in Japan*, p. 154). It was a virtuoso piece. Ebizō first gave it in Edo in 1718 ; this performance was in the eleventh month, 1741. 6. Dealing with the famous vendetta in which the Soga brothers take their revenge on their father's killer ; see Halford, p. 462. 7. I.e., the actors and authors, and those responsible for the finances. 8. 鳴神 "the thunder god." One of the 18 plays of the Ichikawa family ; first played in 1684. For a summary of the plot, see Halford, p. 230 ; *Theatre in Japan*, p. 130. 9. The hero of the play *Kenuki* 毛抜 "Hair tweezers," originally an early section of *Narukami*, but now usually played separately. See *Theatre in Japan*, p. 121.

H. The Secret Tradition of the Kabuki Dance

ITEM I

The movements of the body are in the words, and when the words provide no meaning, they depend upon the style of dancing. Again, when there are no words and one dances to music, one rides upon the rhythm. Because the dance is made from the role that one is performing, one must make reality the basis of one's movements. Whatever happens, one must not forget the meaning of the sort of dance that one is performing.

COMMENT: This Item is in typical paradoxical secret-tradition style, but its meaning is clear enough. The subsequent Items deal with individual subjects and types of dance, and particularize the general remarks made here.

ITEM II

In pieces in which *ōkuchi*[1] are worn, the dance should normally be in the spirit of the *nō* plays, and care taken not to degrade their style. A simplified style is bad.

NOTE: 1. I.e., pieces derived from the *nō*. *Ōkuchi* are the wide trousers worn in *nō* plays, and in their derivatives on the *kabuki* stage.

ITEM III

The sight of a *samurai* dancing violently about, holding his bow and arrows, is unpleasant to see. This is not limited to pieces of this sort, but it is probably the same with all those in which singing in the *nō* style is included. It is bad that all sorts of people should give loud praise to a piece which has connections with the *nō*. It is much better and more pleasant for just one or two words of praise to be proffered.

COMMENT: In shosagoto, and especially those (and they are in the majority) that were taken from nō *plays, any unseemliness and violent activity inconsistent with the original is to be deplored. This applied not only to the piece itself, but also to the audience, who should not indulge in wild applause.*

ITEM IV

In a dance for an old man of mean estate, such as a firewood gatherer or something of that sort, the most important thing is a sort of pathetic excellence that this sort of piece should have, obtained by including every now and then in the dancing a suggestion that age prevents him from doing now what he could when he was young.

ITEM V

In a dance for an old country woman, the most important thing is a pathetic excellence, obtained by including among movements showing that age has restricted her activity, an occasional glimpse of the lively person she was when she was young.

ITEM VI

It goes without saying that old men and women of higher class should be played in the same spirit.[1]

NOTE: 1. Presumably the same spirit as in IV and V.

ITEM VII

It goes without saying that an *onnagata* performance should hold the audience through the heart. When standing, the actor should have his feet turned inwards.[1] The waist should be slender, and the opening of skirts just right.[2]

NOTES: 1. *Onnagata* used a " pigeon-toed " (the text says "crocodile ") stance, which is perhaps still characteristic of Japanese women, especially when wearing Japanese footwear. 2. The kimono opens into an inverted V over the feet, affording a glimpse of the under kimono. It is important that this opening should be neither too small nor too large.

ITEM VIII

In spear dances,[1] the legs should be held wide apart, with one foot considerably bent in. The body should be bent backwards, and regardless of the spear's weight, the movements should be large and rhythmical, and it should be rotated at high speed.

NOTE: 1. These are said to have started with servants accompanying great lords' processions.

ITEM IX

A fox should be played as being afraid of a hunter or dogs. The essential thing about a lion dance is that, since the lion is a king, he should have a courageous heart. With all animals, one should use head-movements.[1] The detail or breadth with which one performs depends upon the type of dance. The most important thing is the use of head-movements.

NOTE: 1. These are not often used in dances of other sorts.

ITEM X

It is essential that there should be seen to be a distinction between methods of performance depending upon the costume one wears, and, of course, this applies to dances performed in ordinary dress.[1] One should avoid in one's performances all feminine movements during a man's piece, and dancing when performing the part of a malignant spirit.[2]   Even though it may win general praise, one should not do anything outside the artistic theme of the piece.

NOTES: 1.   There should be a difference in performance not only according to different types of costume, but also in the same piece done with or without special costume.   2.   This was popular in the Genroku period. and incorporated acrobatics.

ITEM XI

There is an expression " Dancing is done through the eyes."   Dancing can be compared to the human body, and the eye to the soul.   If the soul is not present, the body serves no useful purpose.   Dancing in which the eyes do not take part is called dead dancing, and what is called live dancing is that performed when the movements of the body and the eyes work together to express the spirit of the piece.   It follows that it is of the greatest importance that one should understand what is meant by " Dancing is done through the eyes."   I have no conclusion, so I leave off writing here.

Sadoshima's Diary, the end.

The Mandayū company at the Southern Theater in Kyoto, c. 1680.
The stage is still that of the the *nō* theater, and the musicians and
singers are stationed upstage. The audience sits in side-boxes (*sanjiki*) and on the floor of the house; one of them is having his cup
filled with tea. Over the entrance is the watchtower; to the right
is the ticket-seller, on the other side is the "barker," manipulating
his two fans as he advertises the program.

Appendixes

Appendix I

Glossary of Technical Terms

Ageya 揚屋: a restaurant or tea-house to which a client could summon a *tayū* or other high class courtesan; a house of assignation.

Bon kyōgen 盆狂言: program of the seventh month; see p. 19.
Bushi 武士: another term for *samurai* (q. v.); " warrior."
Deha 出端: strictly speaking is the Osaka term for an entrance, but, since the entrance was often done with a *roppō*, the two terms are often synonymous.

Dōke 道外(化): one of the oldest role-types of *kabuki*, it used comic dances, words and costume. After the early years of the 18th century, with *kabuki*'s increasing sophistication, *dōke* parts lost their independent status, but their tradition still persists in minor roles. Performers of such roles were called *dōkegata* 道化方.

Fuke-oyama 老女形: see *kashagata*.

Gakuya 楽屋: in the *kabuki* theater in the time of the *Analects* this was a large room behind the stage, used for changing, make-up and as a general sitting-room.

Haimyō 俳名: name used when writing *haiku* poetry. Actors usually have one, and at the time of the *Analects* were sometimes referred to by it.

Hakama 袴: Sort of divided skirt worn over the kimono; still worn with Japanese dress on formal occasions.

Hashi-gakari 橋懸り: an element of the *nō* stage, being the passage-way on stage right along which the important entrances and exits are made. This survived on the *kabuki* stage, although its function was assumed by the *hanamichi* 花道, which runs through the audience. See p. 7.

Hōmyō 法名: "Buddhistic name" assumed on retirement from the world or for posthumous use.

Hyōbanki 評判記: these might be termed ranking lists and were of various kinds, the earliest being guides to brothel districts. The first relating to *kabuki* actors appeared in the late 1650's and concentrated on boy performers and their charms, but by the 1680's they were using artistic criteria for their listings. These are of great use as sources for the history of the Japanese drama (see also pp. 10).

Jigei 地芸: at the time of the *Analects* this was the new realistic, non-musical *kabuki* drama, as distinct from *shosagoto* (q.v.).

Ji-kyōgen 地狂言: the same as *jigei* (q.v.). The meaning of "local *kabuki*," which this term usually has nowadays, arose later.

Jitsu-aku 実悪: see *kataki-yaku*.

Jitsugoto 実事: literally "realism" or "serious acting," this term had come to refer to *tachiyaku* parts involving fighting.

Jōruri 淨瑠璃: chanting to *shamisen* accompaniment, and, more particularly, the Japanese puppet drama, which was flourishing at the period in which the *Analects* were written. See Bibliography, Dunn and Keene.

Kabuki 歌舞伎: traditional live popular drama of Japan.

Kagura 神楽: music and dancing performed at *Shintō* shrines.

Kaomise 顔見世: "face showing"; the first performance after contracts had been signed for the year. See p. 19.

Kashagata 花車方: a subdivision of the *onnagata* type of part. *Kashagata* parts were of old or middle-aged women (as against *waka-onnagata*," young *onnagata*") and Sugi Kuhē is usually credited with the founding of this type of role, the name for which came from the technical vocabulary of the brothels. Nowadays such roles are referred to as *fuke-oyama*.

Kataki-yaku 敵役: The " enemy role " was either that of a person who had some grudge or other hatred toward the hero (*tachiyaku*), or else was the target of the hero's revenge in return for some evil deed in the past. This " role-type " was originally included among the *tachiyaku*; but by the time of the *Analects* it had become separated from this category. Alternative names are *akunin-gata* 悪人方 or *nikugata* 悪方, " villain." The *jitsu-aku* 実悪 was one of several later subdivisions, and was the super-villain.

Keisei 傾城：   one of the subdivisions of the *onnagata* type of role；a prostitute.
Originally a term for a beautiful woman, lit. a " castle-toppler," it had come
by the late 17th century to mean a high class prostitute, although it was not
used to designate any particular grade within the brothel hierarchy.   Her
beauty, her extravagant attire and her training in traditional arts such as the
tea-ceremony and flower-arrangement made her an ideal of womanhood and
an ornament to the stage, and the traditional combinations of innocence and
experience, availability (although she had considerable freedom of choice)
and fidelity which were supposed to make up her character made her a challenge both to the playwright and the *onnagata* actor.   At the period of the
Analects, the *keisei* was by far the most important of the female roles.

Kinshu 銀主：   backer in Kyoto/Osaka；see p. 16.
Kyōgen 狂言：   originally this was the name given to the comic interludes between items in the program of *nō* plays, but later the name was applied to
kabuki plays.
Nadai 名代：   theater owner in Kyoto/Osaka；see p. 16.
Niban-me 二番目：   second of two short plays at the beginning of a program,
see p. 20.
Ni no kawari 二の替り：   program in the first month；see p. 19.
Nō 能：   a dramatic form developed out of previous types of performance
in the early 15th century.   From the 17th century it had become mainly
entertainment for the warrior classes, and a new form, *kabuki*, developed for
the townsfolk.   *Kabuki* took its stage and some of its material from *nō*.
Nuregoto 濡事：   see *wagoto*.
Onna-budō 女武道：   one of the subdivisions of the *onnagata* type of role；a
woman of warrior rank, or a woman of warlike spirit, capable of fighting
with a man.

Onnagata 女形 (方):   one of the *yakugara* (types of role) of *kabuki*.   The term came into use when women actors were prohibited in 1629 and female parts had to be taken by men.   Of all the *yakugara, onnagata* became the most specialized, and *onnagata* actors were expected to carry their assumption of feminine ways into their life outside the theater.   *Ayame-gusa*, the third

piece in the present collection, contains much that is valuable for the understanding of the *onnagata*'s art. The term *oyama* is often used as equivalent to *onnagata*, and the *tate-oyama* was the senior *onnagata* in a company, charged with the general control of the *onnagata* actors.   As time went on,   there arose a major division into *waka-onnagata* ("young" *onnagata*) in which the part was of a young woman,   but not necessarily played by a young man, and *kashagata* (q.v.).   An important subtype of *waka-onnagata* was the *keisei* (q.v.).

Oyaji-gata 親仁方: (player of) old men's roles.

Oyama 女形: see *onnagata*.

Rōnin 浪人: a man of *samurai* rank who was without an employer. This could be because he had been dismissed from his lord's service, or because his lord had been killed or for many other reasons.

Roppō 六方 (法): a spectacular acrobatic dance movement, usually to make an exit but sometimes for an entrance. See also p. 139.

Sake 酒: rice-wine; the national and ceremonial drink of Japan.

Samban-tsuzuki 三番続き: three-act play; see p. 20.

Samurai 侍: a member of the warrior class, one of the four classes (warriors, farmers, artisans, merchants) in Japanese society. They had various privileges, such as the right to wear two swords and precedence over the other classes, but also heavy responsibilities, such as loyalty to their masters and the necessity to maintain decorum and set an example to their inferiors. The various *samurai* roles, including the *samurai*'s womenfolk, called for special capabilities.

Sanjiki (*sajiki*) 桟敷: these existed from the early days of *nō* performances, as covered sitting-places distinct from the open viewing area. In *kabuki* architecture they are usually two stories of boxes on the side walls, and in early times the authorities viewed them with some suspicion as places where discreet meetings between actors and their patrons could take place.

San no kawari 三の替り: program in the third month; see p. 19.

Sewa-mono 世話物: play whose theme is taken from contemporary life; domestic drama.

Shamisen 三味線: three-stringed musical instrument which reached Japan from the Ryūkyū islands in the second half of the sixteenth century.   It was, and still is, used for accompanying *jōruri* reciters and, with flute and drums, in the *kabuki* orchestra.   For further information see Malm.

Shosagoto 所作事: sometimes referred to simply as *shosa*.   The signification of this word, like that of many others relating to Japanese arts, has changed with the years.   Its modern use is to indicate an item in a *kabuki* program which consists mainly of dance movements together with formalized, non-realistic acting, and accompanied by musicians including vocalists and players of the *naga-uta shamisen* and the *nō* drums and flute.   At the time of the *Analects*, the meaning was not so precise, but referred to pieces which had a musical accompaniment, but were not pure dances.   Item XII of *The Words of Ayame* is important for the interpretation of the word, and makes it clear that for him *shosagoto* was the older, musical but dramatic, type of *kabuki* piece, as distinct from the more recently developed *jigei* 地芸, the new type of drama, far more realistic that the old *shosagoto*.

Tachiyaku 立役: one of the *yakugara* (types of role) of *kabuki*. This term, in its earlier form *tachikata* 立方, is said to date from the earliest days of this theater, designating then, as the translation of the word indicates, a " standing part " (i.e. a dancer or actor) in contradistinction to the musicians who, as in the *nō* theater, were then seated on the stage. When men had to take women's parts on the stage, the name *tachikata* or *tachiyaku* became restricted to those taking male parts, the term *onnagata* (q.v.) being used for those playing women. Later still, before the time of the *Analects*, the term *tachiyaku* came to be applied only to young or " good " parts as against, for example, *akunin-gata* 悪人方, " wicked roles," otherwise *katakiyaku* 敵役, " enemy roles " (q.v.). It should be noted that the term *tateyaku*, found in some Western books on *kabuki*, does not exist, but arises probably from *tate-yakusha*, meaning the principal actor in a company.

Tanzen 丹前: used in Edo with the same meaning as *roppō*.

Tate-oyama: 立女形: see *onnagata*.

Tayū 太夫: a prostitute of the highest rank.

Teoi 手負: acting the part of a wounded man.

Tsuke-butai 付舞台: forestage, built out from the main stage.

Wagoto 和事: a major division of *tachiyaku* roles, young men in love. Also known as *yatsushi* やつし, *nuregoto* 濡事 or *nimaime* 二枚目. The term most used in the *Analects* is *yatsushi*.

Waka-onnagata 若女形: see *onnagata*.

Wakashu (*-kata*) 若衆(方): one of the *yakugara* of *kabuki*, once separate from *tachiyaku*, but now classified with it. The parts played are usually handsome youths. The term *wakashu*, originally meaning " young persons, " was applied to the *kabuki* that succeeded that of the original female actors, and often carried with it homosexual implications. In the *kabuki* of the time of the *Analects*, a *wakashu* actor often became an *onnagata* as he got older.

Yakko 奴: this word means " slave " or " servant." They appear in *kabuki* as foot soldiers, litter bearers, etc., and often perform comic acrobatic dances.

Yakugara 役柄: *Kabuki* actors tended to play only restricted types of parts, according to their age, temperament, physique, etc. These types of part (e.g. *onnagata*, *tachiyaku*) are known under the general name of *yakugara*.

Yakusha-hyōbanki 役者評判記: see *hyōbanki*.

Yatsushi やつし: see *wagoto*.

Zamoto 座元: we have translated this term as " manager." The systems in Kyoto and Osaka differed from that in Edo, where, from 1657, the *zamoto* was the holder of a license to put on plays and also owned the theater. In Kyoto and Osaka he was the representative of the actors and exercised the function of trainer and general consultant on artistic matters. He very often held the post for only a year at a time. See p. 16.

Appendix II

List of Actors and Others Mentioned in 'The Analects,' with Their Family Crests[1] When Known.

*_Anekawa Shinshirō_ 姉川新四郎 (1685–1749). The early part of his career was spent in _wakashu_, then _waka-onnagata_ parts in traveling companies. In 1710 he made his first appearance in Osaka, as a _tachiyaku_. As time went on his status both as an actor and a personality became more established and in his late years he came to be thought of as Osaka's leading actor. E: X; G: VIII.[2]

*_Araki Yojibē_ 荒木与次兵衛 (1637–1700). He made his name with his performance, in _Hinin no kataki-uchi_ 非人 の敵討, of the wounded outlaw. He specialized in the realistic portrayal of male parts, and was also a _zamoto_ of ability. D: XXIV, XXXIII; E: XV; G: I, VIII.

---

1. The crest or _mon_ 紋 had much the same function as armorial bearings in Europe, except that it was not limited to the aristocracy, and did not have the same possibilities of indicating descent by quartering, etc. Actor families had them, and it was customary to include them on stage costume.
2. The code refers to the piece and item in which a reference to the person in question

Arashi San'emon I 嵐三右衛門初代 (1635–1690).   He introduced a *roppō* into a play in the 1660's, and was famous for this and for his *yatsushi* acting.   He was a leading actor in the 1670's and also did some work as a *zamoto*.   D: XVIII, XXXI;   E: I;   G: I.

Arashi San'emon II 嵐三右衛門二代 (1661–1701).   He was the real son of San'emon I, and took his name at his death in 1690.   He had the same specialties as his father, and, also like him, was a *zamoto*.   C: IV, XV, XVIII;   D. XIV, XV;   G: I.

Arashi San'emon III 嵐三右衛門三代 (1697–1754).   He was the real son of Arashi San'emon II, and took his name in 1705 at an early age.   He worked as a *tachiyaku*, inheriting his father's *roppō*, and later as an *oyaji-gata*. He was also for a long time a *zamoto*.   G: I, II.

Arashi Sanjūrō 嵐三十郎 (? died c. 1750).   He was a pupil of Arashi San'emon II and worked as a *wakashu* actor, first in Osaka, then, in 1695, with Tōjūrō in Kyoto.   He later became a *tachiyaku*, mainly in Osaka, and specialized in merchant parts.   He was a *zamoto* from c. 1710–1720, and later was in a traveling group. D: XXXVI.

---

occurs.   A=*One Hundred Items on the Stage*;   B=*Mirror for Actors*;   C=*The Words of Ayame*;   D=*Dust in the Ears*;   E=*Sequel to "Dust in the Ears"*;   F=*The Kengai Collection*;   G=*Sadoshima's Diary*;   H=*The Secret Tradition of the* kabuki *Dance*.   I followed by a number indicates a page in the Introduction.
Names with asterisks correspond to the illustrations to the left.

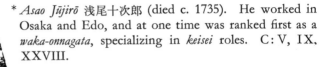

* *Asao Jūjirō* 浅尾十次郎 (died c. 1735). He worked in
Osaka and Edo, and at one time was ranked first as a
waka-onnagata, specializing in *keisei* roles. C: V, IX,
XXVIII.

Ayame あやめ. See Yoshizawa Ayame.
Azuma Sampachi 吾妻(東)三八 (died c. 1735). He was a
dōke actor who turned playwright. He compiled *The
Kengai Collection*. C: XX.

* *Chikamatsu Monzaemon* 近松門左衛門 (1653–1724).
There is speculation about the early life of this, Japan's
greatest dramatist, but about 1680 he was writing *jōruri*
for the chanter Uji Kaganojō in Kyoto, and later he
was to achieve the height of his fame in his work for the
puppet theater of Takemoto Gidayū. During the
intervening period he wrote *kabuki* plays for Sakata
Tōjūrō. Keene's *The Major Works of Chikamatsu Monzaemon* is the best study of his work in English. D:
XVII, XL; I: 10.

Chikugonojō 筑後掾. See Takemoto Gidayū.
Chōjūrō 長十郎. See Sawamura Chōjūrō.
Danjūrō 団十郎. See Ichikawa Ebizō.
Dempachi 伝八. See Sadoshima Dempachi.
Ebizō 海老蔵. See Ichikawa Ebizō.

* *Fujikawa Buzaemon* 藤川武左衛門 (1632–1729). This
long-lived actor (1618 is sometimes given as the date of
his birth) specialized in enemy and similar roles in the
Three Cities, but mainly in Kyoto. C: XXVIII.

* *Fujita Koheiji* 藤田小平次 (died c. 1700).   He started his career as a traveling actor, but later became well known in Kyoto and Osaka.   He is credited with being an originator of the *jitsugoto* 実事 role.   D: XXVI, XXXIII; E: II.

Fujita Magojūrō 藤田孫十郎 Apart from what is recorded in *The Words of Ayame*, nothing is known of this actor.   C: XXVII

Fukui Yagozaemon 福井弥五左衛門 (fl. 1660–1680).   He was an Osaka actor and playwright, and was credited with the first *kabuki* plays in more than one act.   D: XXXIII.

* *Fukuoka Yagoshirō* 福岡弥五四郎 (dates not known, fl. 1700–1730).   His career included a progress through the male role-types of *wakashu, tachiyaku, dōke* and *oyajigata*.   From 1700 he specialized in writing plays, but still acted.   His name disappears from the ranking lists around 1730.   He was the compiler of *The Words of Ayame*.

Fushimi Tōjūrō 伏見藤十郎.   See Sakata Tōjūrō II.

* *Hashimoto Kinsaku* 橋本金作 (dates unknown, fl. c. 1655).   Little is known of this *onnagata*'s life, except that after the incident decribed in Item II of *Mirror for Actors*, he left the stage for a while and is reported to have run a successful tea-house in Ōtsu 大津 near Kyoto. After this, he became a traveling actor, and became involved in another brawl, this time in Iida 飯田, in present-day Nagano prefecture, where he died.   B : III.

* *Hayakumo Chōkichi* 早雲長吉 (dates unknown).   A theater (*Hayakumoza*) was permitted to be established under his name in Kyoto in 1669, and the company that worked there continued to use the name.   C : XXVIII; I : 18.

Ichikawa Danjūrō 市川団十郎 See Ichikawa Ebizō.

* *Ichikawa Ebizō* 市川海老蔵 (1688–1758). He was the son of the first Ichikawa Danjūrō 団十郎, and took his father's name at his death in 1704. His career was outstanding and the plays which were the vehicle for his talents as a *tachiyaku* form the basis of the 18 plays which represent even today the true *kabuki* tradition. In 1735 he handed on the name of Danjūrō to his adopted son, and took the name of Ebizō. In 1741 he went for a while to Osaka at a fee of 2,000 *ryō*. His *haimyō* was Hakuen 栢莚. G: V, XVI; I: 16, 19.

* *Ichimura Tamagashiwa* 市村玉栢 (dates unknown). He first appeared in Osaka in 1700 but mainly worked in Kyoto, as a *waka-onnagata*. At the height of his career he had a reputation only a little inferior to that of Ayame. His name disappears from the programs in the 1730's. C: VI.

* *Ikushima Shingorō* 生嶋新五郎 (?1679–?1733 [?1743]). His main center of operation was Edo, where he was first a *wakashu-gata*, and later a *tachiyaku*. In 1714, he was involved in an affair with a lady-in-waiting, Ejima 絵(江)島 as a result of which the theater at which he was appearing was closed for good, and the two principals were sent into separate exile. According to some accounts he died there in 1733, but others believe that he returned to Edo and lived until 1743. C: XXVIII.

* *Ishii Hida* 石井飛弾. Nothing is known of this man other than what appears in G: XIII; he may, however, be the same man as Yamamoto Hida-no-jō 山本飛騨掾, who worked as a doll-smith in Osaka in the Genroku period.

Iwai Heijirō 岩井平次郎. He was a *waka-onnagata* who flourished in the last decade of the 17th century and worked in Kyoto and Edo. C: XXV.

Jimbē 甚兵衛. See Yamatoya Jimbē.
Jirozaemon 次郎左衛門. See Shinozuka Jirozaemon.
Jūjirō 十次郎. See Asao Jūjirō.
Kaganojō 加賀掾. See Uji Kaganojō.
Kamon 歌門. See Yamamoto Kamon.

Kaneko Ikkō 金子一高. See Kaneko Kichizaemon.
Kaneko Kichizaemon 金子吉左衛門 (died 1728). He became known for his *dōke* acting in the 1680's, and worked with Sakata Tōjūrō. In 1712 he transferred to *tachiyaku* parts, but did not achieve the success he had had in his early days. However, it is possible that he was most important as a playwright, and in particular as a collaborator of Chikamatsu Monzaemon (see D: XVII). His *haimyō* was Ikkō 一高. He was the compiler of *Dust in the Ears*. D: passim; E: XVII, XXI; F: III, VIII, X, XI; G: XI; I: 12.

Kaneko Rokuemon 金子六右衛門. He was a *tachiyaku* who operated in Kyoto and Osaka about 1680, and is reported to have been the teacher of Kaneko Kichizaemon. He was not in the top class of actors, but had some success in fighting parts. He is reported to have died when on tour (see G: XI), but it is not known when. D: XXIV, XXXIII; G: XI; I: 22.

Karyū 歌流. See Sodezaki Karyū.

Kasaya Goroshirō 笠屋五郎四郎. A ranking list of c. 1690 describes him as too handsome for *Kataki-yaku*, and more suited for *jitsugoto* parts. Otherwise nothing is known of him, apart from what appears in the *Analects*. C: XXVII.

* *Kataoka   Nizaemon* 片岡仁左衛門 (1656–1715).   He was the founder of the Kataoka family, which still flourishes, the present Nizaemon being the 13th holder of the name.   He started as a *shamisen* player in the *kabuki* theater, later appearing as an actor in Osaka.   He took the name of Kataoka Nizaemon around 1670, on the occasion of his going to act in Kyoto under the patronage of Yamashita Kyōemon.   Although he did some work as a *tachiyaku*, his fame rests on his playing of *kataki-yaku* parts.   He occasionally served as *zamoto*. C: IV, XX. D: XXXIV. E: VI, XIV, XIX.

Kengai 賢外.   See Somekawa Jūrobē.
Kichizaemon 吉左衛門.   See Kaneko Kichizaemon.

* *Kirinami Senju* 霧波千寿 (fl. 1700–1710).   He appeared mainly opposite Sakata Tōjūrō in Kyoto as a *wakashu-gata* and later as a *waka-onnagata*, especially in *keisei* roles. He is said to have retired from the stage about 1710, and became an oil-merchant.   C: XXVIII; D: XVI.

* *Kokan Tarōji* 小勘太郎次 (died 1713).   He was successively a *wakashu-gata*, *waka-onnagata* and *kashagata*, his greatest success being in the last role-type.   C: XXVI; E: XI.

* *Kokin Shinzaemon* 古今新左衛門 (died c. 1720). He worked in Edo in the 1670's, first as a *wakashu-gata*, and then as a *tachiyaku*. Later he played in Kyoto and Osaka, as an *oyaji-gata* and *zamoto*. C: XXVIII.

Kyōemon 京右衛門. See Yamashita Kyōemon.
Mangiku 万菊. See Sanokawa Mangiku.
Manoya Kanzaemon 真野屋勘左衛門. The only thing known about this man is in Item XXXI of *Dust in the Ears*, namely that he was a *zamoto* in Kyoto around 1685. D: XXXI.

* *Matsumoto Nazaemon* 松本名左衛門. It is difficult to distinguish between the two holders of this name, who were father and son, and it is not known which is referred to in *Dust in the Ears*, XXXII. One or the other of them is said to have introduced the system of yearly engagements for actors. The elder gave his name to one of the Osaka theaters, and was himself an actor who moved from *wakashu* roles to *waka-onnagata*, and to *tachiyaku* in his late years. He died about 1685. His son does not appear to have done much acting, but to have been more occupied with management. D: XXXII; I: 18.

* *Mihara Jūdayū* 三原十太夫 (fl. 1685–1712). He achieved some reputation in Osaka about 1785, having graduated to *kataki-yaku* from *wakashu* parts. He was patronized by Arashi San'emon. He was skillful in all parts within the role-type, and was placed very high in the *kataki-yaku* ratings in 1712, but disappears from the record after this date. E: XII.

* *Mikasa Jōemon* 三笠城(丈)右衛門 (fl. 1700–1715). He was a pupil of Sakata Tōjūrō, and first appeared in Kyoto as a *kataki-yaku*. In 1706 he went to Osaka, and changed to *tachiyaku* parts. His specialty was villains of the merchant class. His name disappears from the records about 1715. C: XXVIII.

* *Miyako Mandayū* 都万太夫 (retired 1710). His artistic career started with *jōruri* chanting, but his voice deteriorated and he was given permission to run the Mandayū theater in Kyoto. He attracted to it men of such standing as Sakata Tōjūrō and Chikamatsu Monzaemon. C: XXVII; I: 18.

* *Miyazaki Giheita* 宮崎義平太 (fl. 1690–1730). He worked in the Kyoto/Osaka area, and specialized successively in *dōke*, *tachiyaku* and *kataki* roles, usually with high ratings; his best work was as an evil *dōke*. His name disappears from the lists in about 1730. E: XXIV.

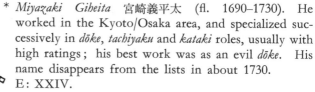

* *Mizuki Tatsunosuke* 水木辰之助 (1673–1745). His acting career came to an early end in 1704, but in that time he traveled along the road of child actor, *wakashu* and *waka-onnagata*. Though his achievements were varied, it seems that he really excelled in *shosagoto*. C: XIV, XXVIII; F: III.

Mogami Tōhachi 最上藤八. His name appears in a program dated 1664, and he is also mentioned as an outstanding *dōke* actor in the 1680's. This is all that is known about him. D: XVIII.

Muramatsu Hachirobē 村松八郎兵衛 (dates unknown). He is mentioned in *Mirror for Actors* as a *tachiyaku* in a performance of a visit to an *ageya*, but apart from this he does not appear in records of *kabuki*. B: IV.

Murayama Heiemon III 村山平右衛門三代 (died 1718). As a *waka-onnagata* (in Kyoto) he became Kozakura Sennosuke II 小桜千之助二代, then was adopted by Murayama Heiemon II, and took the name of Murayama Kurōemon 村山九郎右衛門 as a *tachiyaku*. In 1692, he assumed the name of Heiemon. His later years were mainly spent in Edo. D: XXXVII.

Murayama Matabē 村山又兵衛 (dates unknown, fl. c. 1655–1670). He combined the professions of actor and manager, and was also the senior actors' representative in Kyoto. The Murayama family had been active in *kabuki* in Kyoto since the time of his grandfather, Matahachi 又八. Matabē later changed his name to Heiemon 平右衛門. He is best known for his successful efforts to get *kabuki* started again after a prohibition in the 1650's, an incident which is magnified in *Mirror for Actors*. The Murayama theater in Kyoto was founded by him. B: III; I: 17.

Nagoya Sanzaemon 名古屋山左衛門 (also known as Nagoya Sanzaburō 山三郎). This semi-legendary *rōnin* is credited with starting *kabuki* in Kyoto in the first years of the 17th century, along with O-Kuni from Izumo. D: Introduction; G: I; I: 4.

* *Nakagawa Kinnojō* 中川金之丞. He was a *tachiyaku* who worked on the Osaka and Kyoto stages until 1690. D: XXII, XXXIII; E. XXIII; I: 24.

* *Nakamura Shichisaburō* 中村七三郎 (1662–1708). His *haimyō* was Shōchō (少長). His career started with *wakashu* and *waka-onnagata* parts, but in 1681 he became a *tachi-yaku*. He and Ichikawa Danjūrō I 市川団十郎 初代 were the greatest names in the Edo theater during the Genroku period. He specialized in *wagoto* parts, and, going to Kyoto in 1697, he even rivaled the great Sakata Tōjūrō. F: XI.

* *Nakamura Shirogorō* 中村四郎五郎 (died 1712). His first appearance was in Osaka in 1695, and later he had a brilliant period as a *tachiyaku* in Kyoto, where he was ranked only after Tōjūrō and Kyōemon. C: XXVIII; F: V.

* *Namie Kokan* 浪江小勘 (born 1659). He worked mainly as an *onnagata* in the Kyoto/Osaka area, after starting his career in *wakashu* parts. His name does not appear in the programs after about 1694. C: XXVII.

Nizaemon 仁左衛門. See Kataoka Nizaemon.

Ogino Samanojō 荻野左馬之丞 (1656–1704). In his later life he took the name of Ogino Sawanojō 荻野沢之丞. He was active before 1698 as a *waka-onnagata* and *onnagata* in Osaka and Edo. In that year he retired, but later returned to the stage and acted with distinction as a *waka-onnagata* until his death. C: XXVIII.

Okada Samanosuke 岡田左馬之助 (fl. 1680–1700). He become chief *onnagata* at a theater in Osaka in 1684, and was highly regarded as a *waka-onnagata*, for which he was physically very suited. He was replaced in the popular eye by such actors as Ayame, but maintained a reputation for skillful dancing and manipulation of the halberd, the typical woman's weapon. C: XVII, XXVIII.

O-Kuni 阿国. Accounts of this woman's life are very numerous and contradictory. There is general agreement, however, that she was a priestess of the Great Shrine at Izumo at the beginning of the 17th century, who for some reason or other started a performance in Kyoto that was the immediate forerunner of *kabuki*. D: Introduction; G: I; I: 4.

Osagawa Jūemon 小佐川十右衛門 (died 1731). His first appearances were in Kyoto in about 1690, and thereafter he worked mainly as a *jitsugoto* actor in Kyoto/Osaka. He was being placed high in the rankings by 1708, and maintained his reputation as a *jitsugoto* actor for another twenty years. In 1729 he changed to *oyaji-gata* roles. E: VI, XIV.

* *Otowa Jirosaburō* 音羽次郎三郎 (died 1732). He moved from *wakashu* parts to *tachiyaku* in about 1690, and developed into a specialist in *jitsugoto* roles, apparently attaining his peak as an actor in 1712. He is perhaps better known, however, for his work as a playwright. E: VI, VIII, IX, X, XIV, XV.

* *Sadoshima Chōgorō* 佐渡嶋長五郎 (1700–1757). He was the son of Sadoshima Dempachi, and had the *hōmyō* of Renchibō 蓮智坊. His first appearances were as a *wakashu-gata* in Osaka, but in about 1710 he became a *tachiyaku* and continued as such until his retirement. He specialized, as his father had before him, in *shosagoto*, which he performed both in the Three Cities and in the provinces. He was the compiler of *Sadoshima's Diary*.

* *Sadoshima Dempachi* 佐渡嶋伝八 (died 1712). Although he did a certain amount of acting in *dōke* roles, his main fame rests on his dancing, and on his son Chōgoro. G: III, VIII, IX, XII.

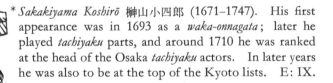

* *Sakakiyama Koshirō* 榊山小四郎 (1671–1747). His first appearance was in 1693 as a *waka-onnagata*; later he played *tachiyaku* parts, and around 1710 he was ranked at the head of the Osaka *tachiyaku* actors. In later years he was also to be at the top of the Kyoto lists. E: IX.

Sakata Ichizaemon 坂田市左衛門. Father of Sakata Tōjūrō (q. v.). D: XXXI.

Sakata Tōjūrō I 坂田藤十郎初代 (1647–1709). He was the outstanding *tachiyaku* actor of his time in Kyoto and Osaka. His father, Sakata Ichizaemon 市左衛門 (or Ichiemon 市右衛門) was a theater manager (*zamoto*) in Kyoto, but little is known of his youth except that for a while he was a pupil of Sugi Kuhē. The earliest printed reference to him dates from 1676, but until 1693 he was not given a very high position in the rankings (see *Hyōbanki*). By 1697 he had reached the top grade in the *tachiyaku* section of the lists. Most of his appearances were at the Mandayū Theater 万太夫座 in Kyoto, and there he often was *zamoto* as well. He was particularly successful in lover's parts in plays by Chikamatsu Monzaemon, and is said to have made enough money to buy a magnificent residence (see p. 125). Although he is said to have worked a scene announcing his retirement into a play performed in 1707, he continued in fact to appear until his death. C: XV, XXVIII; D: passim; E: I, III, IV, VII, VIII, XXIV; F: passim; G: VIII, XII; I: 6, 8–10, 21–24.

Sakata Tōjūrō II 坂田藤十郎二代 (1669–1724). He was a pupil of the Great Tōjūrō, but was far inferior to him as an actor, and did not rise above being the chief *tachiyaku* in traveling companies. He was born in Fushimi 伏見, just south of Kyoto, and for this reason is often known as Fushimi Tōjūrō. E: VIII.

Sakurayama Shōzaemon 桜山庄左衛門 (c. 1664–1714). He started as a catamite in the Dōtombori, then appeared on the Osaka stage as a *wakashu-gata* with the name of Sakurayama Rinnosuke 桜山林之助. In 1696 he changed to *tachiyaku* parts and took the name of Shōzaemon. He was quite well received in this latter capacity, but his best work was done when he played *wakashu* parts. His *haimyō* was Ōzan 鶯山. E: XIV, XVIII.

San'emon 三右衛門. See Arashi San'emon.

Sanokawa Mangiku 佐野川万菊 (1690–1747). He played in Osaka, and changed from *wakashu* to *waka-onnagata* parts in 1715. His preferred roles were in *jigei* and especially *onna-budō*. E: IX.

Sawamura Chōjūrō 沢村長十郎 (1675 or 1680–1734). He was the younger brother of Sawamura Kodenji, and started his performing career as a musician. In 1701 he made his first appearance as an actor, in *tachiyaku* parts, and eventually in the late 1720's became a leading actor in this role-type. C: XXVIII; E: V, VII, X, XV.

Sawamura Kodenji 沢村小伝次 (c. 1665–c. 1705). He was a *wakashu* actor in Kyoto, and later a *waka-onnagata* in Edo, but was better thought of as the former. There is a story that once, when he had a rough journey in a sedan-chair, he complained that it had brought on his period. C: XXVII, XXVIII.

Sawamura Sōjūrō 沢村宗十郎 (1685–1776). His career is described in *Sadoshima's Diary*, V. He was the third Sawamura Chōjūrō. F: VI; G: V.

Sendai Yagoshichi 仙台弥五七　He was a *dōke* actor who worked in Kyoto until about 1700. Some reports say that he was later a traveling actor. Nothing else is known of him. D: XXVII.

Shibasaki Rinzaemon 柴崎林左衛門 (died 1722). In about 1680 he changed from *wakashu* to *tachiyaku* parts and in about 1710 he was at the top of the Osaka ratings. He later achieved the same distinction in Kyoto. E: IX.

Shinozuka Jirozaemon 篠塚次郎左衛門 (died 1717). He started in local theaters, but later moved to Osaka and became a *kataki-yaku*. Later he achieved some fame as a *tachiyaku*. C: XXVIII; E: IX.

Shinshirō 新四郎. See Anekawa Shinshirō.

Sodeshima Genji 袖嶋源次 (dates unknown). In 1699 his playing of a *keisei* role in *Keisei hotoke no hara* 傾城仏の原 was well received, and he continued to play *waka-onnagata* parts until about 1720, when he disappeared from view. He was particularly successful at playing princesses and daughters of great lords, and is also said to have been a poet of some ability. D: XVI.

Sodezaki Karyū 袖崎歌流 (died 1730). He was a *waka-onnagata* of great beauty and ability who started his acting career in Osaka, but went to work in the Three Cities. He was ranked with some of the greatest actors of the time, such as Ayame, and was known as the founder of the *onna-budō* role-type. In the 1710's he changed to *tachiyaku* parts, but also appeared as a *kashagata*. In 1727 he gave up the stage and is said to have set up as a seller of incense equipment in Edo. C: II.

Somekawa Jūrōbē 染川十郎兵衛 (died 1708 or 1711). His career started with country *kabuki*, but about 1700 he began work in Kyoto/Osaka, where he remained for most of his career; he does seem to have gone to Edo on at least one occasion. He specialized in *tachiyaku* parts and was at the height of his achievement in 1707. His *hōmyō* was Kengai 賢外, and *The Kengai Collection* records his recollections.

Sugi Kuhē 杉九兵衛 (dates unknown, fl. 1670–1680). Little is known of this actor's life, except what is recorded in this collection. He is credited with the editorship of *One Hundred Items on the Stage*, and with being a teacher of Sakata Tōjūrō. In Item XLV of *Dust in the Ears* he is recorded as giving advice to Tōjūrō, and in the introduction to the 1750 edition of this work (see p. 13) he is said to have been active until c. 1710, although Gunji is doubtful of the accuracy of this statement. He worked in Kyoto, and is famous for the fact that he was the founder of the *kashagata* role. D: XLV.

Suzuki Heishichi 鈴木平七. He was prominent just before 1700 as a *wakashu* actor, and seems to have played in the Three Cities. His roles also included warriors and *yatsushi*. C: XXVII.

*_Takeda Izumo_ 竹田出雲 (1691–1756). He was the second bearer of the name, and was a manager for the Takemoto 竹本 puppet theater in Osaka. Although he was an expert administrator, his fame as an author (in collaboration) of puppet plays is even greater. G: VII.

* _Takemoto Chikugonojō_ 竹本筑後掾. See Takemoto Gidayū.

Takemoto Gidayū 竹本義太夫 (1651–1714). He came from a family of farmers, but by 1675 he was reciting _jōruri_ professionally, taking the name of Gidayū in 1684. He founded the Takemoto Theater in Osaka, and his collaboration with Chikamatsu Monzaemon produced a series of dramatic masterpieces. In 1701 he acquired the name of Takemoto Chikugonojō 竹本筑後掾. G: VII.

* _Takeshima Kōzaemon_ 竹島幸左衛門. He became a _tachi-yaku_ in 1694 and worked as such in the Three Cities. His most highly regarded performance seems to have been in the _kabuki_ version of _The Battles of Coxinga_. His name disappears from the programs in about 1725. E: X.

Tamagashiwa 玉柏. See Ichimura Tamagashiwa.

* _Tamagawa Handayū_ 玉川半太夫. His dates are not known, but he was acting _nuregoto_ and _keisei_ roles in the last decade of the 17th century. C: XXV.

* *Tamiya Shirogorō* 民屋四郎五郎 (1685–1745). His first appearance was in Osaka, as a *waka-onnagata*, about 1705. He later shifted to acting in *tachiyaku* parts. In 1714 he was involved to a small extent in the Ejima incident (see Ikushima Shingorō), but was pardoned after a year, and resumed his occupation in a traveling group. In 1718 he returned to Osaka and won considerable renown for his playing of *jitsugoto*. His *haimyō* was Kōon 江音. He compiled *Sequel to " Dust in the Ears."*

Tatsunosuke 辰之助. See Mizuki Tatsunosuke.
Tōjūrō 藤十郎. See Sakata Tōjūrō.
Tominaga Heibē 富永平兵衛 (dates unknown, fl. 1670–1700). He worked in the Kyoto/Osaka area, and after some time as an actor, he changed to being a playwright, having the distinction in 1680 of being the first author to have his name on a program. When Chikamatsu Monzaemon began writing *kabuki* plays, Tominaga gradually lost his popularity; he was, however, one of those responsible for the success of *kabuki* at the end of the seventeenth century. He is now remembered mainly as the author of one of the pieces in the *Analects, Mirror for Actors.* D. XXXV.

* *Uji Kaganojō* 宇治加賀掾 (1635–1711). He was born in Uji, in the Kii peninsula, and after some local experience as a *jōruri* reciter, he went to Kyoto and established his own puppet theater, using the name of Uji Kadayū 嘉太夫. In 1677 he took the name of Kaganojō and shortly afterwards Chikamatsu Monzaemon began to write for him. Until about 1685 he had a period of great popularity, but in his later years he was overshadowed by his former pupil Takemoto Gidayū. D: XI.

Ukon Uhē 右近宇兵衛 Nothing is known of this actor apart from the reference in *The Kengai Collection.* D: VI.
Yagozaemon 弥五左衛門. See Fukui Yagozaemon.

* *Yamamoto Kamon* 山本歌門. This *onnagata* actor rose consistently in the rankings from his debut in 1695 until 1721, soon after which his name disappears from the programs. He seems to have worked almost entirely in Kyoto. C: XXVIII; F: III.

* *Yamashita Hanzaemon* 山下半左衛門. See Yamashita Kyōemon.

Yamashita Kyōemon 山下京右衛門 (1652 [?1650]–1717). His early names included Yamashita Hanzaemon 山下半左衛門, and he was, before Sakata Tōjūrō, the leading *tachiyaku* of Kyoto. He was also a great *zamoto* and was responsible for the staging of many famous plays. C: XV, XXVIII; D: I, II, XV, XXV, XXXVI, XLI, XLIV; E: I, XXV, F: V, XI, XII.

* *Yamatoya Jimbē* 大和屋甚兵衛 (c. 1650–1704). He was the son of a *zamoto* in Osaka and first appeared on the stage in a child part, and progressed through *wakashu* to *tachiyaku*, sometimes performing the function of *zamoto*. In the 1690's he went to Kyoto and received a very favorable reception as a *tachiyaku*, but by the turn of the century he was losing public support. C: XXVIII; G: I, II.

* *Yamatoyama Jinzaemon* 大和山甚左衛門 (1677–1721). He was founder of the Yamatoyama family of actors. During his career he moved from *wakashu* to *waka-onnagata* and finally to *tachiyaku*. He was mainly a traveling actor until 1704, when he made his first appearance in a large theater. Sakata Tōjūrō took him under his wing, and he became popularly known as Tōjūrō II (or Kosakata 小坂田), although he should not be confused with the official holder of that name. Tōjūrō, in 1707, as a sign of his retirement, handed over to him a paper kimono such as he often used in Yūgiri plays (see D: XLIV), and it is said to have been this that turned Jinzaemon to *tachiyaku* parts. E: XV.

Yoshida Ayame 吉田あやめ. This actor is mentioned only in *The Words of Ayame*, XVIII, and nothing apart from this is known of his career.

* *Yoshizawa Ayame* 芳沢あやめ (1673–1729) He was born in the province of Kii and at the age of 5 he was already in the Dōtombori pleasure district, using the name Ayanosuke 綾之助. Later he began stage appearances under the name of Tachibanaya Gonshichi 橘屋権七, and received instruction in acting from Mizushima Shirobē 水島四郎兵衛 and Arashi San'emon I 嵐三右衛門初代. After some attempts at *wakashu* and *tachiyaku* roles he specialized in *waka-onnagata* parts. He often appeared in this early period with the *tachiyaku* Yamashita Hanzaemon 山下半左衛門, from whom he also took advice. By about 1700 he was using the name of Yoshizawa Ayame, and was a famous *onnagata*. In the ensuing years the actors' ranking lists had to invent special titles to describe his excellence. In 1711 he changed for a year to *tachiyaku* roles under the name of Yoshizawa Gonshichi 芳沢権七, but returned to *waka-onnagata* parts until his death. He operated mainly in Osaka and Kyoto, but spent a year in Edo from the 11th month of 1713, and charmed the audiences there. His grace and beauty fitted him excellently for his career, and were matched by his voice and acting ability. C: passim; E. XI; I: 6, 9, 26.

Appendix III

Subject List of Important Topics

Actors, cooperation between—A: I, VI; C: XV—XVII, XIX; D: V, VIII, XI, XVI, XXXII, XXXIII, XXXVII; E: VI, XXIII; F: V, XI, XIV; G: V.

Audience—A: I; C: XXVIII; D: VI, XI, XII, XVII, XXII, XXXVI; E: IX, XXIII; F: XI, XIII; G: II, VI, XII, XVI; I: 8, 23.

Authors—D: XVII, XXXIII, XXXV, XL—XLII; E: IX; I: 20.

Backer—E: X; F: IV, IX; G: IX; I: 16.

Comic parts—A: III; C: IX, D: II, III, V, XVII, XXVII.

Costume and make-up—A: VII; B: IV; C: II, XII; E: XI, XIII, XIV, XXII; F: I, VII; G: II, III, VI, VIII; H: II, VII, X.

Deputizing—A: VII.

Homosexuality—B: II; C: XVIII; D: XXXI; I: 5.

Horse—B: I, II.

Jōruri—see Puppet plays.

Maintaining interest—D: XXXII-XXXIV, XXXVIII.

Men's roles:

    kataki-yaku—D: XXXIV; E: VI, XII.

    old men—A: VI; E: XI.

    tachiyaku—A: I; C: X, XI, XXII; D: XLV; E: VI, XXII, XXIII; I: 25.

    young men—B: II; C: XXVII.

Naturalism—C: XX; F: VII.

Nō plays—C: XVIII; D: VI, IX; H: II, III; I: 6, 7, 26.

Official bans—B: III; F: X.

Opening performance—A: II; D: VI—IX, XXX; G: II; I: 21.

Posture—D: IV; E: XII.

Program, annual and daily—D: XLIV; E: III, IX, XVII; F: VI, XI;

Appendix IV

Bibliography

Various books are referred to in this translation; the following list gives particulars of the works concerned.

Dunn   Dunn, C. J. *The Early Japanese Puppet Drama*. London, 1966.

Ernst   Ernst, Earle. *The Kabuki Theatre*. London, 1956.

Gunji   Gunji Masakatsu 郡司正勝 *Kabuki jūhachi-ban shū* (*Nihon koten bungaku taikei* 98). 歌舞伎十八番集, 日本古典文学大系 98.

Halford   Halford, Aubrey S. & Giovanna M. *The Kabuki Handbook*, Rutland, Vermont and Tokyo, 1960.

Keene   Keene, Donald. *Major Plays of Chikamatsu*. New York and London, 1961.

Malm   Malm, William. *Japanese Music and Musical Instruments*. Rutland, Vermont and Tokyo, 1959.

Morris   Morris, Ivan. *The Life of an Amorous Woman*. London, 1963.

O'Neill   O'Neill, P. G. *A Guide to Nō*. Tokyo, 1955.

Scott   Scott, A. C. *The Kabuki Theatre of Japan*. London, 1955.

Shaver   Shaver, Ruth M. *Kabuki Costume*. Rutland, Vermont and Tokyo, 1966.

Shuzui   Shuzui Kenji 守随憲治. *Yakusha-banashi* (*Yakusha-rongo*) 役者論語. Tokyo, 1961.

Theatre in Japan   Japanese National Commission for UNESCO, ed. *Theatre in Japan*. Tokyo, 1963.

一女形風ハ申に及ばす心をつくべきなり。立身に成り候時ハ。わに足に成べし

腰ほそに。すそびらきよし
一鑓おどりハ。随分足を。片わにゝして。ひらけるがよし。身をそりおもた

くと。ひやうしにふりを大きう。又間をせわしくして鑓のまわるがよし
一きつねハかりう人。又ハ犬などに。おそれるやうにすべし。獅子ハ王なれバ。

こゝろたくましく持事。かんじんなり。一さいどれともに。頭をつかふべし。ふりの
しなにより。こまかしく又ハ大間にもすべし。頭をつかふを第一にすべし

一着ながしゝよさハ申に及バず。其身着のまゝにて。それゝにしよさの
仕わけ見へ申やう肝要なりすべて男のしよさに女のふりをする事

又ハをんりやうの中にて。おとりいむべし。諸人ほむるとも。其所作の事わざ
より外の事すべからず

一ふりハ目にてつかふと申て。ふりハ人間の躰のごとし。目ハ魂のごとし。たましい
なき時ハ。何の用にも立ず。ふりに眼のはづれるを死ぶりといひ。所作の気

に乗てふりと眼といつちにするを。活たる振とハ申なり夫故ふりハ目にて
つかふと心得べき事第一也。はてしなき故筆をとめぬ　佐渡嶋日記終

H-XI　　　　　　H-X　　　　　　H-IX　H-VIII　H-VII

○しよさの秘伝

一ふりハもんくに有もんくの生 なき時ハ。品をもつてす。又もんくなく。ふしにてのはす時ハ。ひやうしにのる。なすわざハしよさ成か故にふりに誠を本とす。

一しやうぞく大口事。これら大かた能をする心持にて。風のくづれぬやうに舞ふべし。くたけたる風ハあしく候

一侍の弓矢をたづさへておどりさハぐやうなる八見苦シ。此しよさにかぎらず。すべて謡など入たるか。能がゝりのしよさを。諸人一とうにどよめき。誉るハあしく。只一言二言ほむるハ。ゆかしくてよし

一柴かりなどのやうなる。下々の親仁のしよさハ。ふりの間にむかし若き時の風を年よりて叶ハざるふうの心持。あいたゝゝに入これもしよさがらをしほらしくするを第一とするなり

一婆々の所作。若き時のだて者の品を。年よりてかなハざるふりの間ゝゝに入しほらしきを第一とす

一翁。老女。申におよバず其心持

何によらず其しよさがらのこゝろを。わするべからず。

H-VI　　H-V　　　　　　H-IV　　　　H-III　　　H-II　　　　　　H-I

鳴神上人をやつこがころす事あり。詰に鳴神の亡霊。雲のたへまに。つき

したひがいこつの所作を思ひ付たり。栢莚生得狂言に切殺さるゝ事を忌て

せす予是をさせんと思ひ。四ばんめのがいこつの所。影法師にて拙者勤べしと

いひけれバ。左候ハゝ殺され申べしと相談出来て稽古云合済。初日出せし所に

久米寺弾正といふ侍に成。使者に来りての仕内。あつハれ誠の武士と見へたり

外に此まねをする人なしと大坂中の評判。扨も上手なりと感心し四番めハ

二役鳴神上人の段家の芸なれバ手に入たる仕内鳴神のひゞき近国ハ申に及ハず

遠方よりもいざ海老蔵が鳴神見物せんとわざゝ大坂へ来る人。数を知らず押も

分られぬ大評判大入京の数寄人ハ大坂にて見物したる人多し。然どもつねに京出

勤なく。是のみ残心なり。影に芸ある八奇妙の生得也いづれ妙の字ハ遁れがたし

しかし哥舞妓役者の殺さるゝ役を嫌ふもいか成事か是とても妙なるべし

稀なる物ハ。市川海老蔵なり。予此人を妙人と号たり。中〳〵余人のう

つす事も及バす。玄妙の役者なり。予江戸在住の時。栢莚海老蔵申さ

れしハ。其許太夫本をなさるゝならバ。いつにても登るべしと。いひける事の

有し故。一とせ大坂道頓堀にて座本をせんと思ひ。栢莚を相談に。書状

下せし時。返状に給金弐千両にて。手付金五百両下さるべしと申来る。哥

舞妓芝居始りて以来。給金弐千両取やくしや聞も及バず。稀なる事を

申越されしと。甚おもしろく。手付金五百両調達して差下したり。あの方

にもよもやと思ひしやら。大坂へ来りて其うつり挨拶をせられし故。予答

日弐千両の給金取らるゝ役者古今になし。夫を押出して申越さるゝ

ゆへ。定てそれほどに格別の事。有べしと存なりと申けり予も物数寄

なりと思ふのみ。顔見せハ。ういろう売のせりふ。先めづらしく。大入にて二の替

曾我を出せし所。さん〳〵不当りにて。子息団十郎病気を幸に。十日余り

にて相休。挍三の替の相談何をかなと楽屋おもてとも。彼是申合けれ

ども思案おちず。時に栢莚申けるハ。此次ハ鳴神を出さんといへり。予も鳴

神なれハ。狂言案じるにも及バずと。古き狂言を序へ継合せつゝり。四番め

初日のはり札を出したる事なり。近来ハ替かんばん出し置。俄にかんばんを
かけ替。外の狂言に替る事。折節にあり。是ハ何ゆへなれバ。次の替り狂言
の稽古も出来ざる内先替り看板を出し。抦相談に懸り。役廻りなど打
寄りて申合見る時。何か万事つかへ多く。一決ならず。夫故俄に狂言替り
看板を又出し直す事有となん。初日二三日前より急に稽古して。誠に足本
より鳥の立といはん計の惣座中 甚 さハぎなり。此麁末成事。古今の相
違をかんがへべし

一今時の若き役者衆のいへる事をきけバ誰が仕内ハ古風なり。あれにてハ
当世人々のみこまずなど。毎度人事に付ていふ人多くあり。此事一円
其意を得ざる事なり。狂言の仕内ハ。老若 男女貴賤の人情 をうつす
に古風当流とわかつ事。呑こみがたし衣装 の物ずきハ時々の流行有もの
なれバ。其時々を用ゆべし。心 持に古今の風といへる事あるべからず。すでに
かづらに諸分あり。老人あたま八。古風なりとて。皆黒髪計にても成難し
一役者の仕内に。あるひ八功者根生名人などさまぐ〜に号あり。しかし古今

今二三十年も年立たらバ。芝居大イに衰と成べしと。その時分より。歎き申されし。夫にたがハず。享保年中より段々持なし悪くなり。一向今ハ論に及ばず。今たま／＼古人の教ヘを守る者あれバ。あれハあほうのたわけのと譏る。ものゝみ多かりき。藤十郎存生のうちさへ役者不行義に成たるとて毎度歎申されし。いはんや今におゐてをや

一人形芝居にて八大坂石井飛弾といへる者。尊み申さねバならぬ事也元来操人形ハ。首ばかりにて着物を打きせ。手も足も遣ひ人の手にて仕たるもの。近来まで子供の翫びにでこのぼうといへる物是なり。此石井氏。おとなの手を。人形の袖へさし込遣ひ申故。甚袖見とむなしと工夫して。人形に手を悋付たり。夫より是に習ふて。足をつけ手の指をうごかし。眼を遣ひ眉を動すなど。近来ハさま／＼自由に作るなり。これ石井氏工夫の根元なり。今ハ飛弾の名ハ。浜芝居の名代計に残たり一元禄宝永年中まで。初の狂言して居る内に替り狂言の稽古して。もはや申分あるまじと。替り看板を出したり。それより銘々役柄の工夫して。さあこれでハよいと。おも役者二三人心得すむと。来ル何日よりといふ

終をとるやらん空しき身の上にてぞ有ける

一近来所作事をつとむる人ハ。所作の間〳〵に左右より扇づかひさせ。
又ハ湯をのみ。休息する人多し。これハいかん。見物へうしろを見せ居るうちハ。
正面にて舞より猶大事なり。此間のぬけぬやうに。心遣ひなを〳〵苦しき
ものなりと。古人もいひ置たり。さすれハ湯を呑扇つかひなどせねバ。勤
まらぬならバ。所作事をせぬがよし近来の人を自呵責するにあらず。古人の
教訓を用ゆる人なき故に。書しるし侍る。親伝八予におしゆる時も此湯など
呑事。五歳の時より堅くいましめたり。近年所作事。執心なる人々。物事
聞に来る人に。先所作事の間に湯を呑む事左右より扇つかひさする事
を。最初にいましめ置たり。石橋などの所作事を。舞終り。舞台に打ふし。

後見の人々寄てかいて楽屋へ入。此事一円其意を得ざる事なり。先見物
に対してぶ礼。そのうへ哥舞妓といへる物ハあれほど野卑なる物と。其身
壱人にて。此道の人々をさげしまる〳〵事。芝居道のかきんなり。元来哥舞
妓といふもの。左様なる不行義の物にあらず。古実を能知たる人すくなく。
近来年〳〵に持なし悪敷成たり。坂田藤十郎云元禄の末宝永に至り

一地狂言ハ勿論所作事など。人の工夫して付たる事。後に又すべからず。近年ハ

向ひに出すなんど聞ゆ趣向を。又こちらにもまけじと急に稽古などして。

張あひ仕ける見物同事を二軒見て。何なぐさみにならんや。官女などいと

みやびやか成風俗にてせば。薪を負へる山賤の老たるさまなど然るべし。

一日の狂言にても。堅き武士の詰ひらきあれバ。けいせいの意気地などの

事。又ハおかしき事など。とかく同じ事のならバざるやうにするこそ。此道の

専一なりむかしの当り狂言。仏原浅間嶽因幡松嫁鏡などにてみるべし

一ひとッせ備中国宮内といへる所の芝居へ罷下り。不斗当所にて死去せし

古人金子六右衛門が吉左衛門の古墳に参らんとこヽろざし。少シのよすがを求め

やう〳〵方角を知て。叢の中に分入。ちいさき石塔あり。花をさし水を

手向。それよりほとりにて。人をやとい塚の前の薄など苅とらせ。ほそき

板をひろひ得て。矢立の筆にて金子六右衛門墓と書つけ。さしおき

たり。天地ハ万物の逆旅といへど。取わき役者ハ。一所不住にて。何国にて

悪敷ハ成たり

青江下坂二つ胴に敷腕といひ聞せ。さし付たる刀を。両手に持ながら。左
の方へ引寄。調子を低く。ずんどよふ切れますへゝゝゝとゑしやくする。此
善悪ハ後の芸者かんがへ見るべし

一親伝八予若き時つねぐゝいひ聞せしハ。芸者といふ者ハ金銀に眼をくれる
物にハあらず。一生涯の内。名をひろむるが。肝要なりと。毎度耳かしましき程
さいゝゝ堅く申付たり。此事子供のじぶんより年来聞こみ居しゆへ。
予何国より相談に来りても。つゐに給銀の相対ハ致さず頼なれバ何方
へ成とも二言となく約束極めたり。銘々業相応に給銀のわかち有て。
抱る程の者ハ。夫々に相当せるなるべし。しかれバ給銀相対におよぶ事にあらず

一年中芝居ふあたりにて。年中勘定 ふそくに見へければ。此方より給銀を
まけ。了簡付ヶ出たり。芝居主ハ役者と違ひ。名を上る事ハいらず第一
金銀をまふくるが。其身の肝要といふ物。役者と芝居主との心得ハ。格別
なり。夫に近年ハ。少シの給銀のあやにて。相談不済方多しと沙汰を聞侍
此心底いぶかし。いにしへの役者中途に。出よの出よまいのと。もめる事ハ皆役或ハ
仕内に付ての申分なり。近来ハ金銀の事に付て。もめ粗おほしとかや。双方持なし

八思へども。非人かたき打の狂言ハ。むかし荒木与二兵衛といへる立役仕始たり。其

時のすがたハ。病かづらにて。随分くろ／＼とあぶらを付。顔のつくりも白粉

濃くぬりうつくしく。衣装ハ白小袖の無地。大広袖紅絹うら。花色の丸ぐけ

帯を前にむすび。手足も随分白くして出立せられよし是予が親伝ハ

はなしにて聞つたへたり

愚按　元祖坂田藤十郎申されし非人の心得。やはり自分の考にて

なし。古人申置たる事此荒木与次兵へのせられし非人かたき打の出立

にて藤十郎申されしと附合せり。これをおもへハ。姉川致されし非人

の心得ハ。雪と墨ほど違ふとハ此事なるべし。新四郎非人の仕内よき

ゆへ。人々毎度申出すなれど。ころへハ甚つたなし。是姉川を譏るにハ

あらず。古人の説と合しての論なり。仕内も古人とハ甚野卑なり。ためし

ものに来りし加村宇多右衛門が。せりふに。敵打といふハ命おしさにいふと

さんぐ／＼せめかける時。竹に仕こみし刀をぬきさし付。青江下坂二つどうに

しきうでずんどよう切れますへ／＼と笑ふ。荒木氏始てせられしは

一大坂竹田出雲。子供に六法ふらせたきと。予を頼みに越されたり。所望に
任せ。下りけれバ。出雲殊の外悦び。扨子供に指南仕けるに。振やう首の遣ひ様。鶏の首
思ふやうにゆかず。時に即座に工夫出来。六法のふりやうの程拍子ハ。にはとりの首
のつかひやうに。ひとしと申聞せけれバ。忽に合点して。稽古満たり。物ハたとへ
程よき導ハなし。しかれども是はとても実ならでハ用に立がたし。扨六法の
指南の跡ハ。さまざま古人のはなしなど仕けるに。此時節竹本筑後芝居には
新浄瑠璃かわり目にて。竹田家内ハ。道具立其外万事。こしらへ最中にて。
あまたの人数銘々役々を相勤る。道具立あつらへ方の者。ちよと御出

あれと次の間へまねく。出雲こたへに何の用なるぞと尋しかバ。柳の樹出来
致候。御覧なさるべしと申。それを此方が見るにハ及バず。正真の柳に似さへ
すれバ済む事と申されし。さすが竹田家相続せらるゝ人ほど有て。不断の心
得かくべつなりと感しけり。芝居ハ万端芸の仕内道具立等に至るまで
正真をうつすより外なしと古人のおしへ尤なる事かな。善悪とも不断の事あ
らるゝ物なれバ人ハ常の心得が大事なり
一非人敵打の狂言ハ。中古姉川新四郎此仕内を始て。仕出せしやうに。若き人

さかもあらハさず。今よき身分になれバ。礼を失ふものなるに。其のち大坂へ来り上手と評判をとり。

かくむかしをあらハす人おほからず。其のち大勢の中にて

其暮京都南側の芝居へ十日が間京見物へ目見へに立より。桟敷の

値を上るほどの大評ばん。大入にて近来の賑ひ。江戸へ下り。其暮又上京

し在京の間。上手〱と賞美せられ。其のち又江戸へ下りたり。在京の

間女形の心得に成る書を編たりこれを訥子四十八ヶ条といふ

一近年所作事をする役者。おびたゝしう衣装を着かさね。所作の間〱に

はやし方の並ゐる方へ向ひ見物をうしろになして件の小袖をひとつづ〻

ぬぐなり。所作事に上着をぬぐといふ心ハ。見物長事を見詰て居れば。

なんぼう面白き事にても。すこしは眼にそむものなれバ。其ねふりを覚

さんがために脱ものなるに。中古より余慶着重ねるを全盛にして。余り

さい〱ぬぐゆへ。せわしなく却て眼のさまたげに成なりはやし方に向ィて

衣装を脱だり。又ハ衣紋をつくろへバ。其間見物の眼あくなりとかく。さま

あかぬがよきなり

ともなく。他国めぐりの芝居の笛吹。又ハ何かの助ケなどに頼まれ行。夫より

勢州の芝居へ出にける。其時ハ沢村藤五郎といへり。予勢州へ下り。はじめて

ちかづきに成。仕内をつく〲と打見るに。余の旅役者と違ひ。全躰面白

き芸ぶりあり。後々には立ものと成かねまじき者にてもなしと心を付ケ

けるより。ある夜ひそかにまねき。役者にて終らバ。江戸へ下り精出すまじき

やと申けれバ。答に我も其望なれども。心にまかせずといへるより。当所の

事ハ此方引受申べし。ぜひ当暮江戸へ下らるべしと。すゝめて其年の冬下シぬ。

程なく宗十郎と名を改次第に評よくつるに海老蔵に次ての立者と

成たり。予其後に江戸へ下り。一座に住ゐたりしなれども。今ハ此方より

手をついて挨拶する程の立もの。以前の事ハ鼻息にも出さず居たりし

楽屋にて大勢聞ゐる前にて訥子いハく。扨々めづらしき事かな其元様

と一座致事。思へ八一むかしなり。先年勢州にて御世話に罷成。御陰にて

先今日これほど迄に。立身致たりと予に一礼をいひ扨海老蔵其ほか

立ものゝ役者に向ひ。拙者ハいかゝる恩を請し者など。ふいちゃうしけり。その時

思ふに名をあげる人は了簡格別の事なり。多くの人いにしへの事など。いさ

ほとりの古道具やにて。彼五歳の時勤しごばん人形の唐津焼。店

に出あるおさなこゝろに見覚し人形なれバ。速に価をきハめ。求め
帰りけり。　先年御前御気に入の御側仕の衆。壱つ拝領仕ける。
定て其行すへならめ。これをつくゝ見るにも付ても親の粉骨
砕身せし事をおもひ出し。涙をとむる導と八成けらし

一ある年勢州の芝居へ下り。はやし方など殊外無人。勿論道具
等不都合にて。小鼓一挺あれとも大鼓なし。是にあぐみ居けるを。予細工
に竹を切り。付ケ物をして。大鼓をこしらへ。それよりの工夫にて。一人して二挺
鼓と名付。はやき事など打たりしに。二挺鼓といひならハし。何とやら一曲
と成りたるもおかし

一沢村宗十郎江戸にてハ。長十郎と成。　後二助高屋高介と改誹名を訥子
といふ。此人元 来ハ京都御歴々より出。　若 年のみぎりハ仕官 して由緒
ある血脈なれども。生得心 和らか過て。身を持崩し哥舞妓芝居の役
者と八成たり。初のほど八左もなく流労して。あちこ地と漂泊し。抱らるゝ

るることなきに。評ばんなをりし事ハいかゞと。尋し人あり。此事我に問ふて

我ハしらず。

一予五歳の時より。親伝八所作事をおしへ。東武へつれ下り。碁盤人形

と名付ごばんの上にて我に芸をさせしに。あなたこなたより召され。

春より九月までつとめたり。去御方の御機嫌に入。毎度召れ碁盤の

上の所作を勤ける。御きげんの余り。肥前 国唐津へ。予がごばんの上に

座しゐる人形を焼につかハされ。三つ出来して御とりよせ遊ハされしほど

御興に入たり。其としの十月京都へ登る道中筋ごばん人形の所作を聞

および。宿々にてこれを望む。のぞみ次第に此所作事をつとめたり。九

歳に成たる時最早ごばんの上に乗かぬる時節より伝八工夫仕出して。

七ばけの曲 といふ事を案じ出し。おしへ込シ。後長五郎が七ばけと我か仕出

せしやうに成たり親の厚恩筆に書つくしがたし。思へバ一むかしと成にき

所作秘伝奥に附す

予出 家して。建仁寺御門前に住し。法花経 読誦朝暮おこたらず。

仏 の道を願ふより他事なし。ある時三条新地頂妙寺へ日参の折柄

を振る工夫をして当りを取たるなり。二代目あらし三右衛門三代目と相伝し

て。毎度勤しなり。其のち予又工夫しけり。其振筆に八書取難し口伝

一予始て六法ふりたる八。大坂道頓堀芝居にて。座本より顔見せに六法ふり

くれといふ。是まで三右衛門甚兵衛など振たる跡にて。我等など中〴〵思ひ寄

ずと辞退せしに。ぜひといへるにいなみがたくて。衣装の切付も物数奇して。初日

の夜の顔みせ。六法ふる半ば〳〵より。見物おけやい〳〵と。声々いふより。半畳　五六枚

打こむといなや。追々ばら〳〵と爰かしこより。半畳数多打こみける。夫も

かまハず勤仕廻。楽屋へ入たる時。惣座中首尾能〳〵手を打たんといふ。

予ハ甚其こゝろなきゆへ手を打たず。二日目三日目までおけよ〳〵といひ

〳〵七日つとめ。扨昼に成ても。やハり見物さん〴〵に打こむゆへ。こ八口惜く

当かほみせ六法にて仕損ひて八。後々まで恥を残す事。無念やとなを〳〵

しんぼうして精を出し勤けれバ。いつともなしに評ばん大ィに立直り。よい

や〳〵のかけ声。それより日〳〵に取沙汰よくなり。端々の評判よろしき

と聞し。とかく工夫をこらすしんぼうが肝心なり。しかし初日より仕様替

佐渡嶋日記

蓮智坊 著

一六法といふ風俗は。むかし信州歴々の武門より出たる人。伎芸を好みつるに浪人し。上京しける。其頃名古や山左衛門といへる。武士の浪人もの出雲国の巫女。於国と夫婦に成。京北野にて芝居興行 仕けるに寄彼の山左衛門とひとつに成。江戸さんちや通ひの風俗をして見せけるより起りけるとなん。江戸にて八丹前といひ。大坂にて八出端といふ。それより伝はり其のち立役。荒木与次兵衛。右の六法をふり入を取たるなり。それまで八今の六法のごとく。挙を廻し。振し事八なく。左右ともに真直に振たり。今も江戸に八古風残りあり。与次兵衛より元 祖嵐三右衛門請続是を工夫し。いまのごとくを仕はじめけり。其のち古人大和屋甚兵衛ちんバにて。六法

のせりふおほく。近き比ハ舞台にて二人寝る狂言など粗あり。かやうの趣向を作る作者。古人の示教をしらず。たとへ作者いかやうに作り出すとも。其仕内を呑込勤る役者も同罪なり。藤十郎申されしごとく二三十年過なバやくしやの行義大きに乱ぬべしと未然を察し申されし事。日〻に思ひ当りたり狂言に差合の躰あらバ其場に及バぬうち。いかやうにも仕様あるべし。近来のきやうげんハ。親子兄弟一所に見物成たし。扨々にが〳〵しき事なり

一坂田藤十郎曰。哥舞妓やくしやといへるものハ。人のたいこをもつ気しやうにてハ。上手になりがたし。そのやうに心降ると。後ハ役者同士の出合も。はなはだ疎遠になる物なりと若き者どもに毎度申されし

賢外集終

ぬ。其暮極月廿九日に七三郎江戸の宅の門口に。歩行荷六人して持こむ。
少長此よしを聞。添状を見れバ。坂田藤十郎よりとあり其荷を見れバ。わくに
入たる大壷を出す。少長肝をつぶし。何を送られたるぞ。藤十郎の送りもの
なれバさぞや。心をこめられたる物ならんと。書状を急ぎひらき見れバ加茂
川の水一壷しん上仕候。大ぶくに御遣ひ被下べくとの文躰。少長ほとんど我
を折。さても〳〵我在京の内出会多方こゝろを知りたると思ひの外。此度
の送り物にて心の底深き事。はかりがたしと。家内ハ勿論人々に語り申されし
さしもの少長だに送り物にて藤十郎の心底ふかき事量りかねたり。其
余の人藤十郎の事など一向論しがたし
一山下京右衛門曰。哥舞妓芝居のせりふハ。随分言葉にさし合がましき事。これ
なきやうにこゝろかけ肝要なり。其故ハ親子兄弟一所に来る見物人まゝ
あれハなりと。。若き役者への教訓尤なる事なり
一坂田藤十郎曰。舞台にてけいせい買の狂言を勤るさへ。さし合なり。然レ
ともこれハ是非に及バずと申されし。しかるにいつの比よりか。次第にさし合

ことく今年は少長といへる大敵あれバ。一座の役者ハ勿論。先狂言に骨をおらねバならず。貴様狂言を作らるゝ故。油断もあるまじけれど。一座の者よりも随分貴様勢つよく。狂言工夫あらねバ。芝居の為にならず。顔見せを仕勝しものゆへ。作者の気ゆるみ出る物ゆへ。わけて申とくれゝ内意ありける。さて替りめ度毎藤十郎七三郎が仕内を見物して天

晴の上手なりと云。又七三郎ハ藤十郎が芸を見てさてゝ藤十郎といへる役者ハ聞及びしよりも。いたつて上手なり。我等是までに藤十郎の仕内を見て工夫つけなバ。芸をあげん物を。何をいふても今ハかひなしと悔まれし。藤十郎ハ七三を見て先舞台の行義はなハだ正敷見え侍る嚊。それよりちかづきに成。互に心安くかし不断の身持よろしからんと。心底床しく。それよりちかづきに成。互に心安く度ゝ出合申されし。七三郎元禄十一年同十二年二とし山下座をつとめ同年の暮に江戸木挽町山村座へ下らるゝに相談きハまり。七三郎より藤十郎方へ置みやげを贈りたり。藤十郎餞別に何ぞおくらんとかねて思へとも。あの方より置みやけを贈られたるに。はなむけを又送りなバ。余りしつへいかへしにておもしろからずと。何も沙汰なしに暇乞に行。心よく見立別レ

といふらくしゆ迄。人々諷ふほどの仕損ひ。一両日して追々藤十郎方へ一座の
役者共来り少長ハ七三郎誹名也さん〴〵のとり沙汰あり。又江戸より登り。京
にてやつし事をせらるゝといふ事。大きなる了簡違ひ。そこが下手の
しるしなんど。少長をそしりける。藤十郎申けるハ。成ほど下手なり。京の
見物ハ大ィに下手なり。七三郎ハ先近来の上手。此人の上に立もの当時
壱人もなし。少長のほられしゆへ。我等も精出しなバ。今年中にハちと芸も
あがるべし。顔見せハ此方仕勝けるゆへ。二の替りハ大きなるこハもの也
けつして二の替りにハ仕つけらる　ならんと。顔見せなかバに申居られしが。
はたして翌辰正月廿二日より。二の替りにけいせい浅間嶽といふ狂言を出シ
少長ともへの丞の役。ごばん嶋の羽織をしき茶碗のわれにてひとり碁
を打。太夫奥州とのくぜつの段。いやハや外に。まねの仕手なき仕内
京中の見物うへをしたへかへし。顔みせとハ打て替へての大あたり。さても
七三ハきつい上手かなとの大評ばん。此狂言百二十日興行仕けり隣芝
居の一座さてこそ藤十郎申されしごとく。拔々上手の胸中ハおそろしき
事とかんじぬ。藤十郎金子吉左衛門をひそかにまねき。貞見せより申す

の賜物なるべしと存当り候へども。御名も承らず。ありがたき旨を宰領に

申かへしぬ。我等執心かけし松の樹と思ひ贈り給ハりし段有難き事かな。御大

身とは見請ぬれどちいさき木にてもあらバこそ大木といひ猶以一山へ

届なくてハ。理不尽に掘る事叶ひがたく侍らん扨々有難き御こゝろざし

かなと感心し早く庭へ植べしといひ付けれども。路次口殊の外さハが

しく。いかなる事とたづねければ。先刻の松の木塀ニつかへ路次口へはいり

申さぬよし答ふ。藤十郎聞て。さて〴〵塀もなき事かなつかへてはいらぬ

ならバ塀をこぼち入べし。跡にて塗おけハ済事と男共をしかられける。

此事金子吉左衛門居合せ。上手の名を得し人の心ハ別なりと。ほとんど感

じ此事を人々にはなしけり

一中村七三郎ハ元禄年中。江戸にて上手と諸人に誉られ評ばんを

とりたる。やつし方の名人元禄十年卯霜月京四条山下半左衛門

後ニ京右衛門座へ上京し顔見せハ。坂田藤十郎方。大ィにはやり七三郎甚

といふ

不評判にてよからぬさたのみすくなからす馬の跡あし

一坂田藤十郎鳴物御停止にて芝居休みの間。心安き一座の内の女形
二三人供人引具し。江州石山へ誘ひ行。酒盛して居ける。向ふに武門の
御歴々とおぼしき御方。御忍ひに御参詣遊バされたるや。御近習打まぜ
若殿原五六人。其外附々上下十弐三人御酒宴あり。暫有て。若き侍来。
それなるハ藤十郎ならずや。酒一つふるまひたしと。旦那の仰を達す有難
仕合と。速に御幕の内へ伺公して。御盃を頂戴仕。さまざまの咄シなど申上。殊に
なき御機嫌にて時をうつす。日も西にかたふきけれバ。明日より又芝居
始ますれバ。追付帰宅仕申度と御暇を乞ひ。元の同行の氈の上へ戻る。程なく
若侍かけ来り。何成とも望あらバ申べしと承る。何も所望に無之候へバ。宜敷
仰上られ下さるべしと申せバそれにてハかへつて御機嫌よろしからず是非何
成ともと達而との事ゆへ。左候ハゝ御幕の辺なる松の樹拝領仕たしと申。
其儘皆〱駕籠に打乗京へ戻りける。夫より日を経て表に大勢人声
何事やらんと勝手へ尋ればバ松の木来りしといふ。門違ひなるべしと思ひしに。
坂田藤十郎方ハこれなるかと松の樹の宰領這入。いつぞや石山に於て約束
せし。松の樹送り遣すとの口上。夫にてやう〱思ひ出せり。日外拝領申上し。御歴々

かけす見せ先に立尽しとうふといへるものハいかやうにすれハ
喰やうにハ成やらんと。くわしく尋熟得して。扨もと感心して
立さりぬ。とかくかりそめの事にも麁略にせざる気質信実なる

生得なりと皆人沙汰しあへり

一坂田藤十郎祇園町ある料理茶や。くハしやに恋をしかけやがて
首尾せんと思ふに。件の妻女。おくの小座敷へ伴ひ。入口の灯をふき
消たり。時に藤十郎すぐさま逃帰りけり。其翌朝右の茶や へ
行。妻に打向ひ。御影にて替り狂言の稽古を仕たり。此度の狂
言ハ。密夫の仕内なり。つゐに左様の不義を致たる事なけれバ。甚
此仕内にこまり。此間太夫元よりはやく初日を出し申度と。再三せ
がまれ。日夜此事にあぐみ。密夫の稽古を男に出会もらひて仕たり。其情
うつらねバ。ひとつも稽古にならず。我願ひ成就致けいこ仕たり。今朝
太夫元へ。初日明後日御出しと申遣したりと一礼申されし。一座の人々扨々

名人と呼るゝ人の心がけハ凡慮の外なる事と手を打ぬ

着物等にいたる迄。大概に致し。正真のことくにならざるやうにすべし。此

一役ばかりハ常の心得と違ふなり其ゆへいかんとならバ哥舞妓芝居ハ

なぐさみに見物するものなれバ。随分物毎花美にありたし。乞食の正

真ハ。形までよろしからざるものなれハ。眼にふれておもしろからず。慰にハ

ならぬものなり。よつてかくハ心得べしと常〳〵申されし

一坂田藤十郎金子吉左衛門と連立芝居より帰りがけに。高瀬の橋の上に

立とゞまり。水の流れをつく〴〵詠め居て漸時を移す。金子氏思ひける八

何ぞ下へ取落されしか如何と。共にのぞき。或はふしぎに思ひ供人云く

何ぞおとし給ひたるかと問ふ。答なし暫あつて扨も清〳〵とした物

かなと。高瀬川の流水を感じて。夫より歩行し。其比の宿元河原町

四条上ル町へ帰られしとなり

愚按 儘ならぬもの。加茂川の水双六の籌と申伝へ侍る。此事思ひ

合され侍る歟。元来坂田氏八生得やくにたつのたゝぬの差別なし。

物事を麁略に見ぬ人なり。ある日河原町四条下ル町に。いにしへ

豆腐やあり。最中豆腐をこしらへゐるにふと眼が付腰も

居果より。我家に帰らずすぐさま藤十郎宅へ行藤十郎に向ひ初日の
御批難により。今日又工夫にて致たりしに。やはり其元御気に入らず

此上ハ我力にも及ハず。御指南うけたしといふ。藤十郎左候ハゝ申さう中村
四郎五郎ハ今若手には日の出の役者なり此度の狂言。其元ハ四郎五郎より
さきに役あり。あれほどに当られて八四郎五郎跡へ出て何をかせんなぜ
若手をたすけるやうには心がけせられぬと教訓仕けるに。京右衛門手を
打てかんじぬ

一右近宇兵衛といふ役者旅にて所作事の上手。後に京本舞台へ出たり
沢むら長十郎も元来旅を修行して。勢州の芝居より京本ぶたいへ
出二ばんめを勤。精出し上手に成たり。中古まで二番めハ中通りの役者
出たり近来ハ脇狂言同事に二ばんめも小詰より勤る也これらとて
も古実なく成たり。江戸ハ今に余風ありてゆかし

一坂田藤十郎曰哥舞妓役者ハ何役をつとめ候とも。正真をうつす
心がけより外他なし。しかれとも乞食の役めをつとめ候ハゝ。顔のつくり

あらず。当芝居主。拙者を抱らるゝに。大切成金銀を出し置れ
たり。米に砂あつて若嚙合せ歯を損しなば舞台にて。せ
りふ洩て聞へかぬべし又年ごろのみ付ざる水をのみ若腹中
など悪く成一日にても舞台を引なば。芝居主へ義理済ず
か様に身持養生心を付て。此へ身分に故障 出来ることは
是非なし。よつて斯ハ申付るなりと語られし
一中村四郎五郎若さかりの比。山下京右衛門一座に居けるとき

京右衛門役大ィに出来たり。見物ほめける其夜坂田藤十郎京右衛門
逢ひ今日の初日見物にゆきたり貴様ハいかる下手なりと云京右衛門
諸見物の評ばんとハ大ィに相違したるにより肝をつぶしながら
左候ハゝ二日め見て給ハれといふ。心得たりとて藤十郎二日めも見物
に行たり。京右衛門楽やに入ると藤十郎の桟敷へ人を遣ハし御苦労
ながら楽屋へちよと御出給ハれといひやるすくさま藤十郎かく屋へ
行京右衛門に逢申ける八。貴様御頼ゆへ今日も見物致たり。其元は
とかく下手なりと。昨日にかハらぬあいさつに京右衛門も大きにこまり芝

やがて座敷掃ていて暫く有てこれへお通りあれといひければ。やがて

皆々座敷へ通りみれバ。どんすの鏡ふとんの上に座し茶せん

髪にて提たばこ盆をひかへ。扨一礼すむと。此度の替り狂言は

中〳〵よう出来たるとの噂。どのやうな趣向と狂言の筋を聞かれ

たり。毎日相手の女形に終日の馳走をして帰されけり。此稽古の

間毎日の献立を自身好み。常の女の喰よきやうに取合。女形の

あしらひも。やはり女同前の心得にて。はなしなどもあり甚深切

行義なる事ともなり

一坂田藤十郎高給銀をとり大坂へ抱られし時。京より水を

樽詰にて取寄。飯米を一粒ゑりにさせて用ゆ其事を見聞

人々。扨も藤十郎ハけふがる奢ものかなと。専ら噂ありし事。誰

いひ聞するともなく。耳へ入たるが。ある人に逢ふていハく。私

飯米を一粒ゑりにさせ。水を京都より取寄候事我かこゝろ

しらぬ人ハ。定ておごり者なりと沙汰もあるべし。全く奢に

それはいと安きことなり。其金子ハ此方より遣し申べく間急ニ

囲を御建あれといひかへり。　夫より藤十郎懇意の方へ金五十両

借用申たしと。　手紙にて申遣しけれバ。　早速先方より調達し

て手代持参しける時に。　藤十郎とても御世話に。　歩に被成下

されかしとたのみ。　残らず歩判にして奉書の紙二枚出させ。ひんねぢ

持参して。　件の茶やへ行。　亭主に逢ひ右の歩金五十両袂より

出しあたへけり。　右の金子調達せし人。　一両日して藤十郎方へ来。

件の訳をありのまゝに咄す。　時に用達せし人。　左候ハ歩にて

なくともくるしかるましといふ。　藤十郎云袂より出し。人に遣ハす

金子小判にてハ下卑てよろしからぬと存。　それ故歩にかへ遣候

といひけり

一坂田藤十郎稽古の節ハいつとても藤十郎方へ皆々行ける。

ある時替り狂言の稽古に。　相手の女形水木辰之介山本哥門金子

吉左衛門同道にて。　朝飯後行けるに。　いまだ床あがらざる故。　次の間ニ

待ゐる。　程なく起たるや。　戸の明く音。　又ハ手水の流るゝ音なひ聞

さく致さんと尋ければ一トまわりちいさくと申より。すぐさまあつらへ直し。惣稽古のせつ彼ざうりちいさきゆへ。指にはさみ出られたり。初日にも同じく指にはさみ出る楽屋口に居たる役者名はわすれたり。若ざうりへお足が入りませぬかと。気を付けれバ。藤十郎いはく。此度の草履ハ揚屋の庭にてぬく事あり。舞台にぬぎ捨たる時。さうり大きければハ。ある人此事を不思義におもひ尋ければ。其返答ハ仕ながら。其儘にて舞台へ出たり。諸見物藤十郎ハさてもきつい鍬足なりと見出されてハ。重てけいせい買の狂言ハならざりしと。答られし。すべてか様な事までも気を付。狂言仕ける名人の心得ハ格別の事なり

一坂田藤十郎心安き祇園町料理茶やへ行。これほどの座敷に茶所なきハ如何といへバ。亭主されバの事でござります。何とぞ年比望ますれども。ちつと左様ならぬいはくがこざりますといふ。藤十郎いかほど入候やと尋ければ。五十両程かゝり候と答ふ

228 *The Actors' Analects*

賢外集

東　三　八　述

立役染川十郎兵衛聞覚し事をはなせしを東三八狂言作者也

書置る一冊にして賢外といふ八十郎兵衛法名なり

一坂田藤十郎ハけいせい買の名人と。もてはやされたる稀人。

ある年夕ぎりの狂言に。ふじや伊左衛門役を勤る筈に極り。

今度の狂言にハ上草履いるなれバ。早々あつらへ然るべしといひ

わたしける。扨ざうり出来あがりたりとて見せければ。藤十郎

見て。これハ大き過たり。仕なをすべしと云付ければ。男申けるハ

おまへのお足の寸を取誂候へバ。違ひ申さぬはづといふ。それにても

大きなりとひたすらいひけれバ。買物方の者。これにいか程ちい

かの茶台手におしこみし故。俄（にか）にぬけすいたみ難儀なるをかくし。うろたゆる
思ひ入。見物ことの外面白がり。どよみをつくり誉（ほめ）たりかゝる事にて大当
せしとなり

　　　　　　　　　　　　　　　　　　　　　　　続耳塵集終

せりふはやりけり。　わか立役を女形の誉詞に云〇よう〱　立髪姿（たてかみすかた）に伊達風流（たてふうりう）

股だち袴すそ高く。　たつたの川にあらねども紅葉（もみぢ）の顔にうすげしやう。浅黄羽折（あさぎはおり）

の紐（ひも）きやしやに。　結びとめたる恋のくゝり。目ハありハらのなりひらも。あんまりよそ

にハごさんすまい。　やりたい命（いのち）。切たい小指（こゆび）かゝるなかハらじ二世までと。かはす枕ににく

まれて。浮世（うきよ）も後生（ごしやう）も後（のち）の日も。思ひの淵（ふち）に身ハしつむ。扨も〱見事な御器量（ごきりやう）

でハあるハいな〇又若衆せりふ〇むかふに見へましたハくらま山でこさります

あの山へ心不浄（じやう）なるもの参りますれバ大小の天狗（てんぐ）いかりをなし。悪風魔風（あくふうま）

しきりにして。にわかに引さき梢（こずゑ）にかけ。おきまする。まつた心有侍（さむらひ）ハ僧正（そうじやう）

坊（ほう）に願（くん）をかけ。　これをいのるともがらハ。異国（いこく）のはんくハい長良（ちやうりやう）も。あさむく程

のいせいあり。　なんぼうおそろしき御山なれバ。これよりはるかに御拝礼（こはいれい）なさ

れまして然（ぜん）るへう存ます。かやうのせりふにて大当りせしとかや。其外数多（あまた）

聞伝へ覚へ侍れども。ことしげければこゝに略す

一中川金之丞といふ立役ハ。おかしき事天性（てんせい）の上手也。ある狂言（きやうげん）に使者奏者（ししやそうしや）

物語の所へ。　金之丞茶の給仕役（きうじ）にて出。茶わん差出し引下り。傍（そへ）にゐる内

ふとてんがうに茶台を左の手にさしこみ。　使者用事言付（こと）る所に。金之丞

一桜山庄左衛門ハせりふ付に便有ゆへ。古哥をよく覚しとて。此人三千余首古
哥をそらにて覚たり。それゆへ庄左衛門ハせりふ付上手也と。役者よく用ひ

たり俳名は鶯山と申せし也

一片岡仁左衛門曰俳諧を仕習ふへし。神祇釈教恋何にても役にしたがひ心も
詞も文盲ならず芸のたよりとなるハはいかい也とすゝめしと也

一ある老翁曰。役者に五徳あり。貴き御方の前にもゆるされ出諸人に賞せら
れ自然と古語を覚へ又勤めて脛脉をめぐらし嗜て年若く見ゆ

一凡新狂言相談きハまりて後。一ト場づゝしぐみ立る時。其役人を呼よせ。円居
して。せりふを口うつしにおしへ。一旦はぬる時まで立。又小かへしとて再遍け
いこし。又次を作者せりふ工夫して口うつし立る事也。其座の立者出る場ハ。其
立者狂言を仕組し也。中興狂言趣向むつかしく成てより。執筆頭書せよとて
せりふ付のいひ出しを。一くだり程づゝ書たり。狂言本とてくわしく書事ハ。金

子一高よりはじまりける也

一立役女形等何役にもあれ。出端を誉詞あり。又見渡はやしに景色をつらね

仕のまねにて嫌ひとんだりはねたり太刀打する事下作也とて立者ハせす。

近世音羽次郎三郎沢村長十郎親大和山甚左衛門なとハ。尻からげる事太刀打

は稀也。只狂言の致かたにてよく当り。其前荒木与次兵へ非人敵討の時。

手負の身ぶり太刀打はじめてこなしありしゆへ。珍敷あたりし也

一立合あるひハ太刀打の時。かげを打とて大きなる柏子木にてぐハた〳〵と

たゝく。むかしハか様の事ハなし。或ハ竜をつかふか。鬼神など出合ふ時にハ。たゝきなら

せり。始に八物陰より打ならせし故かげ打といふならん今ハかげ打者。舞台へ

出て打ゆへ。田舎人ハあのやかましく打人ハ何の為じゃと心得ず。当地の見物夫

に答へてアレハ役者のはたらく音の心也といへバ。役者の手足かはたらくとあの様

に鳴ハいかなる事とて。いよ〳〵がてんせざりけり。されバ今ハ聞なれたれハかげ打

ねバ。役者も見物も淋しく。同しく八見物に隠して物かげより打たきもの也

一金子一高曰狂言末になれハ。役者ざれ笑ふ。我ハ末に成ても大事によく勤む。

その故ハ東国西国数百里あなたの人。今日の見物の内に有。其遠方の稀人

は。又と見る事なし。名ある役者のざれて見せるハ。残念の事也。芸者のたしなむ

べき義と。同座の人におしへけり

を切り扨ねりてあるく所大きに見え恐しかりし也。今ハ出端に流義なし。これも

時にしたかふ故ならん

一むかしの役者ハ肌を見せる事なし大はたぬぐ心のときハ上着をぬいて白むくになる也。刀を腹へつきこむといふにも。白むくしにつきまわす。此事は今もあり。然るに白むくごしに腹を切るハ無理也と難する人なきハ。是白むくを肌としてむかしよりつたへ見なれたるゆへ。自然と見物承引するハ。又自然なりけらし

一役者の尻をからげる事。いにしへハ稀也立合のときハ上裙を帯にはさむ計也。それゆへ江戸詞に尻をはしよるといふは端折るといふ詞にて侍る。音羽ハ裙を右へ引上はさみ桜山庄左衛門ハ裙を左へはさみたり誠に尻からけする事ハ小佐川十右衛門より始る。片岡仁左衛門との出合にて。両人ともによき男にて見事也

白糯にて三里紙をあて。足のかざりとす

一狂言の中に太刀打立入する事。只少し立まハり計にて。今の役者の宙返り事水車 かりそめにも立入する事なし。宙返り事とんぼうがへりの類ハ。軽業

一音羽次郎三郎ハ浄るりに仕たる事をつねにせす其故ハ凡 操 上るりハ元来

哥舞妓をまねて語り人形もかふきをまねして行ふ事也然るを哥舞妓

より 操 をまねぶ事かぶきすいびのもとひ也といへり　沢村長十郎も其

心にや上るり事を勤る事嫌ひなりしに。銀主より望 つよく国性爺始めて

竹本座に出せし時新四郎和藤内にて役合ず長十郎かんきの役也元より心

に入らぬ故にやあたらず中の芝居竹嶋幸左衛門希有成役にて大当りせし也

一以前ハ親父方にも。　花車形にも名人有て。一場を受取よく勤し也今ハよき役

なれハ立役よりつとめ。又花車方を若女形も勤むる本意にあらさる事也。　小勘

太郎次といへる花車方三十ばかりの女房の姿 ひらりほうし着て付舞台より替前

に向ふ桟敷の下に立たりしを。　其初日同座の役者も向ふへまわりし時。　彼太郎次か

女姿 の風情よきを見て誠 に見物の女と思ひ。尻をつめりしとかや。　太郎次ハかゝる

名人ゆへ。元祖芳沢あやめ太郎次をまねて。　極上上吉の惣芸頭 の女形となりし

一むかしの役者ハ揚まくより出端を大事にせし事也。　出てむかふを切るに各その

風情流義あり其出る時はや名人と思れ其狂言もしつかりとおもしろく有し

とかや。三原十太夫といへる敵役ハ。小男成しに長き大小をさし。　出端にきつと表

られけるとかや。はたして三ヶ津に名人の誉れ高し

一音羽次郎三郎が曰坂田藤十良せりふのくせとしてかわいや〳〵おれじゃ〳〵
なと〳〵詞を二つ〳〵重ねていへり是ハ大入の時よく聞へさせん為又口拍子
にもよりての事也然るを後に伏見藤十郎といふ役者よく似たりとて
坂田と名のり勤めし狂言に相人地蔵何の仏と問へハ彼伏見藤十郎答への
せりふに。六道能化の地蔵ぼさつじゃ〳〵と長き詞を二つかさねたり是非
に二ついはねハならぬ事と覚しにやおかし

一音羽次郎三郎ハ上手のう〳〵狂言立る事も達者也太平記五日替といふ
狂言をかんばん出し。五日め〳〵に新狂言を替へて出せり又大坂哥舞妓四
軒ありし時。角の芝居にて篠塚次郎右衛門大石宮内の役万菊ハ力弥の役にて外題
は鬼鹿毛武蔵鐙といふて四十七人の狂言を始てしたる時大当りせしかは
中の芝居も又取組西の芝居ハ榊山親小四郎柴崎林左衛門三軒共に同シ趣向
なりけるに音羽次郎三郎ハ東の芝居に勤めし所人まねをせず格別に木會
義仲の狂言を作り出し評判よく当りし也

を聞んと思ひかけなく彼小柄を仁左衛門に見せけるに。仁左衛門色めにも
出さず扨々見事の細工かな随分大切になされよとほめて帰しけれバ
立役も仁左衛門しわさと心得て出せし小柄なれども其色め少しもな
けれバ。相手の仕内いろ々工夫ありて。大出来にてありしなり。まりを
けるに上手より渡せバ請取やすしといふがごとく。敵役ハ仕内なくとも。

此心得第一なり。されバこそ仁左衛門舞台の仕内ハ八千石取とみへたり
とかや。小佐川十右衛門ハ七百石取と見え音羽次郎三郎ハ三百石取とみへし
一元。祖沢村長十郎狂言に。長持のうちに忍ひの者ゐるをしつて。鑓
にてつく仕内ありて。長十郎袴のもゝだちとり思入してつか々と
行。なんのくもなく長持をつきしに。坂田藤十郎其時いふやうは。
扨々長持のつきやう心得がたしちと々工夫せられよといひければ
長十郎其夜工夫して翌日袴のもゝ立ちを取。長持の傍へつか々
と行又跡戻り袴もおろし。そろ々とさし足して長持の傍へ
より。聞耳をたて。内に忍びゐる様すを考へて一ト鑓につきければ。
藤十郎手を打て。さて々驚き入たり。後々ハ其一人たるべしと。ほめ

一或人坂田藤十郎に。切狂言を別に出すとき。の。役者の心もち八いかにと問ひけれバ。初の狂言と八其人が生れかハりたる心にて。切狂言に出へしといひけり。何れ名人の心づかひハ格別とみへたり

一坂田藤十郎説に。女形ハやわらかでわるひハいつぞにハ能成物也

一元祖沢村長十郎旅行の時。道中にて枝ぶりよき並木の松を見て日。直をすける人。此松を植おかバ一しほの詠と成し。此並木の中に交りあれバ。枝のみ邪魔になるとて切とるべしたまく〳〵其長に至る芸者ありといへども。此松のことく却而下手の為に悪名をとらん事残念なりといハれき

一今の敵役にめりはりの差別なく。つつこんて狂言するのみにかゝわるゆへ。立役も又敵役にさそハれてするどきを表とすたとへば蟷螂の友喰ひといふ事あり。たがひにあらそひ手を出してハくハれ足を出してハくハれて。終に八其身をはたすの道理なり。古片岡仁左衛門狂言の序びらきの後々に八我か工みのさまたげになるものと知ッて小柄をしゆりけんに打しを実形の立役是を見あらハして。其意趣

続耳塵集

民屋四良五郎撰
俳名江音ト云

一山本京右衛門ハ下がゝりの事をいふて毎度あたりを取り。坂田
藤十郎ハいはねバかなハぬ場にても。それを底につゝみて当
りをとられたり。　元祖三右衛門ハ見物に。さし合の人も一所にゐ
給ふ事有べし。其まへにてけいせい買をして見せる程さし合
なる事はなし。　狂言なれバこそさし合ある人見ても居たまへ
仕内を風流にして。　言葉にさし合ハいハぬはづと申されしよし
一藤田小平次常にいひけるハ。刀のそりを打つ時ハ。左のひざを
引。　相手の目の内をにらみ付てうたされバ。立派になしとぞ

E-II　　　　　E-I

耳塵集とも思ふべきならし

予つたなき耳につもる塵の言葉書あつめたれバをのづから

まはせバ凡一代の間傾城事を致せり。藤十郎ハ得手成故なるべし。

見物ゆるしてよく見て居たり。尤今実事師ハ一代実事を致

さるゝたぐひならんか。然共藤十郎ごとく同じ狂言を度々致さるゝ

事まれなり。京右衛門曰藤十郎ハ名人にて我得たる狂言いた

さるゝ。我に得たる狂言なし。とかく藤十郎ハ名誉の芸者也と。

芸咄しの折ふしいつとても此事のみなり

〔杉九兵衛坂田藤十郎江示教之事〕

一杉九兵衛といひて花車形の名人あり藤十郎廿余りの時分

九兵衛方へゆき狂言の仕様をならひ度よし申されけれバ。九兵衛曰

我ハ花車形なる故随分女子のまねを仕る。貴殿ハ立役成程に

男のまねを致されよ。今の立役を見るに男ハすくなし。もとより

女形にてもあらず。何やらわけなし。今よりして随分男のまね

を致されよとなり。此詞を工夫して少し芸を仕習ひしと也。

やゝもすれバ右の咄を仕出し。杉九兵衛ハ三ヶ津に有まじき

名人とほめられたり

　　　　　　　耳塵集下之巻終

右の狂言をいだし同廿九日迄大入。おなじく十二月中頃より右の狂言いだせり。是ハ来ル正月二日より夕霧一周忌致さんかため見物におもひ出させるため也。一年の内同狂言を

かやうのけいせい事かぞふるにいとまあらず。又其頃毎年

同三ノ後日壬生大念仏。同後日同三ノ後日の壬生秋の念仏

阿波の鳴戸けいせい仏原。同三ノ後日壬生大念仏。同後日

狂言也。其外けいせい玉手箱又ハ堺大寺傾城江戸桜傾城

右同じ狂言くりかへし致したる事以上十八度。是又珍らしき

正月。同一周忌。同三年同七年同十三年忌。同十七年忌。其外

より宝永六年丑のとし迄三十二年此間に夕霧名残の

霜月朔日藤十郎死去生年六十三歳右延宝六年午年

四度仕る事およそ是はじめの終ならん。宝永六年己丑

の内に二度ハいかゞとおもひ。大磯の虎とかハらん為也。かやうの事を思ひ

七月に曾我を出せり。是ハ春二の替りに傾城事致せし故。一年

一　其比女かた若衆がた立役道外親仁方に至るまで。藤十郎

相手になるもの皆上手に見へたり。其故ハせりふのいひやう

いきつぎ立居に付て藤十郎立てをしへぬ。何も藤十郎に

帰伏して居る故に是をそむかず。をしゆるにまかせ致すが故

格別によく見へたり。しかも藤十郎役すくなくでかしばへ

なき事あり。或人藤十郎に対して曰。狂言ハ面白くはやれ

ども。貴殿役すくなく是のみ残り多しといへバ。藤十郎

打笑ひ狂言さへよくバかんにんあれ。藤十郎が芸の善

悪ハかねて見物よくしれり。全く藤十郎を見する芝居

にあらず。狂言を見する芝居也といへり

〔大坂新町扇屋夕霧追善狂言の事〕

一延宝六年午の正月に新町あふぎや夕霧過行たり。同く

二月三日より夕霧名残の正月と云外題にて則　坂田藤十郎

藤屋伊左衛門といへる買手に成りぬ此時藤十郎三十二才。又

所望有て同六月に右の狂言を出せり。又同十月二日より

のはなしを聞るゝに。我が役の多少にはかまハず。狂言の筋を

能きかれたり

〔山下京右衛門狂言咄を聞事〕

一京右衛門狂言の咄しを聞るゝによしあしにかまハすまづ狂言を
ほめられ作者にむかひせりふ付よくたのむとなり。若気に入ぬ
狂言あれバひそかに作者を呼付今一度聞なをし善悪の
談合有て仕直せりかりにもはなしの場にてあしきとハ
申されず

〔狂言ハなきものといふ事〕

一藤十郎曰。若まづしうして金銀ほしき時。金銀ハぬすみ
ても有べし又道なかに落てもあるべし。狂言計はぬすまん
とおもひても拾ハんと思ひてもねからなきもの也此事を
しらぬハ文盲なる下手の役者なり

〔諸役者坂田藤十郎相手に成上手とみゆる事〕

傘杖にて出る狂言成しが楽屋番にいひ付右の品々
取寄。木履をはき杖をつき傘をさし。さあせりふを付
られよとありし故近松氏予かたのごとくせりふを付一返
稽古を通したり。藤十郎曰扨〳〵よき狂言かな。初て此
狂言の咄しを聞ても又今聞なをしてもわろき狂言
と思ひぬしかれども作者の心に能き狂言とおもへバこそ
役人をよせて咄されたり。我心にあしきと思ひても見物の

ほめる狂言あり。我当年五十に余れども狂言の咄しを
聞て善悪を定めがたし我是をしらバ今時分ハ長者にも
成ぬらん仕手の心作者の心格別なれバ。先せりふを付させん
と思ひ。木履からかさ杖を取よせ。はじめより立て稽古を
せしなり。是縦横のまんといふ心。然るに今作者のせりふ付
によつて正しくよき狂言としれり。兎角狂言の稽古ハ我が
ごとく初手から立たるかよしといへり。此おもひやりハもと藤十郎
能き狂言を拵へられたる故成べしいつとても藤十郎狂言

出端の出立にてせりふを付る事
役の多少を構ハず狂言の筋を聞事〕

一或時替り狂言近松氏我等談合にて楽屋に役人を

集め狂言を咄したるに。我が役よき人ハ狂言をほめぬ
役悪き人ハ吉悪をいはず。狂言のよしあしをしらざる人ハ
いつも顔を見て多分に付べきてい。中にも文盲にして
狂言の心なき人ハ。先一番にはらを立我が家来をしかり
きげんあしく人〳〵にいとまごひもせず立帰りぬ。其ころ
藤十郎座本にてありしが。きやうげんのよしあしをいはざれハ。
外よりいひ出すべき事もなし。藤十郎曰先上の口明より
稽古致されよと立帰られぬ。翌日より稽古にかゝり四五日
の内に上の稽古しまい。其後四番目の口明をけいこする
日に至り藤十郎今一度狂言の咄しを聞なをさんと
有しゆへ又はなしぬ。然れども吉あしをいはず木履をはき

一京右衛門日狂言により中入より出る役人の事を前にいはねバ
つまらぬ事有是よからぬ事也。今する所より外に跡の為に
いふ事其場のさまたげ。口ハ調法なもの中入にていかやうとも

いわるゝものなり。狂言ハいつとてもおもしろく出来る様に致し
たるがよきとなり

　〔前に役人の事を云さぬ事〕

一藤十郎日中入に出る役人の事。前にいわでかなハずバその
役人の事表にいひたて。今のせりふハ次にいふべし。その故は
中入の役人の事前にいふハ見物に能覚させんとの事なり
しからバ表にいひ立よくおぼへさせたるがよし。又今いふせりふ
を次にせよとハ今いふせりふハ則今の狂言にして居るゆへ
見物をのづからよく覚るとなり

　〔近松門左衛門金子吉左衛門相談狂言の事
　　　幷二坂田藤十郎口明より稽古之事
　　　　　狂言聞直す事

致す事をして見物にほめられぬ。我ハ本より外科を
せざる故随分不調法にいたし。京右衛門ハ外科をせざる
ゆへ手負のかん病得せぬ所をよくするといひて見物にほめ
られぬ。いへバいはるゝものなりしかし是誠なり

〔村山平右衛門坂田藤十郎に一礼之事〕

一宝永四年亥の年江戸村山平右衛門京都万大夫芝居登り。
十月江戸へ下る時坂田藤十郎私宅にて立振舞され。予も
相伴いたせしが。平右衛門藤十郎に向ひ御かげ添し。我始て

下りし顔見世より貴公様を手本と致し実事ぬれ事に
よらず一切貴公様の御まねを仕りしに。よき事ハ何国にてもよし。
今江戸二三番切の芸者に成りぬ。是皆貴公の御蔭と一礼申
せしかバ。藤十郎かぶりをふり定而わるからん。芸ハ我性根より
一流仕出したるこそよけれ。我を手本にせバ我よりおとりぬ
とおもへり。今少し工夫致されよと申され其場しらけたり

〔中入より出る役人の事〕

役者附に狂言の作者と書事富永平兵衛初り也。延宝八年
の暮の顔見世成りしが。其当座ハ諸人こぞつてにくめり。

夫より平兵衛打つゞきおもしろからぬ狂言に見物あきはて
ぬ。今一入工夫致され能き狂言を致されよと申せしかば。
平兵衛曰わろき狂言を出すハ能こゝろならねど。座本衆の
大き成ル仕合なり。替る度毎に能き狂言を出し。もし其
よき狂言に見あきなば道頓堀に草はゆべきといへり。
いへバいはるゝものかおかしきへらず口なり

〔坂田藤十郎科医心　得有る事〕
一高野山万燈といへる狂言の中の口明に。嵐三十郎腹を切る。
藤十郎此看病をよくいたしぬ。ある芸者是を見て。京右衛門
に語つて曰。藤十郎ハ常に科医をよく致さるゝ故。手負の

看病自然とよし。外の役者の及ざる所といひしかバ。京右衛門
いわく藤十郎ハ外科をよく致さるゝ故手負のかん病　よく

中川金之丞金子六右衛門其頃若き芸者寄合て。とかく

弥五左衛門が手にかゝらねバ本の上手にハ成がたしといへりとなり

則弥五左衛門曰今上手の中に相手のせりふをいふ内に休でゐる

芸者多しよからぬ事にや。第一狂言ゆるまり其身の

からだ死るなり。とかくせりふをいふ相手の顔をよく見て

ゐるか但耳をそば立聞てゐるがよしといへり

〔片岡仁左衛門落合に念を入る事〕

一片岡仁左衛門敵役致されし時日。いつとても狂言の詰ぎハには

敵役のせりふにゑ〻口おしいたくみし事があらハれた。家来ども

それ壱人も残らず討てとれといふ事ハ。敵役をはじめいづれも

役人狂言の詰ぎハ成ゆへ。麁相になりぬ。一番の狂言の詰

際ハ大事也。我ハそこに心をつけいかにもせりふに力を入さらに

詰ぎハとおもハず別て念を入るなり

〔作者名を番附に初てのする事〕

一冨永平兵衛ハ右弥五右衛門に次での作者にて。今顔見世の

替り狂言のせりふ付のため盃をいだし。若衆が是非悋気
をせねばならざる様に仕かけかくのごとし。いづれも舞台にて
唯今の様にいたされよといへり。是又よき思ひ付なり

古人ハかほど迄心をつくせり

〔松本名左衛門所作事の間心を休めぬ事〕

一松本名左衛門我と人と立ならび所作をするに。独舞ふ時
今壱人ハ囃の前に住ひ居る。此時多く八休湯などを呑り。
我ハ休ず囃の前に住ひ居ても心の内にて舞ふて居る也。
しからねバうしろすがたあしく所作切ると也

〔続狂言作りはじめの事幷相手のせりふを聞事〕

一弥五左衛門といふ有役ハ花車形にて狂言作者の名人なり。
むかしハはなれ狂言なりしが。今の弐番つづき三番続ハこの
弥五左衛門作なり。則非人かたき打の作者也。藤田小平次も
此弥五左衛門吟味によつて実事師の名をとれり荒木与次兵衛

一古嵐三右衛門ぬれ口舌などの狂言の仕組に。相手の役人を
我が内へ呼寄せ。本より酒ずき成ゆへ頓て盃を出し。其座に
懇して居る子どもあれどもそれに八目もかけず。外の子供に
つぶやきさゝやき或ハほうずりつけざし後には酔て正躰
なし。元より若衆ハ悋気して様々のゝしれバ。同子ども
立役あいさつに入中を直し盃させり。此時ハ藤十郎親坂田

市左衛門真野や勘左衛門座本にて有しゆへ。其座へ藤十郎
来り是ハゝそうゝゝ敷事かな。初日も近日ぞや若衆と
口舌所にてハ有まじき事。はやゝけいこをせよと笑ひゝ
申されしかば。三右衛門我も左様に存じ最前より稽古を
致したりと。初而盃を出せし時より今なか直しの盃まで
若衆のりんき人々の挨拶にいたるまで。ことゝゝく皆覚へ
是替り狂言の稽古也と其通に仕ぐみたり。いづれも
役人こハいかにといヘバ。作りたる事ハわろし実よし。その
義をおもふが故に日比ハ稽古の場へ盃は出さねども。此度は

其意を得ず。此度癪をせんと思ひ付しハ見物のこゝろに

いつもの狂言には藤十郎ハよくものをいへり。此度ハ癪故おもふ

事もしかぐ〳〵と得いはず不便の事やとおもハせ見物に泣せん

とおもひしに。今日笑ふたり。是ハ予が工夫たらざる所。明日

より泣せんとあんのごとくなかせたり。ある芸者行て問て

曰。いか成工夫にて今日の様に見物なきたるぞやと。答て

曰。癪ハおのが心に我ハ癪なると思ふが故。人のきくをはづか

しくおもひたしなみて癪ぬ。しかれどもうれしきとき或は

腹の立時我を忘れ癪るなり。夫故今日ハ癪ず嬉敷

ときはらのたつ時ハ又おかしき時に癪る計也。答て日然共

初中後癪の様に見へしハいかに。答て曰口の内にて癪り

いふ所ハ癪ず。口の内にて癪が故それ程せりふのあいだを

ぬく計也といへり

〔嵐三右衛門替り狂言稽古仕様幷酒興に戯るゝ事〕

笑ひ申まじと申せしかど。そこが工夫なり言所によって

わらふべしとなり。其後予がせりふにたゞ今奥様

若君様を御誕生なされしといふを聞て南無三宝

ね耳へ水が入たるやうな事かなといひしに大きに笑ぬ。

かやうのせりふ付格別よかりしとハ此様成ル吟味故歟

〔聾之事〕

一或書物につんぼう八人々寄合て咄有に人の口元を

見て唯にこゝと笑ふとなり

〔あきじり眼の事〕

一大津ならやといふ狂言に藤十郎あきじりなりしが。目

の玉をまん中におけバあきじいの様に見ゆると也

〔瘂の工夫〕

一村松といふ狂言に藤十郎瘂の役なりしが初日に見物瘂ル

度毎に見物おかし笑ひぬ。則能狂言にて評判宜敷ゆへ。

或人初日の夜悦に行。瘂大きに出来たりとほめぬ。藤十郎

一藤田小平次ハ実事に名を得し芸者なりしが。或時刀の
反りを打にハ相手の目の中をにらみ付たるがよしといへり

〔坂田藤十郎道外師心得の教訓并仙台弥五七を嫌事〕

一仙台弥五七といふ道外師京都にて高給銀をとり。並
なき上手なりし故。予道外仕習の時分。ねがわくハ弥五七程の
芸者に成たしとおもふて居たりし折柄。藤十郎曰一向道外
するとも必弥五七まねをいたすべからず。其故ハ此程の狂言
に只今大殿様御死去なされしと聞て皆〻〻おどろく。
弥五七道外に南無三ぼう寝耳へ牛の入たる様な事かな
といへり。いかに笑へバとて道外のいふまじき事也。先道外の
役ハいつとても不調法者麁相あほうなり。ねみ〻へ牛が
入たるとハ或ひ。ハ太鼓もちなどの軽口なり。たとへ帥なり
とも大殿御死去と聞てね耳へうしが入たるとハいふべからず。
ねみ〻へ水の入たるといふハ常なり。同、ハね耳へ水の入たる様な
事といふて笑せたしといへり。予が日左様に申さバ見ぶつ

ぶり。又かたき逃帰りたるとおもハゞ初て手疵苦になる躰。又味方かけ付看病せば口にてハ強き事をいひながら。をのづから気ゆるまりよハりたるてい。又手負の間刀を杖につく

とも小足にあるき度々刀を杖につくハ見へあしく。刀を杖につかバ二足も三足もあるき。又刀を足本より二三尺先へつき立。それも刀に二足も三足も先へあるきこし。又右のごとく刀を二三尺ほど先へつき立たるがよし。刀の長サハつか共に乳切なるがよし。刀みじかけれバ腰かゞみてわろしといへり。尤成ル吟味なるべきか。其時分手負をして大分入たり

〔芸を不レ窺事〕

一京右衛門日。芸ハ狂言のよしあしにかまハず力一はいふんごんで致したるがよし。しかれバ六七分の狂言も十分にも見ゆる也。とかく窺てするハ損也といへり

〔藤田小平次反りを打眼目〕

一中川金之丞ハ藤十郎京右衛門其外心ある芸者が名人と
ほめられし名人。金之丞予にたいして曰人ハ舞台へ出る
度毎日ほめられんと申おもひ。けん物数多くいへども我ハきらひ
なり。一所二所計心をつけ念を入。其外ハうけ返答いかにも
まことしらしくせんとおもふのみなり

〔蘭奢待を手本とする事〕

一或人香を聞習ハ蘭奢待を手本にして。それよりは浅き
濃きあるひハ聞がなきなど〻分別する事あり。芸者もさも

あらん。しかし手本になる芸者ハ誰ならんと問しかバ。側なる
人我も不知と也

〔荒木与二兵衛金子六右衛門手負仕様之事〕

一荒木与次兵衛金子六右衛門ハ手負の名人なり。六右衛門曰手負
とて刀を杖につき息つぎせハしく苦しげにする計にては
有まじく。かたきいまだ近所に居ると思はゞ。随分気を
張り四方に眼をくばり。しかも深手と見へて苦にせぬ身

もくるしからずといひしかバ藤十郎聞ていや〳〵さにハあらず。
役者の芸ハ乞食食袋にて当分いらふが入まいが何にても
見付次第ひろひ取袋に入て帰りたるがよし。入ものバかり用
に立。いらざるものハとつて置入ル時出すべし。ねからしらぬ事ハ
ならぬもの巾着切の所作なりとも能見ならへとなり

〔下手役者の芸入レ念可レ見事〕
一或芸者　曰下手役者の芸を見ても心あらん人とハ修行に
なる也。其故ハ下手を見てわろき所をよく覚〻て我ハせぬ也

〔耳底記之内　一曾が笛之事〕
一耳底記細川幽斎曰。一曾がいふ事ハ小笛に我笛を似せたら
ばくせ事なりといふなり尤也。年寄てと若き時とハ違ふ
べき事也。一曾が曰我も若き時ハゆたりと吹たる也。
又我をしへぬ手をふくならバをしへまじきとなり已上

〔名人より名人と呼中川金之丞事〕

耳塵集　下之巻

〔嵐三右衛門酒好といふ事丼最上藤八鑓の論〕

一古嵐三右衛門常に酒を好で呑るゝ故舞台にても誠の酒をのまるゝやうに見ゆる扨〳〵名人かなと誉る人有しが。かたへの人此度最上藤八鑓にてつかるゝ所実にも誠つかれたるやうなり定てあれも常〳〵鑓にてつかれたるらんと笑ひぬ。

〔芸者善悪を不ㇾ嫌可ㇾ習事〕

一或芸者十二三なる実子の物をならふに役者のならわひでもくるしからざるハ天露盤手跡其外是〳〵ハならハひで

長〴〵とせりふをつけそへなされ候が。ながふせよと八常と
ちがひ七月の見物の御きげん取くるしと申せしかバ。いや〴〵見物に
むりハなし。此藤十郎がさいくにおかしき所と心得たる故也。
高が奥州が心底を聞んがためにいろ〳〵と隙どるしこなし
その気を持狂言すればよしと工夫して。今日いよ〳〵せり
ふをながくつけてせしに。あんのごとくながふ〳〵といふて
なめたり。とかく本心が大事なり。当年五十三になりしがいま
まであがらぬ芸。もふあがらぬ事かとくやまれぬ

耳塵集上之巻終

八郎右衛門が屋敷へしのび入奥州に出合右いけんせしかバ。奥州

大きにはらを立枕をならびやうがならべまいが八郎右衛門殿と

私との詰ひらき。一度女房にやつて置ていらざる御気づかひ

早々御帰あれといへバ。文蔵心に誠をあかさぬ八こしもとども

あまたそばに有故ならん。今お隙をとり奥州とさし向ひに

心底を尋んと。さしてもなき事にいろ〳〵と隙を入ること

おかしき事にて文蔵がしこなし也。初日七月十五日見物この

しこなしにたいくつしておけよ引込よと口々にいひて。其段

狂言わけもなかりしが。芝居はてゝ予藤十郎かたへ礼に行。

貴殿今日おかしき段門左衛門我等談合にてせりふ付たりし

かども。見物其意得ざれ八力なし。せりふ半分御きあれ

かしといへバ。いや〳〵明日狂言の仕様ありと。十六日見物思ひ

多くして有しが。かのおかしきだん大きにおもしろがり。藤十郎様

ながふ〳〵と口〳〵にいへり。其暮に藤十郎同道にて太文字

見物に参らんとさそひに立より。拟々昨日と八違ひ結句は

立女形。我ハそれより二三番目。何ンのその芸になつたら仕勝
てくれん。がく屋の心が舞台へ出る。千寿に仕かたんとおもハゞ

浄るり御前ハ主。十五夜ハ家来なる程に。その家来をいかにも
家来らしく能すれバ千寿に仕勝事もあらん。家来の分として
主に仕かたんとおもハゞ十五夜にもあらず。本より浄るり御前
にてもなく。もし今其様な奉公人あらバ隙をいだすべきより
外なしとしかられけれバ。一座の人々感心源次ハあやまりぬ

〔仏の原三の後日狂言二日目工夫の事〕

一仏の原三ノ後日の狂言に梅房文蔵請出したる奥州といふ
女郎を。家来望月八郎右衛門が女房につかハしたるに。月日かさなれ
どもいまだ枕をならべぬよし。文蔵心に拠ハ八日頃いひかハせし詞
をたがへじと。此文蔵にたてる心中成べし。返て八郎右衛門が

おもハん所もはづかし。奥州に異見をくわへんとはおもへども。
人めをいとひ夜陰に及びかづきをきて女の姿にさまをかへ

一又日嵐三右衛門ハ名人なり。性根もなき狂言に手くせと
してうそらしきせりふをつけ。そも〳〵狂言といふものは
此三右衛門がやうにするもの也といわぬ計に真面になりて
する故。おもしろし。其上芸もゆる〳〵とする事ならぬ
ものなり。とかく我には芸に分別有てわろしとなり

〔山下京右衛門藤十郎三右衛門二人を 指て名人と云事〕

一京右衛門日。我等しならひの時分能心を付て見るに。三右衛門ハ

うそらしき狂言の仕様にてしかも名人なり。藤十郎は
誠にして同名人なり。とかく藤十郎と三右衛門と弐人を
一所にして仕習んとおもひ情を出したるとなり

〔十二段之狂言に主従之論幷霧浪千寿之事〕

一或時十二段狂言仕組の時浄るり御前霧浪千寿。十五夜
袖崎源次せりふの時。藤十郎日源次狂言の仕方心得がたし。
千寿ハ浄るり御前にて主也。源次ハ十五夜にて家来なり。
然るに今狂言の仕様主従のわけ見へず。根心に千寿ハ一座の

ふし所になれバ極て見物ほむる。我々ハ何ほど節をかたつ
てもほむる事なし。されバとて我々が付たる節にもあらず
師匠のふし付をよくならひてかたれどもほめざる事ハふしぎ
といへバ。加賀掾打笑ひさにてハあらず。我ハ何となく浄るり
をすなほに語。ふし所にてふしをかたる。ふし所にてふしをかたり
かたり出すといなやほめられんとおもひ。初手から終まで
面白くかたる故。ふし所に成てもはやおもしろふかたる
ふしなきゆへに誉る所なし。第一ほめられんと思ふて語るハ
わろしとなり

〔見物をわすれて狂言する事〕

一耳底記に細川幽斎の曰。ほめさせんとするハ下手芸也
〔細川幽斎公芸者 考 之事〕

一藤十郎曰。ほめられんとおもハゞ。見物をわすれ狂言を誠の
やうにまんろくにいたしたるがよし
〔嵐三右衛門を鑑とする事〕

答て曰初日ハ大事のものにてハあらず。大事ハ常の稽古
にあり。稽古の時魂を入能覚へ込。初日ハわすれて出るなり。
初日を大事とおもヘバ我芸にあらずと答へけれバ。三益感じ

入たるとなり。予がおもふ事藤十郎日頃仕なれたる狂言にて
稽古を仕覚へ。あたらしき狂言初日にせりふをわすれて
出るとかたられしと。友之進初日ハわすれて出るとこたへ
られしも同意也。名人の詞は自然と当れると

〔せりふはやロ遅口之事〕
一或人藤十郎に問て曰。せりふハはや口なるがよきや。また
おそきがよきや。答て曰はやかろわるかろ大事なし。おそ
かろわるかろなをわるしといふ事あり。同じわろき内
ならバ早きハこらへらるゝ。おそきハわろき中のわろき也

〔宇治加賀掾之事幷弟子問答〕
一浄るり大夫加賀掾弟子共寄合て曰。師匠の浄るりハ。

D-XI   D-X

答て曰我も初日ハ同うろたゆる也。しかれどもよそめに
仕なれたる狂言をするやうに見ゆる八。けいこの時せりふをよく
覚へ初日にははねからわすれて。舞台にて相手のせりふ
を聞。其時おもひ出してせりふを云なり。其故ハ常〳〵
人と寄合。或ハ喧嗤口論するに。かねてせりふにたくみ
なし。相手のいふ詞を聞。此方初て返答心にうかむ。狂言
は常を手本とおもふ故けいこにハよく覚へ。初日には
忘れて出るとなり

〔能脇師高安友之進勧　進能之事并ニ名人の金言〕

一高安友之進といへる能の脇師名人のきこへ有。大坂道頓堀
にて勧進能有し時。初日の前日友達をいざなひ舟遊びに
出。酒にみだれ放埒の躰也。折ふし京より津田三益といへる
医師見廻に下り同船に有しが。友之進にむかひ此度の能御身
独の目当也。則明日ハ初日然らバ今日ハきんがく有べき処に。
油断の躰明日の初日大事ならずやと異見ありしかバ。友之進

芸也とつく／＼顔をうち守り居たりぬ

〔相手役者笑ふ事〕

一藤十郎曰芸者によりて狂言をされ相手にも笑せる有。

是心得がたし。我仕習の時より今日舞台にて仕なれたる

狂言を今日ハ此心にてせん。明日ハかくやせんと。常々舞台

にてけいこせり。其故ハあたらしき狂言の稽古初日は

相手も我もせりふ覚へざるがゆへ。狂言の仕様あらかた也

随分よくせんとハおもへども。なか／＼仕なれたる狂言と八格別也。

夫ゆへしなれたる狂言をされ相手笑ハせる芸者ハ此心なき

やとなり

〔初日より仕馴たるせりふの事并ニ喧哗のたとへ〕

一或芸者藤十郎に問て曰。我も人も初日にハせりふなま

覚なるゆへかうろたゆる也。こなた八十日廿日も仕なれたる

狂言なさるゝやうなり。いか成御心入ありてや承りたし。

一大坂道頓堀にて勧進能ありし時。京よりほねや庄右衛門
とて名人の小鼓 三番目を打れしに諸人こぞつて是を
聞く。尤上手とハ思ひしかどもさのみおどろかず。則 初日の事
なりしに。藤十郎ハ庄右衛門弟子殊に無二の懇 故。見舞かてら
見物して諸人の評 判を聞。すぐに庄右衛門旅宿 へゆき。此度
の能大坂の衆中の心ざす所ハ御身一人。しかるにさのみ
ほめもそしりもせず心得あれかしとなり。庄右衛門心あかれ明日
よりほめられて見せんと有しが。案のごとく二日めより日本第一

の上手とほめたり。藤十郎又行て今日の評 判格別何ンと
心得鼓 を打給ふやと尋しに。庄右衛門日初日ハ大事にかけ
御身が狂言する様にほめられんといふ事をはなれ。まんろくに
打たり。今日ハさらバほめられんとおもひ少し曲 を打たり。それ
故ほめるならん。ほめさすやうにハうちやすきもの。まんろく
に八打にくきものとかたりぬ。予同座に居て是を聞
ほめられふとほめられまいと自由になる八是名人の

一又身ぶりのよしあしを吟味する芸者あり　尤見物に
見するものなれバ。あしきよりよきハよからん。予ハ吟味なし。

身ぶりとて作りてするにあらず。よろこびいかるときハをのづからその心身
にして。よろこびいかるときハをのづからその心身にあらハるゝ。

然るに何ぞ身ぶりとて外にあらんや

〔道外あどといふ事〕

一或芸者藤十郎に向ひ貴殿諸芸達し給ふ中に別而
道外のあど名人なりしとほむる。藤十郎曰道外のあど
とは何ンの事なるや。予ハ道外と狂言する也手前さへ
実らしくまんろくに狂言すれバ道外もしやすく。をのづから
あどになる也。あどゝおもひあどをうてバ。道外師ハ狂言の
邪魔に見ゆるものなり

とかく道外師と狂言を大事にかけよくせんとおもへる也

〔ほねや庄左衛門小鼓之事幷ニ坂田藤十郎問答〕

ねぢたはめられたる事なけれバ。我又人をねぢたハむる
事をしらず。去程に師匠にハたのまれまじきなり
〔実を以笑ハすといふ事〕
一又曰実事をして上手といはるゝハ手がらにならず実事ハ
初心の芸者もその狂言の筋をいふがゆへすこしハまぎるゝ也。
いはんや上手をや誰ならぬハおかしき事也されバこそ耳取て

鼻かむやうなことをいひて笑ハすはあれど。藤十郎ごとく
実をいひて笑ハす芸者ハあらじ
〔実事師心得違之事〕
一坂田藤十郎曰おかしき事が実事也。常にある事をするが
故なり。今の芸者の実事を見るに。互にそりをうち
鼻とはなとをつき合。ぬけぬかんなどゝの詰合。実の
侍のすべき業ならず。此心ゆへせりふづけも又々右に同じ。
是をさして実事といふべき歟
〔身ぶり製に不構事〕

妓の曲をなす 已上

聞書

雍州府志

必能院敬信

【師匠に成まじき論幷ニ造り樹之事】

一山下京右衛門曰。坂田藤十郎ハ天性の名人にして三ヶ津
心有芸者のゆるしたる名人今上手といはゝ立役の
中に藤十郎に及ぶ芸者一人も有べきとハおもハれず。
我も又及ばず。然ども天性の名人成るが故。却而師匠
に八成まじきや。その故ハたとへバ木作りの名人が松
にてもあれさまぐ〜に枝をねぢたはめ。見事に作り
なしたる松と。又天性ふりよく見事に生たる松の
ごとし。余の上手ハ下手をねぢたハめ能芸にいたしたる
上手なり。それゆへ今の上手ハ下手をねぢたはめ能芸
にする事を覚え弟子にをしゆる事あり。其故に師匠
とたのまるべし。又天性の名人ハ生れながらの名人なる故。我

D–I

耳塵集　上之巻

〔歌舞妓之事〕

今の歌舞妓ハ名護屋三左衛門といふ浪人より

始りしとなり其故ハ　雍州府志第八十章之内

一又一種哥舞妓といふ者有。元出雲大社の巫女国女と
号するものあり。神楽を一転して歌舞す。是古に所謂
白拍子の類にして元神楽の変風なり。永禄年中
名護屋三左衛門といふ者あり。元武人にして落魂生也。
京師に有て則国女と密に通ず。苦にこれ謀て歌舞

作者を兼て初心役者を取立し名人也

一冨永平兵衛は元禄年中の狂言作者也元ト金子六右衛門弟子にて金子吉左衛門と八相弟子也此系譜も役者大全に出たり

一荒木与二兵衛藤田小平次元禄年中一名宛有し立役也

一杉九兵衛ハ宝永年中迄出し花車形の名人也坂田藤十郎も此杉氏の口伝を聞上手と八成り名八揚しとなり

已上

一坂田藤十郎とある八宝永年中に鳴し三ヶ津やつし
ごとの開山といひし元祖なり

一嵐三右衛門とある八二代目也中古の新平が為に八親なり

一中川金之丞貞享年中迄居たる名人と呼立役也
近頃死去せし三右衛門為に八祖父なり

一松本名左衛門延宝年中に名高き女形にて近頃迄大坂芝居
名代に有し松本氏の元祖なり

一仙台弥五七元禄年中の道外形なり

一片岡仁左衛門是も元禄年中敵役の一人也其頃八実悪之
部なし敵役と一所に部したる也此系図役者大全にくわし

一山下京右衛門八初〆半左衛門元祖坂田藤十郎同時代の立役名人也

一霧浪千寿袖嶋源次両人共元禄年中の女形なり

一村山平右衛門八元祖村山又八より三代目也坂田藤十郎弟子也

一嵐三十郎正徳年中の立役也享保年中より延享年中迄
居たる嵐三十郎の親なり

一弥五右衛門といふ八福井氏花車形にて延宝年中狂言

耳塵集

凡例

一此書者元禄年中道外形の名人正徳年中金子吉左衛門

古人の説を悉く書置ける一巻にて七部の書の一部なり

則金子氏以て聞書の自筆本を一点も不レ違模写す依レ之

俗言粗有レ之

一耳塵集といへる題号の事ハ往昔細川幽斎法印玄旨

烏丸光広卿問答の書に耳底記といへる哥道極意の

一本有其意をとりて名付るとみえたり則此書所々引てある也

一必能院敬信ハ金子吉左衛門が法名なり

たるにて。花やかなる心のぬけぬやうにすべし。わづか
なる事ながら此若といふ字。女形の大事の文字と
心得よと稽古の人へ申されしを聞侍りし

あやめ艸終

浅尾十次郎。よほどしばゐながら落たり。此芝居こわもの
なり。二軒ハはり合まけになり。万太夫座ハ脇ひらみず
に精を出すなるべし。座がすぎると外を直下に見る
ゆへ。あやうきことあり。これ狂言の仕内第一の心得との

はなし。果してその年万太夫座ハ大入にて二軒ハはきと
なかりしゆへ。座本せきが来て。いろ〳〵狂言の相談有を。
藤十郎いふはいや〳〵こゝをせくハあしゝとて。長十郎を
山形おりべの助に仕立。新よめかゞ見を出されけるに。打て
返すほどの大入。長十郎初て地の舞台へ出られしとき
にて。沢村小伝次おとゝの由ひろうし。新役者へ大役を
させて入をとる工夫。はたして仕当てられしを思へバ。
こゝろへ置べき事と。あやめの物がたりなり
一女形といふもの。たとへ四十すぎても若女形といふ名有。
たゞ女形とばかりもいふべきを。若といふ字のそはり

立役藤十郎京右衛門いまだ半左衛門と申せし時なり。一所に

住べきはづを。夷屋座へ取たて〻座本にせんとの事ゆへ

半左衛門ハ別になる相談より。辰之介とわが身両人早雲

座へすみたり。辰之助ハ夷屋座のやくそくなれども。

半左衛門と入替りの心にてのこと成しが。辰之助をとり

はなしてハと夷屋座へハ。荻野左馬之丞岡田左馬之介

を抱へ。其詰に十次郎かもんをか〻へたり。時に藤十郎

申されしハ。今京都の芝居三軒の内。夷屋座には

半左衛門といふつはものに左馬之丞左馬之介あり。藤川

武左衛門若けれども長十郎あり。此方芝居に八座もと

甚兵衛われら次郎左衛門にそなたと辰之介あり。か様に

牛角なれば。二軒ハはり合ふこ〻ろ出来る物なり

万太夫座にハ。中村四郎五郎を立役のかしらにして

生嶋新五郎古今新左衛門三笠城右衛門女形は霧波千寿

ぎりも仕内下りたるやうなり。それより又膝をたゝいて
すればいき返りたる様にはり合が出来たり。しかれば
癖といふものゝあしき事なれ共。無理直しハならず。無理に
直せば。いきほひのぬける事ありとぞ

一沢村小伝次若衆形にて。藤田孫十郎芝居へすみ。わが身は
都万太夫へ住たる年。小伝次何か腹をたてゝわが身方へ
きたり。涙をながし。同座若衆形鈴木平七と。鑓の仕合
の所へ。女形浪江小勘わけ入て。なだめる事あり。其所へ
敵役笠屋五郎四郎来りャァ〳〵わけまい〳〵。すでつちめら
がほでてんがう。互にてこねさせたがよいとの口上。いかに狂言
なればとて。色をたてる我々を。すでつちめとハわるきせ
りふ。もはや明日より座本へ断いふて。出まじきとの儀
思ひ出せバ久しき事なり。狂言のせりふにすでつちめと
いふが。色の障に成るとある心入。今時の若衆思ひもよらず

一ひとゝせ早雲座にて。座本ハ大和や甚兵衛なりしが

いろ〳〵のめづらしき花共あり。したが今ハ梅のさかり
なり。梅ハめづらしからずとて。ゑもしれぬ珍花共ありて

見物の衆手を打てめづらしがりぬるに。我身ハ梅花を
よく立たるにのみ心とまりたりありふれたる花にて
仕立の上手なるをかんじぬ。仕内もその様な物にて。女形は
女の情をはづさぬやうにするが根本なりめづらしく
せんとて。おかしみをたてとし。つよい事を柱とせバ花ハ珍き
花なれども。いつみてもよき花とハいれまじきなり
一玉川半太夫は上手でハなけれども。すぐ成仕内にて名
を取たる人なり岩井平次郎ハ上手なれども曲が過て
後ハ。見おとされしなり。心得置べき事とぞ

一小勘太郎次くせに。左の手にて膝をたゝく癖あり。去
とハ見苦敷と人々ゐけんせしに。尤なりとて心を付て
たゝかぬやうにせしに。扨仕内にはり合がぬけて。俄に七ぶ

当世過たるとある。過たるの言葉かんしんと申されしと
あやめのものかたりなり

一仕内が三度つゞいてあたると。その役者ハ下手に成もの
なりと。若き衆へ申されし。当りたるかくをはづすまい
とするゆへ。仕内に古びがつくと見えたり

一女形はがく屋にても。女形といふ心を持べし。弁当なども
人の見ぬかたへむきて用意すべし。色事師の立役と
ならびて。むさ〳〵と物をくひ。扨やがてぶたいへ出て。色事を

する時。その立役しんじつから思ひつく心おこらぬゆへたがひ
に不出来なるべし

一女形は女房ある事をかくし。もしお内義様がと人のいふ
時は顔をあかむる心なくてハつとまらず立身もせぬ
なり子はいくたり有ても我も子供心なるハ。上手の
自然といふものなりとぞ

一あやめ申されしハ。頃日天王寺へ花の会を見に行しに

一下手を相手に取たる時。その下手を上手に見する様に
するが。芸者のたしなみなり

一仁左衛門方へふるまひに行しに三八わが身に向ひ。申は
いかヽなれども。ちと新町へ御出候て。太夫のてい御らん
あるべし五年まへと八大きにもやう替りたりきさまの
なさるヽ八五年まへの太夫の躰なり。只今ハよほどそれ
よりハおちたる風なれども諸見物それを見てゐる故。
風があふのあはぬのと申よしとのこたへに。御ゐけん
忝ししかし太夫ハ高上なるがよし。たつた五年の間に
それほど風俗が替りたらバ二十年まへはとつとん
しやうなるべし。よき御異見にて心つきたり。五年まへ
をのりこし。廿年まへの風に致度候けいせい八古風にて
だてなるがよし茶やふろや八当世過てするがよし。此
心得より外はなしと申たれば。　　仁左衛門どの茶やふろや八

ものハ。なまなかに覚てハ狂言の為あしかるべし。なぜに
なれば。仕内ハぬらりと成。又しても所作事が仕たく成らん
か。かぶき方の舞をもよくこなしたるうへに。能もして見
たくば。かつて次第とてをしへ給はらざりしなり。其のち
五郎左衛門さま世話にて。親方を出。三右衛門どの取たてにて。吉
田あやめと。我身よし沢あやめにて。一度に出。吉田に仕
まけぬる事度々なりしが。吉田ハ北国屋さまといふ御方
に。能事を少シ習ひしゆへ。能仕立の所作をもつて。さい〴〵
当りをとらんとせられしに。わが身ハ又地の仕内にのみ骨_{ほね}
を折て勤し。いつとなくわが身名をしられ。吉田ハとり
あへぬる人もなく成て。今は役者もやめたり。さてこそ
五郎左衛門さまの言葉_{ことば}思ひ当りたり。此心わすれがたく。
我身家名を橘やとつき。五郎左衛門さまのかへ名をもらひ
権七とつきたるよし。ひそかにはなし申されし

方を専にするがよしと。あやめ申さるゝハ。鞠を蹴る様
に渡し方を専にはしがたし。相手をそこなハぬやうに
するといふハ。我が当りをと心がけぬことなり。上手に
成るやうに精さへ出さバ。一場のあたりハなくとも。全躰の
人がらにあたりあるべしとなん
一あやめ申されしハ。我身幼少より。道頓堀にそだち。

綾之助と申せし時より。橘屋五郎左衛門さまの世話に成たり
五郎左衛門さまと申ハ。丹州亀山近所の郷士にて有徳なる
御人。いかふ筋目ある人なりしが。能をよく被成たり。親
方ハ三味線方にてありしゆへ。さみせんに精出せと申
さるゝあいゝに。五郎左衛門さまを客にするこそ　幸なれ。
何とぞ能をならひおけと申されし故。二三度も頼まれ
ども。五郎左衛門さまとくしんなく。女形の仕内に精出すべし。
大概人に知らるゝ迄ハ。外の事むようなり。それに心が
あれバ本体の仕内の心がけが外に成べし。其上能といふ

など上手ハ上手なれども。此場の工夫なき様に覚えぬ。
花のさくハ実をむすぶ為なれバ。地を慥にして花を
あしらへと。若き女形へ度々異見せられし
一藤十郎と狂言する時は。ゆつたりとして大船に乗たる
やうなり。京右衛門と狂言する時ハ。気がはつて精出さ
ねバならず。三右衛門と狂言する時は。ひつはつてせねば
間がぬけたがるといふ事。さい〴〵申されしなり
一人の金をかへさずはらひもせず家をかい。けつこうなる
道具を求め。ゆる〳〵と暮す人と。相手のそこねる事
をかまハず我ひとり当りさへすればよいと。思ふ役者
が同し事なり。金をかしたる人何ほどか腹をたつべし

相手になる役者。みぢんに成ことなれバ。つるに八身上の
さまたげともなるなりと申されし
一左馬之助申さるゝハ。まりをけるやうに。相手へのわたし

といふやうなる。女家老の役あり。いかにもしつかりとせぬ
様にすべし。しつかりとして八男の家老がぼうしを着た
るに成べし。申ても大勢立合の所へ。いかに家老の女房
なればとて。心おくせぬ理はなし。身もふるふほどに
あぶな〳〵かゝり。敵役がどつとつゝこんだ悪言をいふた跡
にて。それよりきつとすべし。女は其場に成てハおとこ
よりいひ度ことをいふものなり。但シ少ハ上気したる
ていにて。狂言をすべしと申されし

一女形は貞女をみださぬといふが本体なり。是を以て
ほんの女とおなじ道理を合点すべし。いかやうに当り
の来べき狂言にても断いふべし。女形より役をいぢる
といふは此場が第一なるよし。若き衆へ咄されしなり
一所作事は狂言の花なり。地は狂言の実なり。所作
ことのめづらしからん事をのみ思ふて。地を精出さぬハ。花
ばかり見て実をむすバぬにひとしかるべし。辰之介

られたる躰なるが。其のちわれらにあふて。あやめハ此
道のまほり神と存ると申されしなり

一女形にて居ながら。立役になつたらバよからふといハるゝハ
恥のはぢなり。女形より立役へなをつて。立役にて

ともかくもよいといハるゝは。女形の時ハわるかるべし。立役
に直つてあしきは。女形の時よかるべしと。常に申されし
が。あやめ立役になられてはたしてわるかりしなり。女にも
男にもならるゝ身は。もとになき事故とかんじ侍りぬ

一女形にてゐながら。もしこれでゆかず立役へ直らんと
思ふこゝろつくがいなや。芸ハ砂になる物なり。ほんの
をなごが。おとこにはならぬにてがてんすべし。ほんの女
もはやこれでハすまぬとて。男にならるべきや。その心
にてハ女の情にうときはづなりと。申されしも尤ぞかし

一女形にて大殿の前へ出。夫に成かはつて。事をさばく

つくほど男になる物なり。　常が大事と存るよし。　さい〳〵

申されしなり

一敵役をきめつけることハ。　まづハ女形の役にハめいわく

なる事と思へども。　狂言の仕組によりていやといハれぬ

ばあれバ。　其役を請取る事なり。　かたき役をきめて

勝をとれば。　見物衆ハさてもよいぞと。　その女形を誉る

ものなり。　これにくし〳〵と思ふ敵役を。　よハかるべき女が

きめるゆへ。　うれしがるはづにてハあれども。　これに乗て見物

へのあたりをこのみ。　又しても〳〵此格な事をしたがるハ女

形の魔道なり。　つゝにハ筋道へゆかぬ役者に成べしとぞ

一あやめ十次郎へ申されしを聞てゐたるに。　さりとハ見物

のうけもよくてめでたし。　しかしおかしがらする心持を

止め給へ。　仕内にてしぜんとおかしがるるはよし。　おかしがらせん

とするハ女の情にあらずとなん。　十次郎少シはらをたて

をたてず。又見へによるべし理屈ばかりにて八哥舞妓
にあらず。とかく実とかぶきと半分〳〵にするがよからん
とぞ十次郎もそれより見へしだいにせられしなり
一武士の女房に成て刀を取廻す事。大勢に取こめられ。
たとへバお姫さまをかばふての仕内に八。いかにも男まさりに
刀をさばくべしこゝを大事と忠義の心せまるときは。

さすがものゝふの妻なり。座敷にて敵役をきめるは。
いまだせんのつまりにあらず。刀さばきおだやかなれ
かしと。さい〳〵玉柏への咄なるを聞たり。これ八玉がし八
大勢に取こめられたる仕内。かひなき故の異見とみへたり
一女形は色がもとなり。元より生れ付てうつくしき女
形にても。取廻しをりつはにせんとすれバ色がさむべし
又心を付て品やかにせんとせばいやみつくべし。それゆへ
平生ををなごにてくらさねバ。上手の女形と八いはれ
がたし。ぶたいへ出て爰はをなごのかなめの所と。思ふ心が

すべし。但し武士のつまなれバとて。ぎごつなるハ見ぐるしきつとしたる女のていをする時は。こゝろをやハらかにすべしとぞ

一中の嵐三右衛門吉沢氏と夜ばなしの時。とろゝ汁を出されけれバ。吉沢氏箸を取かねられたり。三右衛門いハく女形は此たしなみなくてハさて〳〵われらあやまり入たり。昼夜心易く致すゆへとの存ちがへとわびことをせられしよし。後に片岡氏に三右衛門あひて。あやめは名人なりと申されしは。かゝることまでに。たしなみふかかりしゆへなり

一十次郎申されけるは。女は右の膝をたて男ハ左の膝を立る。あゆみ出しもおなじ事とぞ。弟子へおしへられしもその通りなるを。吉沢氏ひそかにゐけんせられけるハそれは其通りなれども。見物衆の方へむかふ方のひざ

したること八生れ付て持てゐるなり。男の身にて傾情
のあどめもなく。ぼんじやりとしたる事八。よく〳〵の心
がけなくて八ならず。さればけいせいにての稽古を第一
にせらるべしとぞ

一哥流もと八香竜と書たるを。女形の名に八つよすぎ
たる竜の字と。よし沢ゐけんにて哥流と書替られたり。
哥流あるとき狂言の仕様を尋られしに。よし沢氏曰
家老の女房にて敵役をきめる時。武士の妻なれバと

おもふ心あるゆへ。刀のそりを打事かならずつ八なる
ものなり。武士の女房なればとて。常に刀をさす物に
あらねバ。刀の取まハしり〳〵し過たる八下手の仕内なり。
刀をおそれぬといふ計が仕内なり。何としてかとしてナンと〳〵
いふてぶたいをた〻いてつかに手をかくる八。ぼうしかけたる
立役なるべしと。度〳〵申されしとなん

一吉沢氏の曰女形の仕様かたちをいたづらに。心を貞女に
　後ニ芳ニ改ム

あやめぐさ

福岡弥五四郎述

よし沢氏は古今女形の上手なる故。あれ是へ
はなされしことを聞伝へ。又は自分にも尋ねて
書置ける事三十ヶ条に成ぬるま〻
あやめぐさと名づけ此道のしるべとしふかく
秘して人にもらさず其ヶ条左のことし

一或女形よし沢氏に問ける八。女形はいかゞ心得たるがよく
候や。よし沢氏のいはく。女形ハけいせいさへよくすれば。

外の事ハ皆致やすし。其わけハもとが男なる故。きつと

しづまらす時におくひやう口より揚やのていしゆ。古き浅黄袴の
腰をねぢらせ。てぬぐひを腰にさし。貝しやくしを持て出ェ、旦那お出かと
いふ声の内。諸見物そりや亭主が出たハ。あの顔を見よおかしやと笑ふ
声次のせりふもいひ出さぬ程也。漸笑ひしつまれハ八郎兵へなんとまだ
太夫ハ見えぬかイヤもふあれへもふ追付是へお出と。端かゝりを打詠めアレ〳〵
只今これへ見えますといへハヤレけいせいが出てくるハと見物みな腰を立直し
物をもいハす揚まくを詠めゐる時にけいせいの姿おかしきいしやう金入也。其
時分女形のかづらかくるハたまく〳〵にて。多くハ花紙をひようごわけにつゝみ。只
壱人出て大じんさまお出かへといふを。扨もと悦ひ大じんと互に手に手をとれハ
又笑ひ座敷のあいさつ一つ〳〵こなしをとよみをつくりて誉たり。扨亭主盃
をめぐらし。酒の肴に太夫様一曲の舞所望〳〵とせりふの内頓てはやし形出な
らべハ女形舞の所作有これハ狂言一ばんの仕組なり
　○右に書顕す狂言あまたあれ共事繁けれハ略之　芸鑑

銘々に出錢して食　物を御屋敷の表へはこび又兵衛をはごく
みしが。芝居御停止十三年。寛文八年戊申にかぶき芝居御赦免
なされ。三月朔日より再興の初日出せり。狂言ハけいせい事也。此日ハ
不就日なりとて留めれども。吉事をなすに悪日なしと。おして
初日を出しぬ。十三年が間の御停止ゆりたる事なれバ見物群集
の賑ひ言語に述かたし。村山氏の大功後世の役者尊むべき
事なり

一傾城事の狂言今とハかくべつの風義の違ひ也先其場に口上
出て。只今けいせい買の始りとふれてしまへバ。村松八郎兵衛といふ
立役。買人にて。此出立白加賀の衣装に銀箔にて鹿の角を蜂
のさしたる所を。惣身のもやう也。一尺七寸の脇さしを向へ落る計
にぬきさし。左ハはりひぢ右の手に扇の要をつまみ。端かゝりより
ゆらりゝと出。正面立なからせりふに曰
八まん是が買人でやすと。扇にて脇さしの柄をたゝけバ。見物
一同に。そりや買人の名人が出たハゝと。声ゝに誉る事暫く鳴りも

今ハはや引馬はかりに成たと馬を引よせコリャ馬よ。何と艶之丞が

ふいといた心ハどうであろと思ふととひ給へバ。馬も殿の顔を見て

ついとはいるが幕也〇今思へバか様の狂言大当とハおかしく侍れども。

其時分の見物かゝる狂言をあつさりと面白くおもひ。又役者も

かやうの狂言をよくこなし勤ける也

一明暦二年丙申其比ハ京ハ女形のさげ髪ハ法度にて有しに。橋本

金作といふ女形。さげ髪にて舞台へ出。其上桟敷にて客。と口論し

脇さしをぬきたる科によつて。京都かぶき芝居残らす停止仰付

られたり。これによつて京都座本村山又兵衛といふもの。芝居御赦

免の願ひに御屋敷へ出る事十余年。しかれども御とり上なかりし故

又兵衛宿所へもかへらず。御屋敷の表に起臥して毎日願ひに出るニ

雨露に打れし故。着物はかまも破れ損じ。やせつかれて。人のかたちも

なかりしなり其比の子供役者ども多く八商人職人と成。又ハ他国へ

小間物なと商ひにゆくものあまた有わつかに残りし子供役者

はいれバ。かんなぎお神楽〳〵と呼はりて。侍はいる所へ。艶之丞出。神前に

向ひ柏手打。主君国家大平御武運長久と祈念する折から。茶道

珍才うしろに立。艶之丞が袖を引小声に成て。其元のお為を申さん

殿さまの御寵愛ハ其元お一人とおもひしに此間ハもつはら友弥殿

に御鼻毛を延し給ふ。拙者ハお使に参る。こなたハ神主へ参れと。仰

付られたハ。跡にて友弥と殿さま。契らせ給ふはかりこと。御油断有なと

たきつけてお使にはしり入。艶之丞ハはらをたて。扨〳〵友弥めにくや

腹立やとねたみのせりふ有所へ。殿様御立といふ内に。家来数多

出。奥より殿ハ出させ給ひ。友弥に仰て艶之丞を呼給へとも返事

せず。殿見給ひコリャ艶之丞もはや帰らふこれへ参れハウ愛へこいと

手をとり。引よせ給へバ艶之丞物をもいはず。殿の顔を見てふいと

ふり切。端かゝりへはいるコレハさてきやつもフィト行おつたと草履取を

呼給ひコリャ艶之丞がしかたハどうじやあろと思ふぞと尋給ヘバ。草履

取又殿の顔をみてふいとふり切ツィトはいる。かくの如く家来どもを

一人〳〵呼て問給ふに皆〳〵同じくふり切はいる拠もめんような事

ひよろ〳〵国を祝ひ。礼をいふに舌まハらず小哥ぶし。こなた八馬

上に泪ぐみ。おさらバ〳〵と別れ行。此一段にて狂言大当りせしと也

一むかしの狂言ハ多く衆道の趣向有けり。若衆形の立者ハ若女

形より高給銀也。其時分ハ町〳〵にも衆道はやりけり。むかしの狂言を

又書付侍る。氏神詣とやらん外題をいひ伝し也

殿様氏神詣遊バされ。六法の出所作あり。跡に引馬行列おどり。其

時分の哥二上り殿のお馬ハさび月毛連銭あし毛鹿毛かすげ。しと〳〵

打てハかけあがり。お江戸そだちのひげ〳〵男。お馬の口をしつかりと。つり

りん〳〵ひげ男。つりりん〳〵〳〵つりりん〳〵りん〳〵〳〵りんと

はねたるいさみ馬。つなぎとめたよ恋のせき札　皆〳〵大義じゃ休

め〳〵。家来が手をつき先殿様に八神主方にて御休足と。哥にて皆〳〵

はいる奴共ハけしきを詠め。小性のきりゃうを評判艶之丞がよいイヤ

おらハ友弥殿にほれたと。いろ〳〵噂するを。侍出て。何をたはこと。御小

性の噂今一言いふて見よと。とがめられていりゃこそと。跡をも見ずに逃

はて。おはづかしやと笠とれハ。先ハ御無事てお久しやと互にふり

にし物語　いさゝかの事にて勘気を得られし貴殿。申出さぬ日とて

もなし。何とくらし給ふやと問れて弁右衛門ア、かたしけなき御詞浪

人の身なれバ。朝夕の煙かつゝゝ。習置し諷の袖乞。無念とハ存ながら。

もと諫言過て御勘当。かならず時節を待れよと。其元のお詞を

たのみに。今日まで命ながらへ候也。御上使とあれバ。殿の御名　代御目

見へいたす心地仕る。これを浮世のおもひ出と致す了　簡ずいふん御

無事にお勤あれ。お急ぎのさまたげ名残ハつきずおいとまと。

泪なからに立行をしばしとゝめ仰の如く今日殿の御名　代追付

御勘気御赦免有て。所領　安堵のしるしの盃を致さんハァアこれハ

有かたしと又手をつけ八朶女扇をひらき。途中の馬上　取あへぬ

心ざしの大盃。いざゝゝつげと小性にいひ付れハ同じく扇を銚子とし

つぐおもひ入呑こなしサアいざ参れと弁右衛門にさす。此お盃といひ

お志しの深切いつハ飲ずとてうどたべんと。三度いたゝき呑思入

有て。時刻うつると立さまに。お志しの御酒に酔ひたりと。足元

あみ笠真平御めんと詞の内朶女つく〳〵おもひ入有てﾑ、扨は

し身なれバ。顔を貴殿に見せ申もおそれ有。又面目なく存。慮外の

最前より待うけ。お馬のさきに平伏いたしながら。御勘気をこふむり

わすれ給ふべし。今日此道筋をお通りと承りあまりなつかしく。

先以。大慶至極以前御懇意の拙者なれども。年へたれバ声もき〳〵

用事子細きかんとありければ。彼男謹て。朶女殿に八御堅固の躰

コレそな男。それがしに向ひ用ありげに見へたる八。いかなる人にて何の

躰とみゆれバ。これ全く慮外にあらず。去ながら笠をとらぬ八心得ず

立よらんとする所を主人ヤレまて〳〵。彼者我にむかひて平伏の

を取て片付ろと。いへども更に答なしイヤ推参なと侍 ども

あみ笠を慮外 と申にあらす。お顔が見

御用の道筋馬上八御免。

貴殿こそ以前の傍輩 轟 弁右衛門殿な此方もなつかしく存る。某八

ハあらじと詞かけられ。扨〳〵よくこそ御推慮。いかにも弁右衛門がなれの

たい。お断のだん何かくるしかるべきサア〳〵笠をとり給へ弁右殿ニ違

芸鑑

富永平兵衛著

何事も時に随ふ習ひなるに。わきて狂言の風ハ。時代の品替れりむかし狂言尽の時あたりしと承り伝へ侍る。浪人盃といへる。狂言を左に記するもの也

一萩山の家中高坂采女といふ武士。馬上にて使者におもむく道の景色を称し。旦那より小性家来までせりふ渡り。采女が曰。むかふの館八聲君のお国なれバ。国境より行義正しく。いづれも麁相なきやうにと申さるれば皆領掌の答あり。諷に成る也馬をめぐらし。しと〳〵行むかふへ。深あみかさ着たる浪人もの。あゆみきて。しほ〳〵と平伏すれバ。家来とがめて。何者なれバ。慮外もの。笠

もつて。はじめ一ト足のふみちがひより万里の迷ひとなる也

〇是より下のケ条ハ虫ばみて見えず惜むべし〴〵

舞台百ヶ条終

しそんじあつても取直しできる有。うれい事をする時武士
の妻は声をあげてなくハ見ぐるし。男も声をあげて
なくものにあらず。年より愚にかへるゆへ。思ハずも声あげて
なく事あり。至てうれい事するに。こらへてなく有。おさへて
なく有。おさへてなくハ人目をはゞかりこらへてなくハみれん
にみゆる也。又ちかひ切腹手負なといふ時ハ。一ト調子高し。これとり
のぼす故。前後いふ事さだかならず。次第〳〵に声もよハる也
一見物入なきとて。姿をいとハぬ事。其身のそん也。たとへバ全盛
するけいせいハ。さのみすがたを粧ひなくとも。人目に立風。またはや
らぬけいせいなりとも。衣装はなやかに着る時ハ。おのづから人心

迷ふ也。狂言の役の替りを。人に頼むたのまるゝ事も。人の役故
そまつに勤めても。其身の誤りにならぬと心得るハ。大きなる
違ひ也万一本役の人より。一ト所成とも勝れたる仕内あらバ。
其身の会稽ならずや。おしひかな其壱人に成るべき身を

一芸者其一人となれバ。至らぬ芸者そねみ。あしさまにいふ事ハ。

たとへていハぶ。数百の蟻の。蚯蚓をせ〻るに似たり。甚あさまし

き事也。其長に至るもの八。おのれが心をみがきて。其品に応

ずる妙をあらハせり。甘柿の木に渋柿をつぎて。はやく実の

のるをたのしまんとするゆへ。却て渋柿の悪名をとる。渋柿の

木に甘柿を接合せ。生たつ時ハ本の味をうしなハず。万物も

実ばへより善悪しれがたければ。役者も物になれたる人に。た

より。接穂のごとく修行せば。名誉の名を得べし

一役〻の情をかんがへみるに。けいせいハ位高にして。心ハしゃれ

たるもの也。武士の女房ハ下をあハれむ心有て。人おとけたる

事をいふ時ハ。きつとするかたちよし。よつて武士の妻とみへ

る也。すべて芸者ハ相手の気に応ずるを第一とす音の合ぬ

狂言ハ名人たりとも。心に叶はず。されハ其人の気によつて。せわ

しくしてしにくきあり。又芸のかわる仕内有。又よくおぼえて。せわ

せわしきあり。延過るあり。あるひは拍子きゝにて気のはる有

みづからとよむ恥べし〳〵

一精を出すといふは。ねても覚ても。仕内を工夫し稽古にあく

まで。精を出して。拟舞台へ出てハ。やすらかにすべし。稽古に

力一ッはい精出したるハ。やすらかにしても。少しも間ハぬけぬもの

なり。稽古工夫に心をつくさず。舞台にて計精を出だせば。

きたなく。いやしく成て。見ざめのする事うたがひなし。拟惣

稽古といふもの。初日より二日も前にすべき事也。初日の前

日ハとくと休みて。きのふの惣けいこの事を。ほつ〳〵心におもひ

めぐらし。気をやすめて。初日を始れバ。初日よりおち付て。間のあく

事なし。前日にアタフタと稽古し夜をかけて物さがしく

翌日を初日とすれバ。わるひ事もかなりがけにせねバならず。此

ケ条　大切の事なり

一狂言の実ハ虚よりおこり。おかしき事ハ実よりせねバ無理

あてになる也

一狂言をするハ。心一はいにするをほむへし

舞台百ヶ条

杉九兵衛述

一今の立役のきつはをまハして。かたきをきめるハ。かたち計
にて心のきつはをまハさず。見物衆にほめらるゝ事をのみ
むねに持てまハすゆへ。かたきをきめるでハなくて。見物衆へ
廻すきつハになる。夫故敵役の身にこたへず。よはみの出し所が
はつまぬのみなり。相手仕事なれバ我ハ相手をたて。我も相手に
たてらるゝ様にさへすれば。舞台のおもてしつくりとなる故。
自然と見物衆のあつと感ずる場へゆく也。相手にかまハず。我
ひとりあてんとするを。孤自当といふ孤ハひとりとよみ自は

耳_に塵_{じん}集_{しう}　上手のはなしを金子吉左衛門_{かねこ}書しるす

続_{ぞく}耳_に塵_{じん}集_{しう}　民屋江音四郎五郎事書留し書也_{たみや}_{こうをん}

賢_{けん}外_{ぐわい}集_{しう}　染川十郎兵衛聞覚し事をはなせしを
　　　　東三八_{作者也}書置る賢外_{けんぐわい}といふハ_{言_{ほうめう}}
　　　　十郎兵衛法名也

佐_さ渡_ど嶋_{しま}日_{につ}記_き　むかし今の芸者心得に成べき事を_{けいしや}
　　　　蓮智坊が書置なり蓮智ハ佐渡_{れんち}_{ぼう}_{さど}
　　　　嶋長五郎法名也_{しま}

右七部の書ハ優家の亀鑑なれども梓にちりばめ_ぶ_{しょ}_{ゆうか}_{きかん}_{あづさ}
付録に当時三ヶ津役者芸品定を加入する而已_{ふろく}_{たうじ}_か_{にう}

　　　安永丙申晩秌　　　八文舎自笑述

役者論語

此書やむかしより上手名人と
称ぜし役者のはなしどもを古人
書留め置し巻々なり

舞台百ヶ条
といふ花車形の書置る書也
元祖坂田藤十郎師匠杉九兵衛

芸鑑
冨永平兵衛狂言作者也書置る
元祖むかしの書置

あやめ艸
元祖よし沢あやめはなしどもを
福岡弥五四郎書とめたる書也

翻刻ニツイテノ注記

行移リハ原本ニ従イ、丁移リハ一行アケテ示シタ

「耳塵集」ノ凡例及ビ各項ノ〔　〕ニ入ッタ見出シハ

別本『耳塵集』ノ凡例ト目録ニョルモノデアル

役者論語

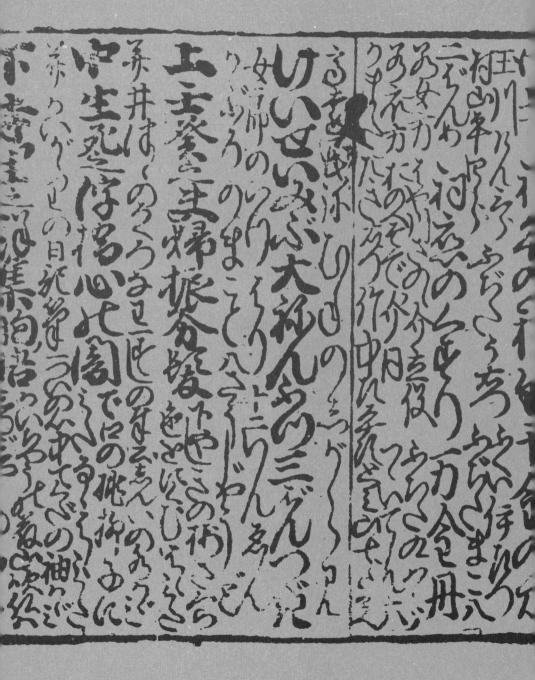